Money, Wealth & War

An Illustrated Guide

by

Robert Shuler

For my son Robert Grandon Shuler

Other books by Robert Shuler:

The Equity Premium Puzzle, Intrinsic Growth & Monetary Policy
Special Investor Edition Dec. 2014
2nd Edition from Tate Publishing 2015
3rd Edition 2016

The Economic Optimization of Innovation & Risk
Expanded 2nd Edition 2015

A Summer Night
The illustrated children's poems of Pauline S. Shuler
Available everywhere as 8x10 paperback
& in keepsake hardback at Lulu.com

Contents

Preface

September 2015 Update

There are three small changes in an update released in September 2015 – not enough to qualify as a new edition. First, the discussion of Russia's role on the "oil war" between U.S. shale producers and Saudi Arabia is updated to emphasize Russia's role as now the largest producer (passing Saudi Arabia in mid-2015, though every other month they change places). Second the discussion of the 7-stage cycle of money, trade and war beginning on page 115 is extended to include fascism and communism. Third, the final chapter which discusses the Greek debt crisis is updated to mention the relation between the way Germany was treated after WWI, and the way it is treating Greece, and the risk this poses of a rise in fascist parties in Greece such as Golden Dawn.

Preface to the First Edition

I hope to make you think about what it means to be human, to be productive, to trade, and about whether we are on the road up or down. And especially about whether anything works as we ordinarily assume it does. Have you thought about these things, or do you take them for granted?

You don't need to want to be wealthy to enjoy this book, and I'm certainly not trying to teach you how to start a war (it's actually quite difficult ... content people with jobs and a life will not readily throw it all away). You may only be curious about how the world works. But it is also invariable that when humans poke around and figure out how things work, they will find some way to benefit, and you may find things I didn't even intend for you to find. However, I also will explain some things about owning your share of the world that I want you to know, because your success in that regard will make the world a better place, for you and for me.

About 1973 I became fascinated with hidden factors shaping humans, things that most people didn't seem to be aware of. I also studied and practiced investing. My father introduced me to investing in high school, through buying stock in a local start-up bank. When other kids were playing sports I was reading books by management consultant and popular author C. N. Parkinson. The dad of a close friend was the town's only stockbroker. We would go to his office and look at big charts on the wall in the heyday of the 1960s. In college I made the first investment of my own in a start-up aluminum company with a couple hundred dollars, worth it for subscription to their annual reports over the next few years. They were alternately filled with optimism, then gloom and doom, something Parkinson had talked about.

One of my friends in graduate school went on to get a PhD in economics, and discovered the equity premium puzzle. His name is Rajnish Mehra. We kept in touch through the years, and one day he began explaining his puzzle. I began looking for ways to solve it and use it, and eventually wrote a book on the subject. Along the way I discovered some uses of the puzzle, like how powerful families accumulate wealth over time, and some rather unpleasant side effects, like war.

What would you do if you woke up one morning realizing you had discovered the cause of war? I asked my wife. She said "Nothing." When pressed she added, "If I wrote a letter to the President it would probably get lost."

It isn't the president who needs to know. He doesn't elect himself, we do! We need to know! The forces I had found are clearly with the people, and I'm not sure any leader can make more than a temporary difference one way or the other.

There was nothing to do but write a book that anyone would understand and want to read. This is it. After all, who doesn't really believe there is some secret method by which the wealthy become the wealthy? And who doesn't believe that masterminds of the world start all the wars?

The paths to wealth and war are more than just mathematical or economic principles. One must have the willingness, character and opportunity. The book contains summaries of different kinds of paths for many individuals and countries. You can draw your own conclusions, and you can and find points of commonality or difference with your own life and character, of which I could not be aware.

Where do You Stand?

Who should read this book?

This book is about wealth and money, and the deep connection of trade and war. If you want your family to be wealthy in the long term, you will want to know how to recognize and minimize the long term threats. So, we will look at the history of money and understand what it is, and at trade to understand what kinds have led to peace and stability, and what kinds have led to economic pressure. And we will look at a number of the world's wealthiest people to try and understand how they got that way. The book is also partly about what to do with money to keep it and grow it. That part is toward the end, and based on the conclusions drawn from looking at wealthy people, as well as the most time tested economic analyses of markets and investing.

I will give you "how to" on investing, but not slogans designed to sell books. You can only use this in combination with having, earning or saving money. My main purpose is to get inside your head and open your mind to the misleading assumptions you have absorbed from culture about what money is, whether it is good or evil, whether it should be backed by gold or printed when needed. When a crisis hits, you cannot be acting on intellect. No one has enough willpower. Emotion rules. You need the quiet confidence to keep your head and recognize what is going on, and figure out whether you need to do something or just ride it out.

That "urge to do something" is the ruin of many a sound financial strategy. We should be doing the right thing to begin with so that we profit from whichever way the economy goes.

Inflation? If you own companies that are providing essential goods and services, they have to keep making money because people cannot live without these. Deflation? As long as you are not over-leveraged (too much borrowing) then it doesn't matter. You will keep your share of the economy.

Your share of the world

Ultimately this book is about getting, keeping and growing your share of the world. Instead of a piece of land on which you have to pay taxes every year and which some big company can probably exploit for more profit than you can, creating pressure to constantly take it away from you, you have a piece of the economic machine that produces all that we have. It produces art, entertainment, medicine, food, transportation, and even philosophy about what it all means.

Since the first stone tools, productivity has been gradually increasing. And since agriculture it has accelerated without end in sight. More and more is produced with less and less labor. More and more the economy is not just like a machine, but is becoming a machine.

The results have been unexpected. Leisure time is far below the 80% of primitive man. Talk of short work weeks from the 1970s and job-sharing from the 1990s has been replaced by people working multiple jobs to make ends meet, and forced to take part time jobs so employers can avoid paying the benefits due to full time workers.

For now, a job may be necessary for you, and maybe you will always want to work. But if you own a piece of the machine which can provide for you, then you can work at what you want to work at. Right now I am not considering whether this book will make more money than something else I could be doing. And so, I am more likely to tell you what I know to be true rather than what you might want to hear. What would you like to do your way, on your terms? Something, I'm sure.

I am appalled by the "theory" of growth stocks that pay no dividends. That theory holds that you simply sell some of them when you need money.

This decreases your total share of the economy. It gives up your birthright. It is like selling your tribe's land in exchange for some trinkets and the promise of mining jobs. You and your clan will get black lung disease working in the mines, and will take to drinking and doing drugs because it is not aesthetically enjoyable like tracking and hunting. And when the mine runs out, where will you be?

The mine always runs out. Every company goes out of business eventually. You and your clan need a better plan than giving up an eternal source of life in exchange for trinkets, or money. Same thing.

Capital assets are those that produce more wealth. The difference between people who manage not only to get wealthy but stay that way, and the rest of us, is they have chosen never to liquidate capital assets. They don't see money to be spent. They see their kingdom. If a king sells off his provinces to finance the palace life, how long will he remain king?

Money itself is just a scale factor for determining relative worth of items in trade. It does not produce anything itself and naturally loses value over time. Do not be too concerned with whether the market goes up or down as long as you keep your share of it and your place in line. You must fight for and keep your share of the world and its bounty. Anything else amounts to just giving up and quitting.

I believe if more people had more stake in the world, say 10% to 20% of us owners instead of just the top 1%, that the world would be a more pleasant place in which to live. That's why I am writing this book. The very wealthy are immune to many practical considerations, and though they may be charitable and intend well, they cannot know everything, and their actions cannot be democratic. There are simply too few of them. They have an unduly large influence on our society. America was founded on the idea that it would be governed by a population of free landowners, farmers and ranchers. As more people give up their land and become employees, with their future tied to the interests and whims of one industry or another, the model of America's governance becomes arguably weaker.

What is your share of the world?
source: all-free-download.com

Your life plan

Maybe you already have a life plan. You are the only person who can decide what it is. I do not know your circumstances, skills, desires, and so forth. I do know that Americans are obsessed with individualism, and this leads to the destruction of wealth. No matter how much you enjoy self-indulgent hedonism in your youth, it will be a faint and unsatisfying memory by the time you are 50 or 60.

Here are some thoughts to consider as you ponder your life plan. If you do not have to accomplish the whole transition to wealth all at once, it gets a little easier. Push your family situation forward one notch and perhaps your children will push it forward another, and next thing you know you will be the movers and shakers in the world, instead of being the moved and shaken. It is a recipe that many waves of immigrants have followed to success. Sometimes those of us who have been here longer forget it.

If a job has a role in your life plan, that's fine. I worked for 42 years. I carefully chose my job to have security and enough degree of interest to keep me occupied. I didn't get rich quick, but I steadily progressed until I am very comfortable. My children should have a more secure starting point and the ability to take more chances.

Many people who suddenly come into money go broke, whether they got it by lottery, from a business windfall, or a high paid career like acting or sports. Usually they were following a life plan to do something they were passionate about, without really planning for the money except to spend it. People vastly underestimate the skill required to hold on to money. Perhaps part of your life plan should be to acquire some of the attitudes and basic knowledge of what types of financial instruments are available, and practice using them?

If you suddenly came into a lot of money what would you do?

Your style of approaching challenge

There is no right or wrong style. All styles of human behavior are evolved to meet needs of survival. However, reading a book written for a style that is not your own, and trying to follow that other style, may not be your strongest approach.

While there are many ways of analyzing style, not all of them are helpful, maybe even not any of them helpful. I want to offer one that at least has some explanatory power. I encountered it many years ago in a 1980 book by psychologist Joyce Brothers, *How to Get Whatever You Want Out of Life*. Determining your style by this method can be a little confusing, so I will alter her question by giving more explanation, at some risk of biasing your response.

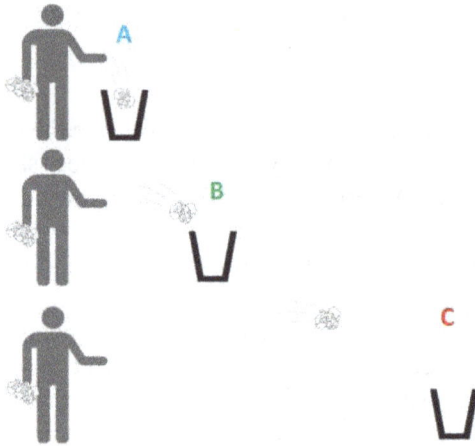

Some possible choices in Joyce Brothers' personal style test

You should actually do this simple exercise, not just look at the picture and make a choice (Brothers didn't even provide a picture). The task is this. You do it any way you want to:

- Crumple up three pieces of paper
- Choose a standing position relative to a waste paper basket
- Toss the crumpled paper pieces into the basket one at a time
- Record your position and the results of the test

Later I will tell you what Brothers said about the styles and also what my own style is. Do NOT look ahead as that removes any usefulness of the information. Stop now and do the exercise.

Where you stand on the wealth scale

We hear a lot about the top 10% or the top 1% and most everyone thinks "those people" have unobtainable status. Or maybe you think you are already there. Do you actually know where you stand? Take a moment right now to find out by going to this website:

NET WORTH PERCENTILE CALCULATOR

Here's a calculator to rank your net worth to specific age groups to see where you stand or where you project yourself to be in the future. Use the percentiles to compare your net-worth to US households using data from 2013.

Edit: As of 9/14/2014, this calculator is now using SCF 2013 data instead of 2010.

From Age: 60

To Age: 70

Networth : $ 1000000

SUBMIT

A networth of 1000000.00 for ages 60 to 70 ranks at .82.4%

This means that for every 100 people there are about 82 who have less or the same

http://www.shnugi.com/networth-percentile-calculator/

If you use the default setting of 18 to 100 years, you will see your percentile ranking among all U.S. households. This is a ranking of families therefore, not individuals. Since wealth naturally increases toward the end of a working career, and then diminishes if one draws it down to live on, it might be more meaningful to look at an age range close to your own.

I have elected to find the ranking of a hypothetical household with a net worth (assets, including real estate, stocks and retirement plan, less debts such as a mortgage) of one million dollars, near the end of a working career. Thus the age range I used was 60 to 70.

The ranking of 82.4 percentile means that this household is NOT in the top 1% or even the top 10%. They are barely in the top 20%. You can play around with this calculator and try to guess how many of your neighbors are rich or poor. My conclusion was that I am doing okay, but not nearly as wealthy as I thought I was. I have to include young people in the age range even to get in the top 10%. When it comes to IQ, I am much higher than that. Of course, it has long been known that IQ is not necessarily correlated with wealth. Yet the notion persists, especially among wealthy people themselves, that they are somehow really "smarter" than the rest of us.

My suspicion is that for most of you, your prior opinion of where you stand will turn out to be too high. Even if you think you are poor, you will turn out to be poorer than you think. Most of us are actually falling behind where we think we are or should be. And the really bad news is that often the harder we try to catch up, the more mistakes we make and the farther behind we get.

If you are ahead of where you think you are, maybe even where you want to be, you are doing fine already and should take a break and enjoy life.

Analysis of the style test

There are really four styles, not three. If you peeked ahead before taking the test, your style is cheating. You cheated yourself out of really knowing what your own style is. I'll not pass judgment, but just let you figure out what to do with this information. But beware of possible insider trading charges.

If you selected A, and stood over or very near the basket to be sure you got all the papers inside on the first try, you are like most people. You will succeed at most things you try, and will not try things at which you cannot succeed. Your best bet for accumulating wealth is the normal path of getting an education, a stable job, and investing. Moreover, this will work very well for you. It does not work so well for the other two styles.

If you selected B, and stood far enough to make it challenging, but at a distance where you were likely to get at least 2 in and possibly all 3 if you pay attention, then according to Brothers you are the type most likely to succeed in business. You like a challenge and are not content with following directions. At the same time, you are realistic about what you might accomplish, and will be careful to avoid bankruptcy, or starting a business for a product no one wants. You will do okay at investing, and possibly quite well, but you will be tempted to vary from the standard advice of patiently waiting for index funds to grow, and research has suggested this is not a high percentage play. Knowing this, however, you will probably focus on business, in which you can gain proprietary returns not subject to public market theory (more about that later).

If you selected C, you are bored with the mundane and want to accomplish something exciting. Perhaps you have been told by parents or friends this is expected of you. I have never seen an explanation of why these styles arise. Perhaps it is just hormones.

C is my style. I'm not satisfied with just accumulating wealth for myself. I'm writing a book with the goal of making millions of people wealthy. But the chances of success are small. I spent my career working for an organization trying to put humans on Mars and other exotic places. Nearly everyone who works there has the C style. As a result, our plans were always too grand and impractical to get off the ground. Literally in many cases. With investing, I am always trying to beat the market, with the result that I often miss the basket. Hopefully by knowing my style I can reign it in a little bit. But if boredom sets in I am lost, as any style C person will be. I guess writing a book gives me something to do besides tinker unnecessarily with my portfolio.

Where others stand and how it changes

In this section we look at what typically happens to people at different percentile points as they move through life: whether they move up or down, and whether the changes are primarily driven by investments or salary. You can use this information to figure whether you are getting ahead or behind where you should be, and see if there is an opportunity that fits your life for getting out of the pack and moving ahead. Doing so will almost certainly require you be a little different than your peers. If you are driven strongly by the need to blend in, then perhaps this section will still be useful to make sure you are not falling behind.

income percentile (all tax filers 2010)

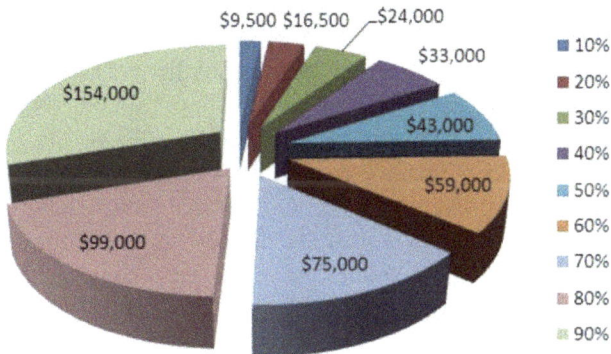

The pie chart above shows income of all taxpayers. It does not include people who did not file a tax return. The 90th percentile (90%) means people who make $154,000 per year have more income than 90% of other people, but less than 10% of other people. The "top 10%" might have a considerably larger average annual income. The pie slice for the 90th percentile graphically illustrates relative income size compared to other percentile points. The 10th percentile number of $9,500 is more than 10% of people but less than 90%.

The difference between the 10th percentile and the 90th percentile is about a factor of 15, which is large, but not as large as we might expect. The top 50% can all pay $1000 a month rent, drive a decent car, eat, raise a family and still set aside something for savings even if in the 50th percentile it is not a lot. So what do these people actually do in each group? How does their wealth, their net worth, change over time?

net worth age 34-36 (2014)

■ 10%	
■ 20%	
■ 30%	
■ 40%	
■ 50%	
■ 60%	
■ 70%	
■ 80%	
■ 90%	

($10,000) $6,800 $15,000 $30,000
$500 $50,000

$400,000

$110,000

$195,000

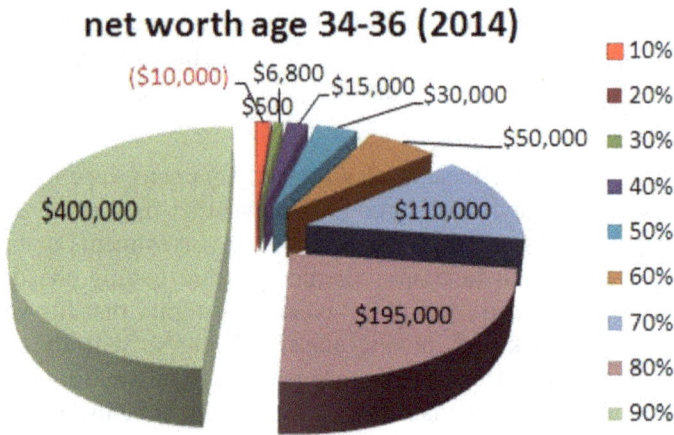

We start at an age in the mid-30s, when a person is hopefully established in a career, has paid much of their student debt, but has not yet earned a lot from their job. In the chart above it is obvious that there is a much greater difference between the percentiles for net worth than there was for income. The 90th percentile starts out with money they cannot have earned. They must have inherited it, I presume. Even the 70th and 80th percentiles are not likely to have earned their sizable nest eggs. Remember that people are taking on new home and car payments, having babies, and trying to outspend their peers at this age. Everything is about expenses in the mid30s. We see the dominance of expenses at the 40th percentile and below. These people have accumulated little, and the bottom 10 percent are in debt for around $10,000. This exceeds their annual earning power of $9,500 (if we assume the percentiles are roughly correlated between the charts).

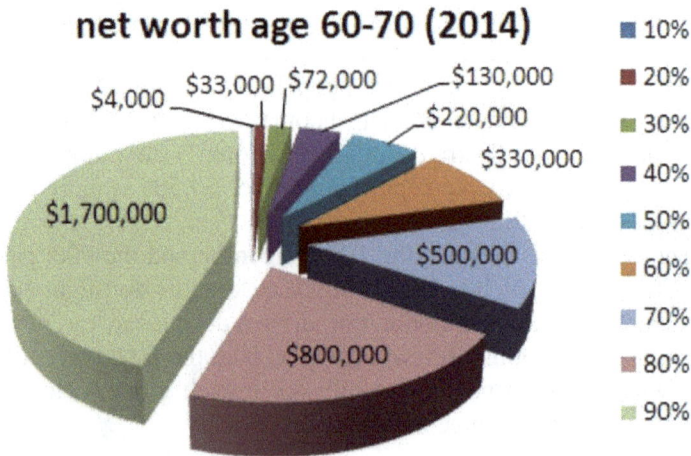

net worth age 60-70 (2014)

■ 10%	
■ 20%	
■ 30%	
■ 40%	
■ 50%	
■ 60%	
■ 70%	
■ 80%	
■ 90%	

$4,000 $33,000 $72,000 $130,000
                            $220,000
                            $330,000

$1,700,000

$500,000

$800,000

Now we fast forward to 30 years later and look at the 60 to 70 age bracket, around retirement age. The top group has surprisingly lost ground. Even the 50th percentile is worth nearly a quarter of a million dollars. This may mostly be home equity, but bankers are expert at helping you extract that equity if you want it for something. If you spend it, of course you immediately drop to the bottom of the pile in net worth. Later we'll consider what you might do, but remember that extracting too much home equity partly led to the 2009 financial crisis.

The 30th percentile at a net worth of $130,000 could possibly generate as much as $26,000 a year in investment income (with a lot of risk, we'll see how this works later). That's about as much as they were making in salary in their mid-30s. In theory it doesn't consume the $130,000 to do this, and other retirement income might be available. If the $130,000 could be passed to a single child, the next generation would automatically move up 20 points to the 50th percentile (see age 34-36 chart). The nest egg could be split among as many as three children and they'd move up about 10 points to the 40th percentile.

In every case, retaining rather than liquidating the retirement nest egg provides reasonable investment income and moves at least 2 children up 10 points to the next bracket.

The central claim of the wealth side of this book will be that you can move up at least one bracket at each generation by switching from retirement planning to a generational wealth building strategy. The cost is you give up a little extra income in the early years of retirement, but as we will see later the cost is no more than 1/3rd of your self-managed retirement funds, which is probably not your only source of income.

The war and money aspects of the book will attempt to convince you not to pursue trade and fiscal policies (with your votes and your civic affiliations and persuasion among your friends) that will lead to economic disaster and war, and that the natural instincts you have for such things are probably 180 degrees off course. This is true whether you are liberal or conservative. This book attempts not to take a political side, and criticizes extreme policies of either type. Building a broad wealth base generates more tax revenue without raising tax rates. The chapter on unexpected results explains why going directly for a policy goal in a complex society often produces the opposite results of what you want.

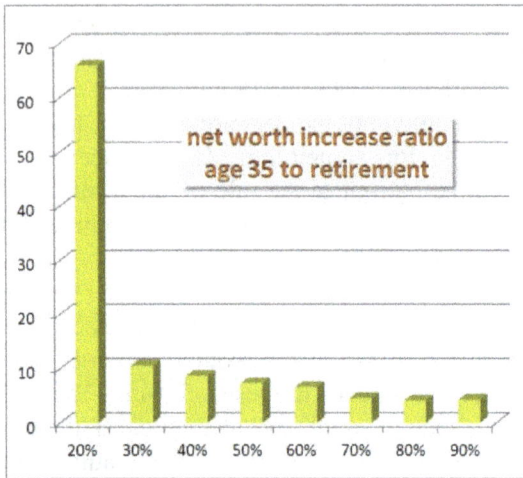

The net worth increase ratio chart above shows the ratio of the net worth at retirement to the net worth at mid-career. The bottom 10% is omitted because their net worth at mid-career was negative, a debt, so the ratio is not meaningful. The surprising thing is that the lower percentiles are consistently able to increase their net worth faster. This agrees with the "catching up" we saw in the two net worth pie charts above. Apparently the old adage about the rich getting richer does not apply to an individual in their working career. At least, they do not get richer as fast as the poor do, oddly enough.

If we look closely at the net worth pie charts, we see that the high net worth starting position of the young rich - the money they got from their parents - is completely missing in the lower percentiles. This generational transfer is where the rich behave differently and get ahead. They are not obsessed with the idea that they should disinherit their children and leave them to fend for themselves, or save only for their own retirement, or beg the government or some corporation for a good start in life for their kids.

A friend of mine, on reading this section, pointed out that the lower percentiles do not necessarily narrow the absolute dollar gap with the upper percentiles, and that most of their equity is in their homes. I concede both points, and counter with the following. It is the percentile that matters because you absolutely *can* move your family up in percentile by preserving wealth across generations. And because the future growth of that wealth is based on a percentage return, not a fixed salary. It is the attitude toward work as the justification for existence which separates the masses from the wealthy, whose existence is justified by the wise management of their assets to enable more production in society. You might think the smaller salary income of workers affords less flexibility, but only at the lowest percentiles. In most cases, it provides the perfect cover for increasing wealth without increasing expenses. Wealthy people think they have to buy a lot of unnecessary stuff.

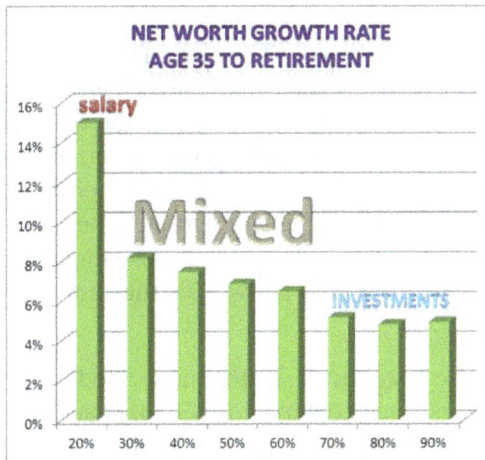

Above I plotted the same ratio, but in terms of the annual percentage increase as if the increase were evenly spread over 30 years, from age 35 to 65. In an Excel spreadsheet you can do this with a power function. For example, for the 20th percentile's ratio of 66, the annual growth rate of 15% is found by the formula "=POWER(66,1/30)-1" or 66 raised to the 1/30th power. That comes out to be a number like 115%, and subtracting 1 gives the usual way of writing it, 15%.

Few people are making 15% reliably in the stock market, and the 20th percentile people likely aren't investing in the stock market. Their wealth increase is entirely due to their salary. They must keep working, it is their only choice. They also pay very little taxes on their salaries. While the very, very rich, probably well above the 1% bracket, may have access to complicated tax dodges, even the 90th percentile generally does not.

The top three brackets have an annual percentage increase rate in the 4% to 5% range. They could get this from relatively safe corporate bonds while spending their entire salary. Most likely some of them do spend their entire salary. It appears they could move up the wealth scale much more rapidly than they are by making two adjustments:

- Consume a little less and invest more.
- Use a better investing technique that has at least a market average rate of return.

We'll learn what market average rates of returns are later, as well as investing techniques. If these people are investing at all, the trouble probably isn't that they are investing too conservatively. The usual problem, and the problem I certainly had at that age, was chasing supposedly rapid wealth building strategies, like stock picking, options or derivatives, that often result in long-term returns of 1% or 2% or even negative returns. We'll discuss that in the last chapter on Mistakes Everyone Makes.

The people in the middle brackets from 30th to 60th percentiles are probably using a mixed strategy. They are accumulating some from their salary, but it is not effective because they already have a good next egg, and the salary with their saving rate doesn't change the nest egg a lot each year. This is a problem for anyone as they get near retirement, and can't easily make in salary what they have accumulated over their lives. Since this group doesn't have as much to invest as the top groups, they are probably investing it in index funds and actually doing better at investing than the hot shots who are already wealthy and think they know what they are doing.

The plan of this book

Warren Buffett still lives in the same modest house he had many decades ago. Nicholas Cage bought a lot of houses and then had to sell them. Here are two examples that could happen to you:

- One young man lived frugally, joined the Navy, saved and invested, and became a millionaire by age 30.

- A lottery winner took a relatively small amount to splurge and give away, then invested the rest in a balanced portfolio and still has it many years later.

After looking at paths to wealth, and some paths to war, and the origin of money and our unconscious feelings about it that are buried there, we will examine the real effects of trade, and the causes and consequences of war. These most often underlie the upheavals that would rob you of your hard earned place in the world. We will look at contracts, coins and central banks to understand the powerful institution that regulates our economy, the Federal Reserve. That gives us the ability to understand debt and equity, the difference between them, the issues of trust that cause people to favor one or the other and invariably make wrongheaded decisions, the way the Fed's regulation affects each, and the reasons why one of them works surprisingly better than the other. We will learn that the Fed, or its historical equivalent, expired once and was abolished another time.

With an understanding of money, debt, equity and banking we can look at companies vs. economies, and why you should be more interested in economies than companies. Most of the time whole economies move up or down together. Finally we will cover the mechanics of wealth, how one actually goes about managing an account and finding investments that have the characteristics we have learned about.

Does this approach make sense to you? Ready to begin?

Paths to War & Wealth

Wealth is a family habit

Do you aspire to be wealthy but have not an inspiration for flipping multiple internet businesses like Elon Musk, or picking stocks like Warren Buffett? Are you willing to proceed down a path to becoming wealthy which is fairly sure to work, but might take most of your life? Do you want to understand financial policy well enough to elect policymakers that will enable prosperity and avoid calamity?

A lot of people will answer no. The cost is too high. The time frame too long. They would rather have someone else to blame. But if you answered yes to any of these questions, this book is written for you.

Most wealthy people did not make it from scratch. To be sure, we worship those that did as some kind of Americana deities. And if you can do that, more power to you. But such people do not need a book. And generally speaking, they have had limited impact on the world. Families that retained their position in future generations like Rockefeller, Walton, Hilton, Adams (two presidents) and Bush (also two presidents, maybe three someday) have shaped American life, politics and culture for three centuries. More than one president was the son of a president. America's real power, though, is its middle class. And I would make the middle class wealthy.

Sam Walton's father was not a farmer all his life. He entered the farm mortgage business and repossessed farms during the Great Depression. Bill Gates' father was a prominent lawyer and his mother served on the boards of a network of banks and the United Way (perhaps giving rise to Bill's charitable interests?). Warren Buffett was the son of a Congressman.

Steve Jobs' biological father was a university professor and his biological mother had an advanced degree also. Jobs' mother was forbidden by her father from marrying Jobs' father (when her father died the next year they did get married) so the baby was adopted by Paul and Clara Jobs of California. His mother insisted on a college educated couple. Paul taught his son to work on electronics, and his adoptive mother was an accountant. They lived in Mountain View California. It was the perfect recipe for starting a tech business.

Take the case of the Koch brothers, David and Charles, whom politicians love to complain about. You might have seen David Koch on a Barbara Walters special in 2014. He insists he was born well off but not wealthy. That may be true by his standards now as 9th richest person in the world, but his father Fred Koch founded and owned an oil refinery. I expect that would qualify as wealthy to most of us. Nor did things simply begin with Fred. The grandfather Harry Koch worked in newspaper printing in Europe before coming to the U.S. in 1888, and owned a newspaper. Most of us never even got as far as owning a newspaper. From there he gave his son Fred an education at Rice and MIT as a chemical engineer, and Fred was able to improve the cracking processes to make smaller refineries more competitive. Nor was it easy. He was challenged in numerous patent lawsuits.

So none of the three generations exactly started from poverty. And as for politics, Fred founded the John Birch Society. His sons had seen it all done and knew how to do it. Now they are "having their say."

I know you can cite examples of people coming from poverty to wealth. I will tell you a secret. Out of billions of people in the world, sure a few will become wealthy, by innate talent or luck. But I was picking the names above at random! I was just thinking of people who are admired and wealthy. I got tired of picking names before I hit on one that had started out poor. Our romantic notions of rags to riches are not realistic. Those stories are possible, but I am writing for the rest of you.

Paths to war

I want you to have your say. Even if you don't care about becoming wealthy, I want you to have the knowledge of how money really works, not just old wives tales and superstition, so that you can get the results you want, not some surprising negative outcome as is so often the case when new policies are tried. Do we balance the budget or not? Do we end the Fed or not? (Hint: It's been done twice in our history, the second Free Banking Era ending only with the Civil War.) Do we change the way the Fed works? What effect would it have? Low interest or high interest? Inflation or deflation? What kind of regulation of markets do we want? What has led to stability and prosperity in the past, and what to war and chaos?

The oil war

As I write this, we are embroiled in one of the most expensive wars in decades. Not Iraq or Afghanistan or the new spat with the Islamic State. I am talking about the energy war. Energy producing countries do not want the energy consuming countries to develop their own resources, or invest massive amounts in electric cars and renewable energy. So they are fighting where they have the advantage, in the oil market, where they can pump oil at $20 a barrel if necessary.

The war in Ukraine

The war in Ukraine has always been about money. The Ukrainians wanted to join the European Union to improve their economy, and Russia was afraid of losing its trading hegemony. Sure, the Russians complain about NATO, but NATO was not a factor until after the split over economics. With NATO pondering reinforcements, that's not the outcome Russia wanted. One reason Russia hasn't taken the whole country is probably that Ukraine paid

Russia $385 million for a billion cubic feet of gas in early December, enough to last them only 5 weeks, and if Russia takes over Ukraine then I guess they would have to foot that bill themselves.

Donetsk Airport before & after destruction
Wikimedia commons (before), frame grab BBC drone video (after) [102]

The economic war with Russia

NATO chose not to respond militarily when nonmember but close neighbor Ukraine was invaded in 2014. We are being realistic here, not quibbling over uniforms. Russia allows training camps for volunteers on their soil, and has supplied regular troops and heavy arms, including the missile that downed MH17. Instead they started an economic war with Russia. No one thought sanctions would have much effect that I knew of. Of course no one knew OPEC was going to start an oil war. Or maybe the American shale oil producers started it.

Or actually, Russia is aging it on, never agreeing to production cuts in their pre-conferences with OPEC, and as of July 2015 having passed Saudi Arabia as the world's largest oil producer. Russia, Saudi Arabia and the U.S. account for ¾ of world production of around 40 million barrels per day. Per year, about 4 million barrels per day go out of production due to well depletion and have to be replaced. Compared to that, a potential additional one million barrels per day from Iran is not all that alarming. Oil consumption is still growing, albeit slowly, but even when economies otherwise contract like in China in mid 2015. Anyway, the oil component is a war of wealth, by wealth, on wealth.

In early November 2014 I saw a chart of the amounts of Russian corporate dollar-denominated bonds due by month. There was a big peak in December 2014. No one knew exactly what would happen, just that something would. *Then oil collapsed, but weaker oil exporters than Russia* had no currency crises. However, Russian companies could not simply reissue new bonds as they normally would do. Companies often borrow long-term capital in the short term capital market because interest rates are lower. They have to roll it over every few months to a year. With sanctions, they could not borrow new dollars, and could not roll over their debt.

So the big government controlled oil company Roseneft borrowed 10 billion Rubles, and used the Rubles to buy dollars on Monday the 15th of December. The Russian central bank accepted the 10 billion Ruble note as "collateral," a code word for fiat money creation, itself a code phrase for the trigger of hyperinflation. The currency markets found out about it and essentially didn't accept the newly printed Rubles. They were worth nothing.

Medvedev made a show of saying that Russia would not institute capital controls, that in the past that was a mistake and they would use market means to stabilize the Ruble. That is code for saying that they have to let the companies with bonds expiring buy dollars with their Rubles, and that the Russian central bank will sell however many dollars it takes to stabilize the market. In other words, the Russian central bank will accept worthless Rubles and cover the maturing bonds, as long as the Russian central bank has dollars. When they run out, the jig is up. I don't know how this will come out. I should disclose that I am long Russian equities. No, I am not smart enough to figure this is the bottom, and that is not the kind of advice I am going to give you. That's just a reflection of the fact that I made 6 trips over there and married a Russian and became overly optimistic about the country.

That the entire Russian power hierarchy is motivated entirely by money was forcefully presented in a Frontline documentary which you can watch online.

http://www.pbs.org/wgbh/pages/frontline/putins-way/

According to Frontline, 110 people own 35% of Russia. Allegations, the credibility of which you can judge for yourself from interviews on both sides, are that they have started wars and faked terrorist attacks to manipulate elections and secure protection of their power. Perhaps not all of them feel equally. In an interview in the film, Khodorkovsky (whom we'll discuss later) states: "*I thought he [Putin] would choose the European model and I was not the only one thinking that, because it was obviously more beneficial for the country.*"

In 2018, presumably Putin will step down as planned. Perhaps Medvedev will run again and little will change. But in fact Russia was slightly different under Medvedev even with Putin pulling the strings. As I will discuss in a later section on the 7-stage cycle of money, war and trade, former communist countries (e.g. Russia, China) do not seem to have as much clarity in their transformations as former fascist countries (e.g. Germany, Japan), though at the height of their ideologies there are many similarities.

Paths to wealth

Now I want to surprise you with the less well known aspects of some of the paths to wealth. I'm not advocating you take any of these paths, rather just let you know what they entail if you want to embark on them. I won't try to talk you out of them either of course, it's your business.

Elon Musk's path (Tesla, SpaceX and formerly PayPal)

Personally, I do not want to flip internet businesses to become wealthy. I have tried it. I wrote some zip software that sold well, called Zip-n-Go. It allows me to use multiple computers and keep all my files synced. My files are far too big to sync over the internet. I have close to a thousand technical papers as PDF files, and hundreds of large CAD files (computer aided design). I think no one figured out what Zip-n-Go really does. The sync routines provided by Microsoft and others are terrible, no control, just one big folder that gets synced, and not combined with a standard compression format like zip that can be accessed on different types of machines, and different operating systems. Like with many other types of software, Microsoft includes just enough capability in Windows that no one buy separate zip software anymore. I started several other internet businesses. A large-format print business with an image sizing wizard operated for ten years. No one offered me millions of dollars for it, and after losing and replacing an operational partner once, on the second loss I shuttered it. This is the story of the vast majority of internet businesses.

Elon Musk
Picture by Dan Taylor http://www.heisenbergmedia.com
Used under Creative Commons Attribution 2.0 Generic license

Musk was the son of an engineer and a model. You can tell he gets his pretty boy looks from the model. He learned programming at age 12, but he did not study either programming or engineering. He made his way from South Africa to Canada, taking advantage of his mom's citizenship there, then to the U.S. for school. His first degree was in economics. We don't know the details of his family finances, but he felt no compulsion to quit school and pay off student loans, so I assume he didn't have any student loans. He then got a degree in physics. He signed up for a PhD is physics but quit after one day to go to California and join the internet boom.

Immediately he failed. He spent a day hanging around the lobby of Netscape and could not get an interview. If he had succeeded, probably he would have amounted to nothing but an average silicon valley programmer. People now entering college have never heard of Netscape. It was a victim of the sort of Microsoft throat cutting that I experienced with Zip-n-Go, Desktop Referee, Scrap and TextFind, except on a seriously large scale with the Justice Department involved. Everyone was rooting for Netscape. Microsoft won.

Instead Elon got with some friends and founded Zip2. If you go to Zip2.com today you'll find a generic search page. I tried to think of something cool to search for and typed in "what is" and it suggested "What is ISIS" so I clicked that. I got a video on Bible downloads, links to information about an Egyptian goddess, and several people named Isis. Nothing about the Islamic State. Whatever Zip2 was is gone. Actually it was a city directory and sold for $302 million, of which Musk's share was 22 million. It has been made obsolete by CitySearch. CitySearch tried to acquire Zip2 and Musk talked his friends out of it. Instead they sold to Compaq. Teenagers now entering college will not remember Compaq as an independent company. They, um, oh, what did they do? Oh yeah, Compaq invented the portable computer. I have four laptops. None of them are Compaq. Cleverness wasn't enough. Even Houston oil money wasn't enough to keep Compaq going. They hired a generic CEO who ruined the company, and it was acquired by HP. Nothing ever came of Zip2

Elon took his $22 million and started a company called X.com. No, Musk did not start PayPal as is often reported. If you type in x.com now it rolls over to eBay. One year after founding, before anyone had heard of them, they merged with Confinity which had already started PayPal. Musk had the good sense to drop the name x.com. The real founder of PayPal, Peter Theil, was appointed CEO. Musk was credited with a "viral marketing campaign" that allowed PayPal to grow. That is a strange way of putting it, "credited with." Why not just say he did it. Unless there is some doubt? Maybe he did it, and PayPal grew, and no one knows if there is a relation. I have a PayPal account and you probably do too. Why? Not because of viral marketing. When running those other internet businesses I opened every type of payment account I could find, including software registration services, a regular credit card account with online processing, and PayPal. I was actively searching for payment options as was every other internet business. Nothing viral about it.

Beyond the point of selling PayPal Musk was already extremely wealthy, and while his further exploits may be interesting, they are not part of his path to wealth. His secret was provided to us by Kenny Rogers. Musk knew when to walk away, and when to run. He walked away from South Africa, ran from Netscape and Zip2, and prudently walked away from PayPal. My trouble is I stick with things much too long. I've made a profit on nearly every investment I ever made, but many of them I didn't sell. When you sell, you have to figure out something new to buy because life doesn't end there, and it is a real problem. More about that later. Musk knew when to sell. He also knew when to hold in 2009 when the chips were down, and kept both of his current companies (Tesla and SpaceX) when everyone else was bailing on everything.

One more thing to notice about Musk ... he didn't fall very far from the tree, so to speak. His dad was an engineer and Musk learned programming and made his money in programming, regardless of what he does now that he is rich. His mom was a model and he dates and has married women that certainly look like models. Another way of saying this is, the real key to his success was his family pattern. He mostly held on to it. The only obvious thing he left was South Africa. Of course if your family doesn't have a good pattern, you will have to let go of more things, and figure out what to replace them with. It probably isn't buying lottery tickets you'll want to pin your hopes on, because if you get the money without a good family habit of holding on to and increasing wealth, what do you think will happen?

You will have to figure out how to adopt the new pattern for yourself. There are self-help books for that if you need them. I have never belonged to an investment club, but I imagine that would work too, just like Alcoholics Anonymous. If you have a gambling tendency, you will have to get rid of it, or get very good at it like Elon. He is like the roulette winner picking the correct number four times.

Growth & Total World Capital

Four of the people on Forbes Top Ten ranking for 2013 were Walton's. If added together, their wealth would be more than twice that of any other person on the list.

Forbes Top 10 Ranking for 2013

rank	investor	worth $B	source	Δ 2012	%Δ
1	Bill Gates	$72	Microsoft	$6	8.3%
2	Warren Buffett	$58.50	Berkshire	$12.50	21.4%
3	Larry Ellison	$41	Oracle	0	0.0%
4	Charles Koch	$36	Diversified	$5	13.9%
4	David Koch	$36	Diversified	$5	13.9%
6	C. Walton fam.	$35.40	Wal-Mart	$7.50	21.2%
7	Jim Walton	$33.80	Wal-Mart	$6.70	19.8%
8	Alice Walton	$33.50	Wal-Mart	$7.20	21.5%
9	S. Robson Walton	$33.30	Wal-Mart	$7.20	21.6%
10	M. Bloomberg	$31	Bloomberg	$6	19.4%

The total rate of increase of their wealth is even more striking at $28.6 billion over the previous year, an average growth over 21% after taxes. If your wealth grew 21% a year, you would soon be wealthy too. Starting with $100,000, after 12 years you would have a million dollars, after 24 years 10 million, and if you can keep going 48 years you would have a billion dollars. No one actually keeps such a steady pace of above normal growth, of course. After a century it would produce a net worth of 10 trillion, and after just another 12 years 100 trillion.

Currently the total world capital is $118 trillion. [57] One might theoretically grow by acquiring a larger share up to that point. Once one owns the world, then the growth rate is limited to what the world economies can sustain.

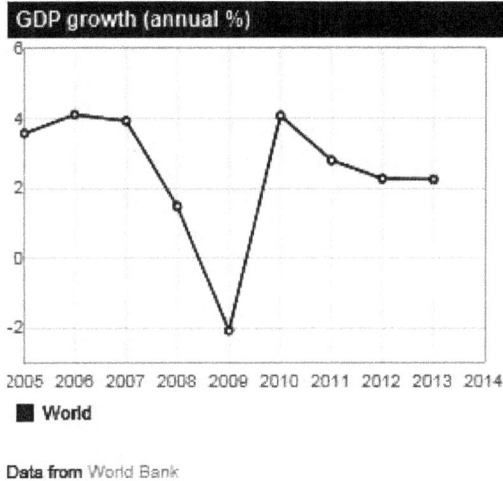

GDP growth (annual %)

World

Data from World Bank

As you can see from the preceding chart, the world economic growth rate typically fluctuates between 2% and 4%. Since the 2009 dip to -2% it has been hovering at the low end of that range. This low growth rate causes high unemployment not only in the U.S. but even more so in Ukraine, Libya, Syria and other trouble spots, leading to wars of desperation or wars to obtain a neighbor's wealth. Usually when there is a drop to negative growth, in following years there is excess or above-average growth, so that the average rate catches up. You can see the world never caught up from the financial crisis of 2009. People who lost out have been under strain for a long time and it is breaking things. They are breaking things. Most people don't leave good jobs to fight wars over ideology.

The highest individual country growth rates, other than following a dramatic drop the year before, are only about 10%, and only in small undeveloped countries. The U.S. growth rate closely matches the world growth rate, not only because we account for a large share of the world, but also we buy from and sell to the world. The only large nation with a consistently higher growth rate is China, and we know that at least some of their reporting is misleading, such as construction projects which remain unoccupied.

I guess the Walton's will have to settle for lower growth once they take over the world. Exactly how they get higher growth in the meantime is an interesting puzzle. Some of which is accounted for by strategies you can use. But if they wish, they also have access to private capital markets. In theory, private capital markets should do better, but a minimum wealth is required by regulation for one to enter private capital markets and the risk of loss is great. Most of the Walton's wealth is in equity, that is stock, and increases faster because of the equity premium, which we'll discuss in later chapters. In a nutshell, stocks do better than bonds or savings accounts, but only over long periods, and best of all when an entire economy is represented in the portfolio, not just a few handpicked companies. The theory of private capital is different, however, as it utilizes not only handpicked companies, but those whose stock is not yet available to the public.

What we can get from this chapter is, I think, that wealth usually involves:

- A family habit and a good start (some exceptions, but we haven't run across them)

- Rapid growth, at least more rapid than the economy generally

- A sense of how long to hold on to things and when to start something new

- Being in the right place at the right time, which might be partly maneuvering but also partly luck (as in Elon's failed day at Netscape)

Origins & Methods of the Forbes 10

There are wealthy people living near you, perhaps on the same block and you do not know it. On my ordinary little street of small three bedroom houses built 40 years ago, a low profile couple died a few years ago. They had no children and both worked. It was discovered they owned millions of dollars worth of stock.

We can find news articles about people who had surprising and unknown wealth, perhaps leaving a hundred million or more to their favorite charity. I don't count these stories for much because I don't know how unusual they are. But when people in my neighborhood turn out to be wealthy, without the usual trappings such as inherited wealth or some high level job, it tells me that it is an attainable goal.

However, we do not have much information on these people, and I personally do not necessarily aspire to be like them. I would rather have a little more of a voice in the world, which probably explains why I've gone to the trouble to write several books. I do not necessarily aspire to be like the very wealthiest people either, but there is a lot of information about them, and because they have become so unusually wealthy, looking at their origins and methods may provide us some understanding of the factors that produce wealth and power. These factors must have been distilled to their essence in these people.

In order to control for selection bias, I'll take names from an established list, the Forbes Top 10 of 2013 in the previous chapter. If I just pick people I randomly think of, I might be attracted to certain personality types that would skew the conclusions. While there are ten people on this list, there are only six families, which is the way I'll organize them, starting like Letterman from the bottom of the list.

Michael Bloomberg's path
(Mayor of NYC, investment banker, business information provider)

Bloomberg is the grandson of immigrants from Russia on one side and Belarus on the other. His father was a real estate agent, who apparently had enough money to send him to college, and of course Michael must have had the smarts to get admitted. He has an electrical engineering degree from John Hopkins (which surprised me, I have an EE degree and most EE's are not rich), and an MBA from Harvard (ah, that explains it). Within seven years of graduating he was a partner at Salomon Brothers investment bank. When it was bought by Philbro he was given a $10 million dollar severance package. He would have been in his mid-to-late-30's about then, at a reasonable peak of personal energy and understanding of the business world.

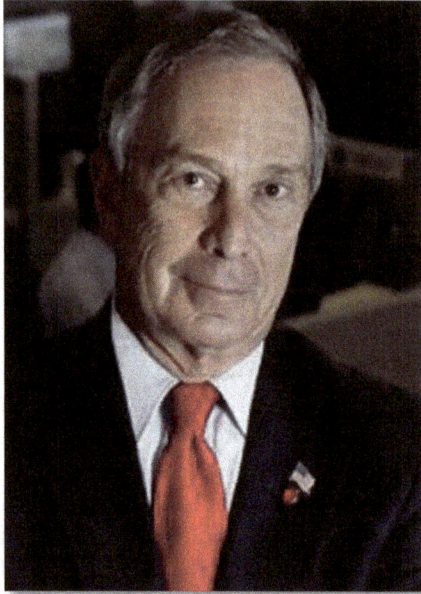

Michael Bloomberg
Wikimedia commons

He decided to become an information provider to the financial world and started Bloomberg News. Merrill Lynch became the first customer and invested $30 million. Exactly how he got from there to a net worth of $30 billion is not clear to me, but he wrote an autobiography which you can read if you are curious. At that point he resigned the CEO job and entered politics.

I have found less information and have fewer observations on Bloomberg than any of the others. It would be pointless to comment on that before comparing to the others, so I'll save my speculation until the end.

Sam Walton
(Wal-Mart)

Do you think the Walton's want to take over the world?

I cannot answer for them, but I can say that Sam Walton's actions suggest he might have had a large share of the world in mind. I infer that from his tactics, which I assume he got from his father. By now you know that I assume heavily that people will behave in a manner they learned from their family, consciously or unconsciously. The reasons why people do these things are not my concern. They may not even be aware of it. I haven't interviewed any of them and I am not assigning motives, just observing connections.

Sam Walton in high school yearbook
Wikimedia commons, from un-copyrighted source

Yes Sam did come off the farm, so to speak, but not in the way the expression usually implies. His father gave up farming because it didn't make enough money. So his father was more ambitious than he was tied to tradition. Sam would have been very familiar with farmers and the small towns of America, but wouldn't necessarily have identified with them. Sam's father Thomas left farming in 1923 and returned to a previous job in his brother's company, Walton Mortgage Company. So there was a family history in a financial business. Sam graduated from high school 13 years later in 1936, in the middle of the Great Depression. What Thomas Walton was actually doing from 1929 to 1936 was repossessing farms.

We do not need to have a lot of detail to understand what this was likely to have been like. My mother was in the 1960s still telling stories about people who bought property in tax sales during the depression, right along with how they kept their wives tied up in the attic. Probably the man was simply protecting her from being killed by the people who disliked him. Hopefully Thomas' wife Nancy had no such problems. We haven't heard of them. Sam got along well enough in high school to have been voted "Most Versatile." He would have absorbed a lot about finance and bankruptcy from his father and uncle, just as I absorbed electronics and engineering from mine. Perhaps more importantly, he would have been exposed to many different personalities in that business, and among the people they dealt with, just as my father's associates made strong impressions on me. He probably liked some of them and disliked others. We aren't privy to the Walton's family conversations.

Sam did leave a memoir, *Made in America*. He had just finished but not yet published it when he died. It is "light on biography" and contains a defense of accusations he ran the competition out of town.

Ah, two reactions to that:

- It does not matter whether he *intentionally* ran other merchants out of town. He did it, over and over and over. He was willing to keep doing it. It wasn't a one time thing. He didn't take any corrective action. He may as well have intended it. Any defense is empty before it starts. I'm not saying good or bad (yet), just that he cannot talk his way out of it.

- He didn't run other merchants out of town exactly. He ran them out of business. They either went bankrupt, or voluntarily ceased operations because they realized they were going to go bankrupt. In other words, he did the same thing his father did for a living, bankrupted people, just on a much grander scale.

Your takeaway point is that to get really wealthy, you have to be willing to take it away from others. You do not need to do it as aggressively as Sam Walton. You do not need to be as rich as he was. But at the very least, you have to be willing to hold more wealth than other people have, otherwise you will be compelled to give it away until you are no longer wealthy. If you think you are going to end poverty on Earth, go for it, but this book will not help. Even Jesus could not figure that one out, saying "*The poor will be with you always.*"

Maybe Sam started in small towns because that's where he was. That's what he knew. The effect of it, once he got going, is that the competition did not have deep pockets. Many of the stores in small towns were specialized - clothing, toys, hardware. Their suppliers were middlemen. This allowed a depth of expertise and, as I recall, assistance in these stores was legendary. But if even 20-30% of their business was captured by lower prices on a smaller selection of inferior merchandise at a "general" shop-for-yourself store, that would be enough to undermine their profit margins and send them into retirement.

Probably Sam Walton believes as he wrote in his memoir. His motivations were positive. He was helping people by providing better products and services and wider selection at affordable prices. He was helping people by providing better products and services. This is true. Wal-Mart remains a very useful store. I shop there a lot.

When I was a kid growing up, there were no Wal-Marts and until I was in high school there were not even discount stores. Many of my friends' parents owned or worked at local stores. The store owners would sponsor awards for students and promote community activities in a way that Wal-Mart does not. Will my son's friends' parents work at Wal-Mart? It seems likely. And what will my son do for a living?

Sam graduated in 1940 from the University of Missouri with an Economics degree. He had been in ROTC and, since World War II was ongoing, he served until 1945. With a $20,000 loan from his father and $5000 saved from his army salary, Sam purchased a Ben Franklin variety store in a small town in Arkansas. This was interesting to me because my uncle, John Sloan, owned a chain of Ben Franklin variety stores in neighboring Mississippi. I remember going into them when I was very young. They were large, well stocked stores. I can definitely see them as a precursor to Wal-Mart. I do not remember going into them when I was older because uncle John worked himself to death, dying of a heart attack at age 49. This is another takeaway point. You must have the physical constitution for whatever path to success you choose to follow in life, or you will not live to enjoy it.

Sam's leaseholder would not renew. He wanted Sam's successful location for himself and his own son. So Sam sold the inventory and fixtures and bought a new location in Bentonville, where Wal-Mart's headquarters are today.

Sam actually had two stores, 220 miles apart. That was quite a bit farther than my uncle's stores, and Sam was forced to learn to delegate. I'm not sure "learning to delegate" is the right word. I have had that trouble myself and see it in practically every manager I ever worked for. When you don't take care of things yourself, or at least monitor them closely, they fall apart. It must be something else, like learning who to delegate to, or how to set up goals and rewards? I frankly do not know and do not ever expect to acquire this bit of wisdom. But it might be the reason why Sam lived and my uncle didn't. My uncle was constantly running between stores.

One trick Sam and his brother (who helped him) used was to encourage managers to invest in an equity stake in the business. As much as $1000. It doesn't sound significant, but it would be about $8000 today. The strategy could be part of the trick of delegating and motivating others. Another thing to notice is that Sam had a trusted helper in his brother.

I have never found such a helper for longer than the duration of a particular project, usually a few months. The method of investing I will cover in later chapters will be much slower than Sam's method, or that of any of the other biographies, but it will not require helpers, delegating, skills at electronics and programming, etc.

As for "made in America," presumably Sam was referring to his fortune. Eventually, after his death, this store chain based on the lowest prices sought out the lowest cost supplier, communist China, with its child and prison labor, pollution, and absence of living standard or worker benefits. This wasn't Sam's decision I'm sure. It was a consequence, an inevitable consequence, of his business model. In a later chapter we'll look more closely at unexpected, or unintended consequences.

The Koch Brothers
(David and Charles, sons of Fred, Koch Industries)

Their great grandfather was German ship owner Johan Anthon Koch. Someone back in the family must have been a cook, because *koch* is the German word for cook.

Johan shipwrecked near the Dutch town of Workum and married the mayor's daughter, having 8 children, 6 of whom survived childhood. One of them, Harry Koch, worked as a printer's apprentice and came to the U.S. in 1888. Two years later he moved to an east Texas railroad town and bought one of the local newspapers. He also was a founding shareholder of a railroad line. How he saved this much money out of a printer's salary, I do not know. He promoted libertarian politics and his own railroad in his newspaper, and did not like Franklin Roosevelt. He did not like trade unions, retirement pensions, or bank regulation. You can see where this is going already, if you know anything about the Koch brothers.

Harry had two sons, Anton who continued in the newspaper business, and Fred who went to Rice and then to MIT to study chemical engineering. Fred worked in Port Arthur, for a time in England, and then joined a former MIT classmate named Keith in Keith-Winkler Engineering in Kansas. Keith left and it became Koch-Winkler Engineering. Where you go to school determines who your associates are, and sometimes their business success becomes yours. This is why so many families are so desperate for their sons and daughters to go to Harvard or Yale, not necessarily because the education is markedly different there. For Engineering MIT was the equivalent of Harvard, located near Harvard in fact, and educating many of America's future leading scientists and engineers.

At Koch-Winkler Fred developed an efficient cracking process that allowed small refiners to compete with larger players. The larger players filed 44 lawsuits. While Fred eventually prevailed, Koch-Winkler was meanwhile effectively barred from the U.S. market. Fred went to the Soviet Union during the height of our depression between 1928 and 1932 and built 15 cracking plants there (refineries). So there is a connection between Koch and Russia's industrial base and oil economy today in the 21st century.

Fred did not like communism. This did not keep him from working for the Russians and taking their money. He came to feel that the methods of communism posed a threat to America. Many of the Bolshevik engineers he worked with were later purged. Fred helped found the John Birch Society (JBS), a conservative anti-communist political group in the U.S. that still functions. The JBS was often mentioned when I was growing up in the 1960s. Some people were more afraid of it than the communists, as it became associated with the fringe American right-wing. Koch wrote: *"The colored man looms large in the Communist plot to take over America."* He thought the communists wanted to *"get a vicious race war started."* He thought welfare was a secret plot to attract blacks to eastern cities to vote for communist causes.

Fred Koch
Wikimedia commons

There is no doubt that in any democracy since democracy was invented (almost certainly in the unknown past before writing and historical records, since primitive tribal organization often features a council and election of leaders), there are schemes, secret or not, to manipulate demographics and policy to get more votes. No one denies that. But no trace of communist plotting on welfare legislation has ever been found. And it is not as if people didn't look for it, for example Senator Joe McCarthy. But if Fred had friends and coworkers in Russia who had been purged, he would naturally be a little paranoid. When I first traveled to Ukraine and Russia to find a wife, my family thought I would possibly not safely return, and that was in 2010-2012, after the fall of communism in Russia. Welfare was no doubt conceived in response to the policies of communism, to head off unrest among the poorer classes in western countries.

We had a depression going on here, and the government of a major European power had been toppled by rousing the downtrodden peasants to revolt. Most of the countries of the world implemented some degree of socialism in response, to head off problems. Businessmen feel threatened by either socialism or communism. Russia had nationalized industries and re-educated or killed the upper class and business class. Fred had been there. I can understand that he would feel threatened. He was also under attack in the courts in the U.S. by sniping large corporations trying to squelch technology he had invented. Wouldn't you feel a little paranoid?

In 1940 Fred created the company which would become Koch industries. (By then he was too old to be drafted into World War II.) His sons Charles and David each own 42% of that company. Charles is CEO and board chairman. David is executive vice president.

Charles also studied chemical engineering at MIT. He wrote a book on Market-Based Management called *The Science of Success*. It is really more about organizational management than markets, and has five main *"dimensions."* These are *"vision, virtue and talents, decision rights, incentives, and knowledge processes."* He thinks Wall Street causes public firms to be too focused on quarterly profits, and so he has kept Koch Industries private. He also thinks public firms attract lawyers and lawsuits, and are over regulated. He says Warren Buffett and George Soros *"simply haven't been sufficiently exposed to the ideas of liberty."* In 2011 he wrote in an opinion piece in the Wall Street Journal:

> *"Government spending on business only aggravates the problem. Too many business have successfully lobbied for special favors and treatment by seeking mandates for their products, subsidies (in the form of cash payments from the government), and regulations and tariffs to keep more efficient competitors at bay. Crony capitalism is much easier than competing in an open market. But it erodes our overall standard of living and stifles entrepreneurs by rewarding the politically favored rather than those who provide what consumers want."*

His brother David is not simply a carbon copy, and though they get along well now they didn't always. Some of you may have seen a recent interview with Barbara Walters. He described himself as socially liberal and fiscally conservative. He supports gay rights, but wants to balance the national budget. Many people were critical of Barbara's "softball" interview (gee, that's what she does for a living, softball interviews!) but she did point out he financially supports the fiscal conservatives as a priority over fiscal liberals who are also social liberals. For the record, any list of David's accomplishments focuses on his charitable contributions to various organizations where social liberals are likely to hang out, so I think he accurately described himself. The apparent contradictions are forced by American politics.

It is clear that children in this family follow closely in the business and political views of their parents. It is also clear they make changes from time to time, to move to a location where they can make more money (even doing business with the Russians), or expressing their unique slant on things, like David's gifts to liberal-associated organizations.

Larry Ellison
(CEO Oracle Corp.)

If you don't really know what Oracle does, you are not alone. The reason is that their products and services, mostly large database software and hardware, are sold only to businesses. In the 1970s there was IBM and an array of companies competing with more user friendly and capable database services that were easier to program. My first full time job was to set up one of these databases. I did not care for it and moved on to something else. I was peripherally aware that Oracle eventually won the competition, but I have no idea why. Their products appeared just as stodgy and difficult as IBM's to me.

Larry was the son of an unmarried mother and an air force pilot and was put up for adoption. Considering that Steve Jobs was also adopted, we find there are no impediments to the financial success of adopted children. Larry is the 3rd richest man in America and 5th richest in the world. Maybe I should have stuck with the relational database systems?

His adoptive father made a small fortune in Chicago real estate, but lost it in the Great Depression. Apparently there was enough money to send Larry to college and he attended University of Illinois at Urbana-Champaign, dropping out near the end of his second year when his mother died. Then he attended one term at University of Chicago before moving to northern California. That is a code phrase for somewhere near Silicon Valley. He worked for Amdhal Corp. and then for Ampex which was doing a database for the CIA.

In 1977 he founded one of those small relational database companies that I mentioned which renamed itself a few times eventually becoming Oracle. Larry wanted to be compatible with IBM's System R database system, but IBM wouldn't give up the code. In 1990 while I was exploring the frustrations and higher salary of management, Oracle nearly went broke. There were lawsuits associated with overstating earnings. In the next few years several companies other than IBM dominated the database market for the new mid-sized and smaller computers. IBM took its eye off the ball with regard to smaller computers, as is well documented. But Oracle was not the leader. Sybase was.

Ellison's yacht Rising Sun
Wikimedia commons

Sybase lost focus in a 1996 merger and then sold the Windows version of its database system to Microsoft. This is now Microsoft SQL Server. Informix took over the rest of Sybase and became Oracle's main competitor. In 1997 Informix revealed a revenue shortfall and the CEO was imprisoned. IBM absorbed their business. Oracle was the clearly dominant player for a few years, but IBM and Microsoft remain strong competitors. While Larry's approximately million dollar salary is enviable, it accounts for little of his wealth. By 2010 he was collecting only a nominal $1 a year. In college we always used to talk about rumors that certain professors had a lot of patents and were dollar-a-year men. I don't think any of it was true. But here it turns out the third richest man in the country is a dollar-a-year man.

However, Larry was paid seven million stock options several years in a row. He must have sold some of that stock to diversify as he now has large holdings in biotech, pharmaceuticals, and 98% of the Hawaiian Island of Lanai. In other words, while he got a good start from his salary and a better boost from stock options, Larry made the final leg of his trip onto the Forbes Top Ten through investing.

But at the root seems to have been the move to northern California. I was never willing to do that. Too far away. Too high a cost of living. I don't even like the Silicon Valley area.

By the way, Lanai is not some micro-island. It once produced 3/4 of the world's pineapples, and has two luxury resort hotels. Larry's adoptive father took the name Ellison after his point of entry into the United States at

Ellis Island. Now on the other side of the world Ellison's Island is Lanai. It is the 6th largest Hawaiian island at 140 square miles, and has a peak elevation of 3,366 feet.

Warren Buffett
(Berkshire-Hathaway)

For a while Warren was the richest man in America. He's certainly one of the most public and well known. In reading books about him one sort of gets the impression he came out of nowhere as a financial genius, or perhaps he learned it from Benjamin Graham. That is not so.

Warren's grandparents Ernest and Henrietta owned a grocery store. They were business people. They had French origins as you might guess from the name Buffett, but came from Huguenots and were Protestants, in fact Presbyterians.

The impulse to ascend the scale of human evolution seems to have been strong in Warren's father Howard, who started a small stock brokerage. As a kid Warren spent time in a regional stock exchange near his father's office. It has been my observation that one of the root causes of career floundering today is that kids are not able to hang around where their parents are working as farm boys did, or nearly anyone did up until the mid-20th century. I received a severe reprimand for invading my father's place of business one day to converse with the programmer there. But the influences on young Warren did not end with exposure to stock brokering.

Howard served on the school board, getting a taste of political wrangling and influence. He ran for Congress in 1942 as a Republican and was considered a "sacrificial lamb" during the Roosevelt administration. But he won! Sounds a lot like today's politics. The more I learn about politics in America, the more it seems that it repeats the same themes over and over. People who are aghast at the levels of animosity today are forgetting that not long ago we fought a Civil War, which occasioned the first national budget over one billion dollars, and which was the first war using submarines and other mechanized engines of destruction.

Howard was not just a Republican but a libertarian, and also an advocate of the gold standard. [58] According to his biographer Roger Lowenstein, he was "Unshakably ethical, ... refused offers of junkets and even turned down a part of his pay." His wife said he considered only one issue when deciding whether or not to vote for a bill: "Will this add to, or subtract from, human liberty?" Apparently Charles Koch had not checked his facts when he alleged that Warren had not been exposed to the concepts of liberty. Here is what Howard said about war:

> *"Even if it were desirable, America is not strong enough to police the world by military force. If that attempt is made, the*

blessings of liberty will be replaced by coercion and tyranny at home. Our Christian ideals cannot be exported to other lands by dollars and guns. Persuasion and example are the methods taught by the Carpenter of Nazareth, and if we believe in Christianity we should try to advance our ideals by his methods. We cannot practice might and force abroad and retain freedom' at home. We cannot talk world cooperation and practice power politics."

"When the American government conscripts a boy to go 10,000 miles to the jungles of Asia without a declaration of war by Congress (as required by the Constitution) what freedom is safe at home? Surely, profits of U.S. Steel or your private property are not more sacred than a young man's right to life." [59]

Howard Buffett spent four terms as a U.S. Congressman, and took his family to Washington with him, including Warren, who graduated from high school there with the annotation on his class photo *"likes math; a future stockbroker."* They might not have been rich, but Warren was close to power and, like young Sam Walton, must have absorbed the ways of power from his environment and his father's associates.

After a degree in business administration Warren tried and failed to get into the MBA program at Harvard. Instead he went to Columbia and studied economics. He says that knowing Benjamin Graham and David Dodd taught there influenced him. Columbia is to economics what MIT is to engineering. My friend Rajnish Mehra who discovered the equity premium puzzle got his PhD from Columbia. I met Rajnish at Rice where he was at the time studying electrical engineering. The first book I ever wrote was on the equity premium, not on electrical engineering, or even physics in which I've done some novel work. The people you meet in school make a lot of difference. I don't actually know a physicist or engineer that has a stature in those fields comparable to Mehra, so my first breakthrough was in economics.

Buffett wanted to work on Wall Street but Graham refused to hire him. So Warren returned to Omaha to work as a stockbroker and investment adviser. He also began to teach investing classes even though he had no particular track record at this time.

Many books have been written about Buffett and you may have read one of them, as have I. What can we distill out of it? The first dozen years did not entail rapid progress. By 1962 he was only just becoming a millionaire. The way he did it though not overly rapid, was significant. He mostly used other people's money. The story of his partnerships is legend, and in my opinion not only financially important but also psychologically important. Warren was practicing his skills at persuading other people to go along with his schemes. Now his following is cult-like.

Continuing in this vein, he used the partnership money to buy a lot of stock in a particular company which made maps and also held other investments. He then pointed out to the other investors their stock was trading for less than the value of the investments they held, and the map business was counted as nothing. This got him appointed to the board. So from very early, Warren did not make money by picking companies and trading their stock on public exchanges. He made money by persuading other people to do things, and taking over companies either to restructure them, or for their cash flow.

In 1965 Buffett's partnerships began aggressively acquiring Berkshire Hathaway at under $15 a share, knowing that the company had working capital amounting to $19 a share. How he found this out and no one else knew it or took advantage of it is a mystery to me. I'm not sure I will ever believe any simple version of it. Warren actually claimed the textile business had been his worst trade, and began selling off the mills, moving into the insurance business, and using Berkshire as a holding company to acquire other companies.

Warren Buffett doesn't just own a jet, he owns NetJets
Wikimedia commons

Companies generate a lot of money. The shareholders never see most of it. It gets spent theoretically on growing the business, but in truth management's inspiration on growing the business is usually either to buy more locations to do the same thing, or to try something new they know nothing about and fail. Meanwhile most of the money gets wasted on corporate jets and other executive perks. Warren does not believe in paying any dividends at all. He takes over whole companies though, so that he can control all the excess cash they generate. This is what he likes about the insurance business.

In other words, Warren *does not allow* the companies that he acquires to do as he does, and not pay out their cash. Isn't that interesting? The lesson I take away is to do as he does and acquire cash from companies when possible, not to do as he says and permit management to keep it all. He only advocates that when he is the management.

The one area in which I recommend modifying the strategy deduced from study of the equity premium is to include cash generating companies, or indexes [125] which pay dividends. I do not trust all-growth. There is too much risk one bad manager may squander or even steal the accumulated profits. I know for a fact I will not sense the "right time to sell." I would rather write physics papers or fantasy novels than worry about timing the exit of my investments. My friend Rajnish Mehra invests primarily in income producing investments, not growth investments, even though he discovered the equity premium.

By the way, Buffett does invest in some companies that remain public, including Coca Cola, Wells Fargo and IBM (but not Microsoft). Coke pays a respectable dividend of 2.8%, Wells Fargo 2.7%, and IBM 2.8%.

Warren comes from a family that appears to have noble ideals. Some of the tactics he has used, such as the breakup of Berkshire-Hathaway, resemble the methods of the hated restructuring artists of the 1980s. Maybe this is why Warren said that he felt Berkshire was his "worst trade?" He could have created a new holding company. Maybe he didn't like selling off pieces of a company. He did not repeat the pattern of restructuring companies, that I know of. I'm guessing at his motives of course.

In dealing with Warren's companies (NetJets, GEICO) I find that they are pretty much run like any other company in their industry. When my wife ran off the pavement in the grocery store parking lot, misjudging the position of the front wheels, and invoked our roadside assistance coverage to have a tow truck return the car to the pavement to avoid damage (and there was no damage), GEICO recorded it as an accident claim and raised our rates. We now have Allstate and only carry the state minimum. I am convinced that insurance companies intend to profit by not paying claims and using every excuse to overcharge. Warren's GEICO is no different.

Bill & Melinda Gates
(Microsoft, the Bill & Melinda Gates Foundation)

William H. Gates II (now Sr.) was a prominent attorney in Seattle, and also a philanthropist. It is impossible to become noted for giving away a lot of money (philanthropy) unless one has a lot of money to begin with.

Mary Maxwell Gates was on the University of Washington board of regents, the board of the First Interstate Bank of Washington, and was the first woman to chair the national United Way's executive committee. Her various activities are much too numerous to mention. She has a degree from the University of Washington where she met and married law student William H. Gates II. At one point she served on a United Way national campaign with some IBM people, and it is sometimes speculated Bill's IBM connection may have come from there, or at least some family knowledge of IBM's organization and who to contact.

The product of their marriage was the boy-faced man who wanted his software to control every desktop computer in the world, who became and still is the richest American, and who was the richest man in the world up until just this week, Bill Gates. (Gates and Carlos Slim have changed places several times.) He may have dropped out of Harvard (hey, he got in Harvard at least!) but he sure didn't start from nothing. And that he would end up as a philanthropist seems, in retrospect, utterly predictable despite his aggressive business persona that might have led you to believe otherwise if you were one of his competitors, or even one of his customers.

Bill Gates at 59 still looks boyish
Simon Davis/DFID via Wikimedia commons

Early talent and character

Bill's first computer program was tic-tac-toe written in BASIC. The computer time had been bought with donations from the Mother's Club, which I gather is something like a PTA. When the time was used up, Bill and three other guys including Paul Allen hacked the system to get more time. They were caught and banned from using the computer. When the ban ended, the boys offered to find and fix the bugs in the code that they had exploited.

So Bill was a hacker. It is no wonder then that Windows is so friendly to hackers. Thereafter he and Allen and sometimes the other guys took several jobs, including one for the school administrators, at 17 years of age, which involved writing the program to schedule the school's classes. He arranged for it to schedule him in classes with a large number of interesting girls. Apparently the guy never played on the level. Sure it's "cute" in a high school student, but he was hugely rewarded for his computer gimmicks and I see no negative experiences in his record that would have prompted reform. Gates wrote: "*It was hard to tear myself away from a machine at which I could so unambiguously demonstrate success.*" [60]

These guys who used the school computer to set themselves up with girls are the guys we trust to safeguard our financial account data on our PCs? Certainly youth pranks are normal. What concerns me is that Bill and Paul were rewarded with jobs, and that their pattern of behavior repeated. Do you know of any personal anecdote that Bill ever told that indicated he had "grown up" and out of this phase? Is it possible part of his business strategy would have been to exploit his total control of our PCs to his advantage? I think it was more likely inevitable.

We'll explore his business strategy in a moment. Certainly Bill and Paul seem likeable and not evil in any way. Most of my friends in high school were into sports, not computers or electronics. I enjoyed them but I had to accommodate their interests. I met friends like Bill's in the science fair, but they lived too far away in other towns to spend time together. And having such friends, whether a brother or a childhood prank-mate, we have already seen is key to success - but not only "success." It is a key to simply getting the most out of life.

I can relate to Bill's early exploits. I am a little older, so computers were not available in high school. In 1966 I declared I was going to make a computer for a science fair project. My parents wondered how the heck I was going to figure that out, and frankly I did too, but I studied some books on arithmetic circuits and came up with transistors wired on green-painted pegboards, a big relay, and a row of red lights (painted with nail polish) to show the results. Unimpressive now, but it was good for 1966 and I won a week-long trip with it.

By college we had computers and a group of us did figure out how to enter the system privileged mode, but we did not do anything so clever as scheduling classes with girls. I had all the computer time I wanted when the night operator would declare the machine broken and go home (often), as I had figured out how to get it to work even when he couldn't. It just had a few faulty switches on the front panel that could be bypassed if one knew how.

Education or lack thereof

After reading a Popular Science article about the Altair 8800, Gates dropped out of Harvard to start a computer software company with Allen. His parents were supportive. I cannot even imagine what mine would have said if I'd dropped out of college for any reason. I felt I had great parents but they would not have been supportive. They would have been nervous as heck about failure, and would have advised me that I'd regret the lack of a college degree no matter how successful I became. What would your parents have said?

I had an economics professor my sophomore year who directly advised us that we would obtain greater wealth by dropping out of college and investing the cost of the college education. The trouble with that was, no one was going to give me the cost of my college education to invest. That was considered gambling, and despite the books my dad was reading, I realized no one in the family knew how to invest. My uncle John with the Ben Franklin stores had already died from overwork trying to run a business. The culture and trajectory of a family makes a lot of difference in whether one is able to reach billionaire status. However, many people can become wealthy, and from that position you can lay the groundwork for your children to be on the Forbes list, if you wish it, by following the examples here.

I'm not adverse to dropping out of college to go into business, partly because of my economics professor, partly because I have had some success at writing physics papers even though I have only had a few formal courses in physics and no degree in it. Even difficult academic things can be done without the degree, and in fact Einstein did not have a PhD and was not working as a physicist when he wrote his three famous 1905 papers. However, I labor endlessly to make up for the lack of a degree in physics, reading hundreds (maybe thousands) of technical papers and bouncing my ideas around with friends and colleagues (mostly on ResearchGate). I also have the benefit of having an advanced degree in the related field of electrical engineering, holding several patents and having published many papers in that field.

By contrast, Bill has formal training neither in business nor in computer science. He is missing, perhaps, some of the fine points of business ethics (assuming "business ethics" is not an oxymoron), about which I can mostly just speculate because I do not have a business degree. However I have an electrical engineering degree which was at that time mostly computer science already, and I can say definitely what is missing from that standpoint.

DOS and Windows are both terribly unsophisticated, not only by modern theoretical standards but by the standards of their day. Time-sharing and security had both been fully studied in the early 1970s, a decade before DOS was written. Viruses were already known and had been spread by removable media. I seriously doubt any company would hire a programmer or designer, much less a project manager, who was not trained and well versed in these subjects. Bill's wife Melinda had a degree in computer science when she was hired by Microsoft. But Bill did not.

Not only did Bill not have the theoretical knowledge of how to make a system secure - something that is not as easily acquired by self-study as finding a security hole or solving an algorithm - he had a tendency to want to see what he could do with back-door software, like scheduling classes for himself. This, or something like it, led Microsoft to leave a lot of hooks in Windows so they could update it or control things in their favor. It eventually led him to bury browser features in the operating system so that Internet Explorer could not be removed. And it has given hackers a large number of opportunities to exploit by discovering the back doors that Microsoft created.

Bill's business strategy

86-DOS, referring to the 8086 Intel processor, was written by Tim Paterson in 6 weeks. It was essentially a clone of Digital Research's CP/M. I recall using CP/M and remember noticing later that it was identical to *PC DOS*.

Responding to a request from IBM for an operating system (OS) to run on the IBM PC, Microsoft bought 86-DOS for $75,000 and hired Tim Paterson in mid-1981. They developed several flavors of it. PC DOS ran on IBM PC's, and MSDOS on clone machines.

Remember Larry Ellison's desire to have compatibility with IBM's database system? For a time IBM controlled 80% of the computer market. Software was bundled with IBM's computers at no extra charge until a lawsuit by the Justice Department persuaded IBM to unbundle it in 1969. The Justice Department never actually won the lawsuit, but IBM operated under the severe handicap of this ongoing Federal antitrust lawsuit until 1983. Amdhal and other companies made IBM compatible computers, and they needed software to run.

DOS application (Lotus 123)
Wikimedia commons

Microsoft's MSDOS was an enabling platform. Other manufacturers could make PC's which were similar to IBM's PC, and use MSDOS. The point of compatibility for further applications then became the operating system software layer, not so much the actual hardware. So-called device drivers could be provided by manufactures of displays and modems and other devices to provide an application interface. All of a sudden, the former monopoly field of business computing was actually wide open.

This inspired many people to start companies to develop applications, such as...

- *WordPerfect* - Developed in 1979 for Brigham Young University, the authors retained the rights and formed a company to port it to MSDOS in 1982. It rapidly took over from applications such as WordStar and became a standard by 1989. Its use was required for file interchange in fields such as law where collaborative document production was important.

- *Lotus 1-2-3* - Lotus was founded in 1982, partly by personnel from VisiCorp, the distributors of Visicalc, to develop a spreadsheet program for MSDOS. Lotus 1-2-3 was highly innovative and captured the spreadsheet market just as WordPerfect had captured the word processing market.

Lotus 123 Spreadsheet for DOS:Release 4 DOS Software
$37.46
Was $49.95
or Best Offer

25% off

source eBay.com – DOS software still selling!

- *Stacker* - Early disk drives had capacities of a few megabytes and later a few tens of megabytes, just not enough, but processors rapidly became fast. Microsoft's software releases and larger applications were straining against high disk drive costs. Five Caltech graduates started a company to develop compression technology and in 1990 released Stacker, which performed this function in software, effectively doubling disk drive capacity.

- *Harvard Graphics* - This was one of the first programs to allow mixing text, graphics, charts and data from such programs as Lotus 1-2-3. It was the market leader through the late 1980s with 80% market share, and was extensively used in the office where I worked at the time.

Harvard Graphics 2.0 NEW OLD STOCK SEALED 1993 DOS 3.1 or WIN 3.1 SHIPS FAST
$9.98   1d 13h left (Wednesday, 2PM)
9 bids
$19.98
Buy It Now

source eBay.com – DOS or Windows, no bids though

- *PKZIP* - Floppy drives were much more constrained than hard drives, and data communications proceeded at the not-very-blazing speed of 9600 baud (roughly but not exactly bits per second - not bytes, bits). Several compression formats were developed for data transmission and offline storage and archival on file sharing services. The most popular was Phil Katz Zip (PKZIP) released in 1989. Phil obtained a patent. Zip became a standard.

- *Netscape Navigator* - Netscape was founded in 1994 to capitalize on the emerging World Wide Web. They developed a clone of the Mosaic browser developed by the National Center for Supercomputing Applications (NCSA) and initially called it Mozilla, for Mosaic-killer. Shortly the name was changed to Netscape. Release 4 supported Javascript and encryption and many other features we take for granted today. Within a year it was the dominant browser and everyone had a copy. Awkward teletype interfaces were replaced by this cool new graphical, hypertext interface and people began to build virtual worlds online, supported by new faster communications technology. The internet boom began in earnest.

Microsoft was differentiated from Apple in that it was an open system. Microsoft encouraged anyone to write any kind of software for it. Steve Jobs wanted a controlled user experience for the Mac. I remember looking into the Mac and being repulsed because there was no easy or affordable way to program it. One had to join an expensive developer association to get tools to develop for it, and the tools were expensive themselves. While a compiler didn't automatically come with MSDOS, they were cheap, fast and readily available, such as TurboPascal and later Boreland C. LISP and many exotic artificial intelligence languages were available for the PC, though sometimes the capabilities were more limited than for workstations.

Apple also made changes which rapidly broke old software. Microsoft was much slower to break old software, at least at first. In theory some old DOS programs can still run, although special means of accessing peripherals, keyboard input and the display don't work. Microsoft enabled both hardware and software vendors to cash in on the computer revolution that IBM had kept to itself for ages. The modern computer age was effectively born. In addition to the popular mass-market applications I have listed, thousands of commercial software packages, sometimes selling for thousands of dollars a copy, were developed for this open platform. Now I cannot consider going to a Mac or a Linux machine because I use several of these packages for chip design and programming, and they are only available for Windows.

Then Bill turned on the software developers that had made his operating system not only a success, but a required universal standard. Microsoft had been tinkering with its own applications since 1981, but they were not well developed in the DOS days. Windows was a new and very complex interface to program, even though it was a much easier interface to use. Microsoft was developing Windows and the applications for it jointly, sharing information between the groups, much like Apple had developed its closed system. Probably Microsoft was trying to copy Apple.

The effect was devastating on the ecosystem of the market:

- WordPerfect could not be immediately converted to use all the Windows features, while MS Word had years of co-development. It raced ahead of WordPerfect in popularity.

- The name of Microsoft's spreadsheet reveals that the strategy was hardly an innocent accident. Excel's symbol is the letters XL, which stand for "kill Lotus" much like Netscape's Mozilla killer.

- Harvard Graphics released a windows version in 1991 but never approached its old market share, and was replaced by PowerPoint which was "bundled" into Microsoft Office. It was impossible to be interoperable among applications in Windows in any practical way (via cut and paste) without adopting Microsoft's data formats, which it could change or obscure at will.

- In 1993 MSDOS included a disk compression program DoubleSpace, bundled IBM-like at no cost. How could Stacker compete with that? They couldn't. There was a patent lawsuit with claims and counter-claims. The jury found fault on both sides. The net result was in Stacker's favor and produced an investment in Stacker of $40 million by Microsoft, and additional payments in royalties of $43 million. Today, however, no one has heard of Stacker.

- Many people ripped off Phil Katz before Microsoft got the chance. It has often been speculated in the shareware industry that the alcoholism that caused his death may have been aggravated by the issue. I got an "open source" zip program from InfoZip, supposedly which did not use the PKZIP patents, and produced a Windows zip/unzip program because I was dissatisfied with how WinZip worked and I thought there should be a less expensive program available. By the release of Windows 98, Microsoft had included zip capability in its OS, though not turned on by default. With Windows 2000 it was, and sales of the other zip programs fell rapidly Even the dominant WinZip has vanished. This story illustrates that Microsoft is not the only villain, indeed just as teenage Bill Gates was neither the first nor the last hacker. But basically Microsoft and Bill are the biggest hackers. I had an application called Desktop Referee which Microsoft had the nerve to purchase a copy of without concealing their identity, and two years later the capability showed up in their OS.

- The contention between Netscape and Microsoft will probably be remembered by more readers. Netscape not only advertised that "the web is for everyone" but they intended to "level the playing field" among operating systems. This was very threatening to *Microsoft*, so M*icrosoft* "bundled" their own browser with Windows in 1995. By version 3 it was feature comparable with Netscape, and by version 4 it was more stable on Windows than other browsers. I will skip the lawsuit details. The gist is that Netscape as a company is no more. There is a group of never-say-die programmers maintaining and improving Firefox Mozilla for free. It is a pretty good browser. At home I still use Windows XP. It is much faster than Windows 7 and I like it better. Since it is no longer supported by Microsoft, I am using Firefox to write this book at Nookpress.com. I'm not even using MS Word!

I have retreated from the software business because I do not feel it is worth my time to fight so hard over computer programs which will be obsolete in a few years anyway. I would rather write books which I hope have more lasting value, and work on the problem of inertia and finding a simple explanation of curved space-time. Larry Ellison also had a very competitive life. I get the sense that the Koch's had it a bit easier as their father did most of the fighting (though I don't have detail on their own battles), and I admire Fred for taking away from big corporations rather than start-up entrepreneurs.

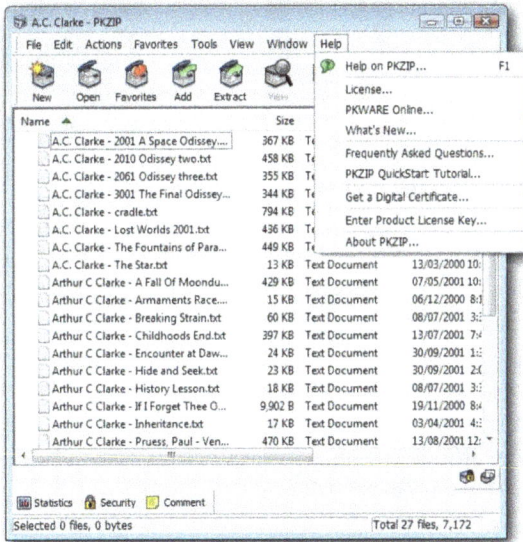

PK Zip - Windows version
source: pkware.com

Phillip Walter Katz programmer
Wikimedia commons

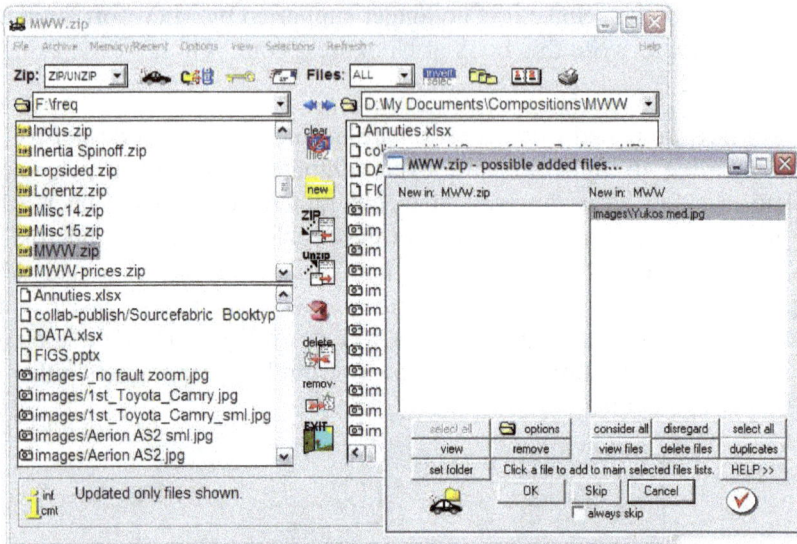

Zip-n-Go - the author's multi-folder zip and sync program

There was a limiting downside to Bill's strategy. It was a failure to realize who the real customers were, or maybe a jealousy of the real customers you could say. No one buys a computer to use its operating system except a developer. Microsoft's customers were application developers and hardware developers. But the incentives for Microsoft were unclear. On the one hand if a software developer selected their platform, they were paid very little directly by the developer, but primarily by the developer's own customers. Thus Microsoft came to view the end users as its customers, and undermined its developer clients. *You* can imagine how opposed hardware developers would be whenever Microsoft would experiment with marketing its own hardware.

After the success of coupling Word to the Windows platform, and later Internet Explorer, Microsoft began to change the basic structure of Windows faster and faster to give themselves an advantage. By changing it rapidly, other developers could not keep up with the changes. Microsoft pretended this was "innovation." Not all the changes were visible to users. Device drivers were made obsolete at each new release even if applications limped on. Printers, scanners, modems, digitizers, all kinds of cool devices were suddenly nonworking. Manufacturers and retailers were initially delighted. They could drop support on old devices and require users to buy new ones even when nothing was wrong with the old ones. Eventually sales of new Windows PCs dropped.

Lots of cool new devices like smart phones and tablets were developed. Microsoft's tablet flopped. Microsoft's phone flopped. No one would pile on and develop apps for a new Microsoft platform because they had been burned by Windows. The mass appeal apps were "confiscated" by the platform owner, Microsoft.

New big players like Google acquired their own platforms, such as Android, from start-up developers, just like Bill had acquired 86-DOS. Microsoft tried to develop a new interface for modern "apps" in Windows 8, but had to restore the old interface because it turned out all people want Windows for is to run their old legacy apps. This situation is unrecoverable because it is not due to technical flaws. It is due to the reputation of Microsoft with respect to competing with its customers. No other extremely wealthy man has walked away from his business in his prime the way Bill did. I believe the reason is because he figured out the situation was not salvageable.

The impact of Bill Gates

Microsoft's strategy didn't just affect itself. It set a style and precedent that was quickly adopted by other companies following the leader. Adobe, for example, has used automatic updates and the idea of providing a platform to not only take over the ad market (most ads use Adobe Flash), but to completely take away control of the user's PC from the user. Can you imagine a video playing on your PC and there is no OFF or PAUSE button? Well, try stopping an ad video. Try configuring Flash not to automatically play videos. It can't be done. If you disable Flash, you can't play YouTube videos.

Microsoft could easily stop this. For that matter any browser could provide an off button on any plug-in, on each specific instance of it. However, most of the browsers are enslaved to the requirement for complete visual compatibility with the Microsoft browser. So it would be up to Microsoft to stop it. And why do videos play on tabs that are not currently being viewed? They are useless. Is it a deliberate attempt to make me get a faster connection that can play multiple videos, in order not to slow web browsing? I suspect that instead it is because the advertisers can be charged for displaying multiple ads, even though the user cannot view them all.

For that matter, why does Windows run *any* code from the web or email without my authorization? It is not necessary. I could just click on any ad windows I wanted to animate. And then it should still be impossible for them to modify my hard drive, and they should be automatically stopped when I click on something else. PC web ads are like the old Outer Limits TV series which claims "*for the next hour we control your screen.*" Except that it is not limited to an hour. Given Bill's often quoted early desire to have his software run on every desktop, one has to wonder if he planned this? I emphasize again, I don't think Bill is evil, just clever and has the personality of a trickster.

It is almost impossible to imagine the computer world without Bill Gates. His impact has been both good and bad, like most people. One can easily imagine the computer world without Steve Jobs. It would be almost exactly like it is now, but without Apple. Without Bill, possibly IBM would have retained more licensing control of PC DOS and there would be fewer clones. They might have had their own operating systems, resulting in less of a universal platform to spur application development. My guess is that by the mid-1980s Intel's chips would be powerful enough to run Unix, and a Linux-like OS would have become the standard platform. Eventually it would have a graphical interface. The graphical interface was invented at Xerox PARC and both Apple and Microsoft simply appropriated it. That was Xerox's fault, as they were too attached to their paper document business to exploit it.

Regardless of what you think of Bill, removing him would, in my opinion, make a larger change to humanity's timeline than anyone else on our list. Although, Sam Walton is a close second, and second only because discount stores were already a trend. While PCs were a trend, a cross-vendor OS platform was not a serious trend, and that's what Bill did. The second thing he did, coupling the apps to the platform vendor in the style of Apple, was a giant step back toward being IBM-like. While Google to some extent has again uncoupled the apps, Google retains tight control of the apps, and runs its own advertising agenda much more aggressively than Microsoft. They also run the auto-update agenda more aggressively, forcing the obsolescence of both apps and devices. Bill's attitude of let the apps do whatever they want was not entirely bad. It had an element of liberty and freedom in common with the Koch's and Howard Buffett.

Family, retirement, philanthropy

Bill left Microsoft in 2008 and quit his post as chairman in 2014 to devote full time to the charity he and his wife Melinda founded in 2000, following in his father's and mother's footsteps as a renowned philanthropist. Bill is doing a lot of good in the world, and from reviewing his history and thinking about TV appearances I've seen, I imagine I'd quite enjoy spending an evening over dinner with him.

There were no women on the Forbes list. It was a controlled sample. I didn't pick them. There is of course Bill's wife Melinda, and it is obvious from the family histories that several women played key roles. Melinda was from Dallas Texas and was valedictorian of her class. She has a degree in computer science from Duke and an MBA. She was project manager of Microsoft Publisher, Microsoft Bob, Encarta and Expedia. They got married on Larry's island, Lanai, and have three daughters and a son. I'm sure a future generation will hear from them.

Recap

Helpful family background

Having some kind of helpful family background and consuming interest is a common thread. All these people kept most of their family characteristics and only made a few changes. No one in this club completely made themselves over.

Willing to take people's money

Being willing to take people's money is, well, a prerequisite, though most of the people here had some larger purpose in life and did not envision themselves as merely misers. In the next chapter we'll meet the richest man in the world in the mid-20th century and the world's first billionaire, who did consider himself a miser. Ruthless competition and willingness to lay employees off and shut competitors down, and viewing most everyone as a competitor, is a characteristic of at least 8 of the 10.

Changing the paradigm

Most of these people changed the typical pattern of how things were done, the so-called paradigm, or at least climbed on board a new paradigm very early. For some what they did is not so obvious. For example, lots of people climbed on the PC paradigm, the shift to PCs from mainframes, but Gates figured out how to enable 3rd party hardware and software vendors. There are lots of investment companies, most operating under the classification of investment company and are required to pay most of their earnings as dividends. Warren Buffett used an ordinary company like an investment company, perhaps at a tax disadvantage, but was not required to pay any dividends (and doesn't). Fred Koch enabled smaller refineries to compete. Sam Walton put big discount stores in smaller towns, and though he wasn't the only one he certainly had the biggest stores with the broadest selection. Bloomberg innovated several concepts in financial news delivery. Ellison was in the relational database paradigm very early, but like Walton, I'm not completely certain how his approach differed from others.

Connections

I promised to come back to Michael Bloomberg. It was hard to really see how he got his start, why other people invested so much money with him and how he parlayed it so quickly that he could retire to a political career while still young enough. All the others (in the case of the Waltons or Kochs, their fathers) except Gates could have been ordinary upper middle class people at the start. And Gates is fully explained, I think, both as to his origins and his methods.

Bloomberg is not fully explained. So I tentatively suggest that he must have had connections, probably through his family, that are not entirely obvious. It may not be so, but one would expect to find this somewhere, and among New York bankers is a likely place. I'll also mention in passing that the elder president Bush was son of a Wall Street banker and Senator from Connecticut, and likely got a rapid start in business from those connections, which enabled his family's subsequent political careers.

Still, it's heartening to realize that "connections" are not required or even evident for 90% of the Forbes list. Even if you didn't have the high powered start in life of most of those people, there is little preventing you from giving your children such a start if you are determined and have just a little luck. It appears connections are required to be both wealthy and have a career in politics, from our very limited sample anyway. If so, that only requires one more generation to set up.

Having a lead customer

Warren had his initial partners. Bill had IBM. Fred Koch had the Russians. Bloomberg had Merrill Lynch. Sam Walton had two successful stores branded by another chain. Ellison had the CIA. By a "lead" customer I mean not just a first customer, but a trendsetter who will lead other customers to follow.

Warren's initial partners were prominent physicians. IBM led to the clone PC makers. Fred's foreign clients would have meant credibility with domestic customers. Merrill Lynch was at that time the premier financial services company. A prominent and well liked store in one small town would lend credibility for hundreds of miles around. And how much more confident and high-tech can one get than building a database for the CIA?

Beyond America

If you were a wealthy merchant in Rome in about 300 AD, but knowing everything you know now, what would you have done?

You could go into Europe, but it was essentially a barbarian mess and degenerated into unstable fighting for centuries. Finally, in the Renaissance, businessmen and bankers again thrived. You would not even have been completely safe as a monk.

Probably you should wait 30 years for Emperor Constantine to found Constantinople, and open a branch in the new eastern capital. You could transfer one of your sons there to run your operations, and keep your family's options open. During the 300s it was not at first obvious whether the eastern or western regions would be the most stable. However, in 409 Alaric sacked Rome, and though the city remained, the western empire was doomed.

Your descendents in Constantinople would be relatively safe even through the Middle Ages and the rise of Islam, as the city never fell to the Arabs. The city was safe for over a thousand years, until 1453. Then somehow you would have to survive the arrival of the Turks and the Ottoman Empire Most likely you would send one son north, perhaps beyond the Balkans, to Moscow which wished to take up the banner of Rome, or toward the east to Iran or China. Your other son you might have sent closer, perhaps to a subsidiary of your business in Syria or Lebanon.

Each son would have to survive further upheavals of course, and probably not by hunkering down in one place. But if they kept working at your plan, one of them might someday be the richest person in the world, or at least in their part of the world. Would the new location have lasted until our present day? Let us imagine that this story is true, and see where your descendents wind up.

Lebanon to Mexico, Carlos Slim

The Lebanese merchant

In 1902 Khalil Salim Haddad Aglamaz emigrated from Lebanon to Mexico. He was 14. His reason for coming? It was a tradition. Young men left Lebanon to avoid conscription in the Ottoman army, which became a possibility at age 15. To blend in he took the name Julián Slim Haddad. His wife Linda Helú was also of Lebanese descent. Her parents had emigrated in the late 1800s. They brought with them a printing press and published Arabic language magazines for the Lebanese-Mexican community.

As yet unmarried, Julián started a dry goods stored in 1911, *The Star of the Orient*. You can see his flair right there. It is a mystical, romantic name that invites me to explore inside, especially if I discover it in Mexico

City. By 1921 he had enough money to buy real estate in the growing commercial district, and these two enterprises made him wealthy. He married Linda in 1926 and had four children, one of them named Carlos.

Julián insisted his sons learn business skills. At age 12 Slim (Carlos) bought shares in a Mexican Bank. My father persuaded me to buy stock in a bank, but he did not teach me business skills. He was an engineer and taught me electronics. It is interesting to think about these slight turns of direction and combinations of skills. Several of our American billionaires started with electronics or programming skills. They all seemed to have a source of business skills as well.

Carlos Slim
Wikimedia commons

The richest man in the world

By 1996 Carlos Slim was already worth $40 billion. The ups and downs of the Mexican economy slowed the growth of his wealth. In 2007 he edged out Warren Buffett. Since then Carlos and Bill Gates have periodically switched places according to how the winds of fortune blow. The majority of his wealth is from América Móvil, Latin America's largest cell phone company. He has 6 children.

Some Lebanese friends of our family owned a dry goods store in my hometown. It was named Antoon's. My grandmother worked there for a while, and Mary Evelyn Antoon was a classmate in school. There must be a strong merchant gene among the Lebanese.

Several of the members of the Forbes Top 10 served in the military, mostly in World War II due to the time frame of the list. Carlos' father avoided war. The Ottoman Empire was dissolved after being on the losing side in World War I, and Lebanon fell into dire chaos in the 1980s. Julián made the right move. Now Mexico seems to be falling into disorder. I do not know of course if Slim descended from some wealthy merchant of Rome or Babylon, but I wonder if this family will move again?

In an interview in July Carlos said he thought people should work only three days a week (although 11 hours a day), and take more time to enjoy life. [61] This, he thought, would help them work until 70 or 75. He himself is now 74. The article did not say if he follows his own advice.

Uzbekistan to Moscow, Alisher Usmanov

The name Usmanov is almost certainly the inspiration for the fictional Udinov family in the TV series Nikita, the richest family in Russia. Alisher was born not in Russia but in Uzbekistan in the capital, Tashkent, son of a state prosecutor. We can only imagine what that was like. Uzbekistan is just north of Iran. Keep going north and there is the large country of Kazakhstan and then the larger country of Russia. To the east is the mountainous country Kyrgyzstan, and then China. Uzbekistan was part of the Ottoman Empire, and our merchant's son could have traveled there easily.

Uzbekistan & surrounding countries
Google maps

Alisher did not want to be a prosecutor. He wanted to be a diplomat and so he moved to Moscow and entered the Moscow State Institute of International Relations. He got a degree in international law in 1976. I suppose that is consistent with his family vocation, and it is about time a lawyer showed up among our list of wealthy occupations. He then was appointed to the Foreign Economic Association of the Soviet Peace Committee. So he must have gotten some economic insight there.

But Alisher was on both sides of the law, deservedly or not. Someone thought he got too much economic insight and he was charged with corruption and spent 6 years in jail. Time in jail seems to be a merit badge that Russian businessmen must endure. He was released in 1986, and 14 years later the conviction was "vacated" and ruled unjust.

Little detail on how Usmanov came by his business success is available. He has investments in telecommunications (e.g. MegaFon), mining (Metalloinvest), technology and media. He married Irina Viner in 1992, a gymnastics coach who is reputed to be close to Putin, having introduced Putin to his current girlfriend. Usmanov must have already had some wealth, and Putin was not powerful at that time, but it seems he was hanging with the right friends.

In December 2014 when Putin asked Russian businessmen to bring their capital back to Russia in response to the fall in oil prices and Ukraine sanctions, the next day Alisher made an appearance saying that he had pulled most of his stock back into Russian-incorporated entities. He also gives his thoughts on how the world economy will develop in an interesting video interview in a Yahoo news article. [62]

That is the end of our little game of imagining how our merchant might survive the fall of Rome and endure and prosper to the present day. But I have a few more people I want to introduce you to before we move on the roots of money and war.

Huiyan Yang - richest woman in China/Asia

Huiyan's father brought her to board meetings when she was in middle school to train her in the ways of business. He gave her most of his stock in his upscale real estate developer Country Garden Holdings before the stock was offered to the public (before the IPO). At 33, she is also the youngest billionaire on the list. There is a beautiful picture of her where I found the story about her father taking her to board meetings, but unfortunately nothing I can include in the book. [63]

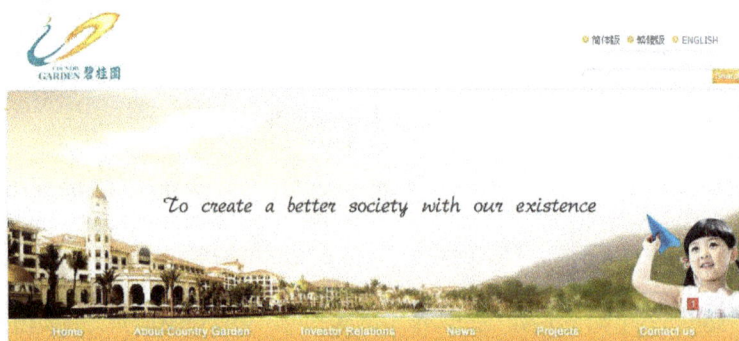

Country Garden Holdings website
http://www.bgy.com.cn/enn/

Little further information is available about this stunning woman in western language media. I did see an article that she married recently. But from what little we do know, we see how important it was to Yang to not just pass his wealth within his family but to train his daughter to handle it competently. And to begin that training at about age 12 or 13.

The world's first billionaire, J. Paul Getty

Getty was an oilman and an icon in the 1960s. His father was an oilman and thought J. Paul would ruin the company. He only left J. Paul five hundred thousand out of his $10 million estate. Nevertheless by 1966 the Guinness Book of Records listed J. Paul as the world's richest man. He is thought to be the first billionaire. That is somewhat an artifact of inflation as he is only the 67th all time richest American, but still impressive.

J. Paul Getty
Wikimedia commons

Getty had made his first million in 1916 and in 1917 announced his retirement and went to Los Angeles to become a playboy. You can see why his father might have been annoyed. But in 1919 Getty returned to business.

Getty prided himself on being a miser and installed a payphone in his mansion. He was often compared to playboy Howard Hughes, but Getty did not engage in philanthropy and Hughes was generous.

In July 1973 in Rome his 16 year old grandson was kidnapped and a $10 million ransom was demanded. The boy's father begged J. Paul for the money but Getty wouldn't pay it. Even after the ear of the grandson was delivered and the ransom reduced to $3 million, Getty only agreed to pay $2.2 million, loaning his son the remaining $800,000 at 4% interest. It seems $2.2 million was the maximum that was tax deductible.

The grandson became a drug addict and had a stroke in 1981, brought on by alcohol and drugs, and was thereafter unable to speak. Nevertheless, Getty defended his decision, saying that to submit to the kidnappers' demands would immediately place his other 14 grandchildren in great danger.

He also added a rationale that echoes current U.S. and British policy toward negotiating with kidnappers or terrorists: "The second reason for my refusal was much broader-based. I contend that acceding to the demands of criminals and terrorists merely guarantees the continuing increase and spread of lawlessness, violence and such outrages as terror-bombings, 'skyjackings' and the slaughter of hostages that plague our present-day world." (1976) [64]

The negative side of wealth

There have been a few other high profile kidnappings, such as the Lindbergh case, and Patty Hearst, but perhaps not as many as you would think. There is a reason for this. None of them ended well. The kidnappers are mostly dead. The victims and their families did not fare well either, but it has become pretty clear that American and British families and governments are going to choose the end in which the kidnappers die, regardless of the consequences. Their belief is like Getty's, that otherwise such practices will get out of control. Not everyone understands this.

I was recently reading a collection of stories about Middle Eastern lands written about 100 years ago by Otis Adelbert Kline, who fancied himself somewhat of an expert on the culture of the region. He portrayed desert warfare as a sort of polite sport among the sheiks. Not that it couldn't be deadly, but ordinarily it was not supposed to be excessively so. If one was outnumbered, one either ran away, or put down one's arms and submitted to capture. Kidnapping was common. A ransom was to be paid, and the victims were safely returned. In some cases kidnapping was for the purpose of slavery, in which case the victim must find their way as a slave in another country.

The British, they complained, did not understand the system. They would not pay the ransom and came in with troops and started killing people. There was no middle ground between the cultures.

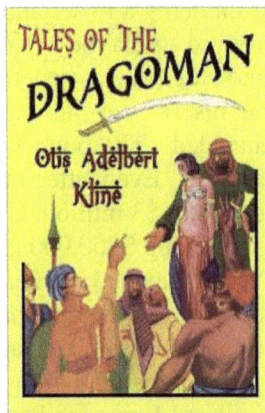

Tales of the Dragoman
Otis Adelbert Kline

To this day the kidnapping rates in the U.S. and Britain are low compared to many countries. Some countries such as Columbia have endured extremely routine kidnappings. When Americans are kidnapped, the results are almost always unpleasant for the victim, either years in captivity, occasional release by special forces, or lately a beheading on YouTube. Nevertheless, there aren't any rewards for the kidnappers.

There are more mundane drawbacks to wealth as well. I am not talking about the "fame" side either, in case you should become that wealthy, but much more ordinary things. Jealousy is very easily provoked. I have known wealthy individuals who were disliked for giving away too much money. It was felt they were gaining too much control. Every little club or school or business or church has its organization and its pecking order and if someone comes in and disturbs that, people get upset. Then there is the old problem of wondering if people like you for yourself, or for your money. While I don't want to be like J. Paul, I can see that by being a miser he did not have to worry about this. And I suspect that is why he did it. His three years in L.A. probably cured him of ever trying to buy anyone's affections.

There is the question of family too. It is much easier if families rise or fall together. Most any personal finance book will tell you not to lend to or borrow from relatives. Better to make it a gift. How are you going to collect a loan from your brother without alienating him? And he will avoid you because he can't pay you. Leave lending to the banks. Much of the gist of this book will be that equity investments are superior to lending anyway.

Some things might work out differently than you expect. As your wealth and influence increase, you will experience a lot of things for the first time, and that's what we'll look at in the next chapter. But first, a man who is very up front about the negative side of wealth and its obligations.

Jack Ma

At this writing, Jack Ma is the richest man in the largest and fastest growing country in the world. China. A country in which until just a few years ago private wealth was taboo.

China is also the fastest growing large economy, and has maintained its fast growth already for more years than seem possible by western standards. Controlled and sustained growth is the equivalent of nuclear weapons in economics. No one yet realizes this except myself, at least they have not said it out loud.

Now let's listen to what Jack Ma has to say, for he has been talking. But first, who is he and what did he do?

Early life & education

Jack was born in 1964. His parents were musicians and storytellers. What a fascinating and unusual beginning for the richest man anywhere, especially if he isn't an actor or singer! It immediately tests all our theories.

Ma has never written a line or code or made a sale to a customer. According to comments in 2010, he never encountered a computer until he was 33. That would have been in 1997! I had already started two internet businesses by then, and written hundreds of thousands of lines of code and made at least a few thousand sales. But my business didn't grow. I guess Jack's did.

I have not been able to find out much about what Jack's childhood was like, especially the level of wealth or poverty. We know he worked. But his parents weren't farmers. And he did not work in a factory. There is basically no escape from working in a factory because it constrains the mind in space and time and wears out the body with exhausting tedium. A farm is slightly better because at least the work is outside amid nature. We do know that Jack had a tremendous desire to learn English.

If he rode his bike 45 minutes to a hotel, to converse with foreigners and practice English, leading them about town, this qualifies as a job, but clearly it was also an opportunity. At least, he made it so. Jack was determined to study English further, and persisted even though he twice failed his entrance exam to the Hangzhou Teacher's Institute. This seems to be different than the stories we've heard of Chinese education where failure is completely devastating. But it is consistent with the biographies of other famous people who are not necessarily successful right out of the starting gate.

Jack is certainly educated. How this was arranged or paid for by musician parents I do not know, but he obtained a graduate degree in business in 2006. What he has done since then is amazing on several levels and makes me feel like a dullard. While we were all concerned about technical jobs being migrated to China, Jack Ma, a man who never wrote one line of code, started building websites for Chinese companies. Who actually built the websites? Friends of his in the U.S.! How did he even get friends in the U.S.?

Business ventures

Well it was not like he had done nothing but go to school. He had started China Yellow Pages in 1995, thought to be the first Chinese internet business. And he had other businesses. So he probably paid for his own graduate education. It is very interesting that he took the time to go back to school. I have often thought of going back to school, and taking a class or two here and there, but have never been willing to enter the level of serfdom required to get another degree.

Before that, for a decade he had been a lecturer in English and international trade. He is the first professor-turned-businessman we have seen, another data point outside the mold of wealthy people.

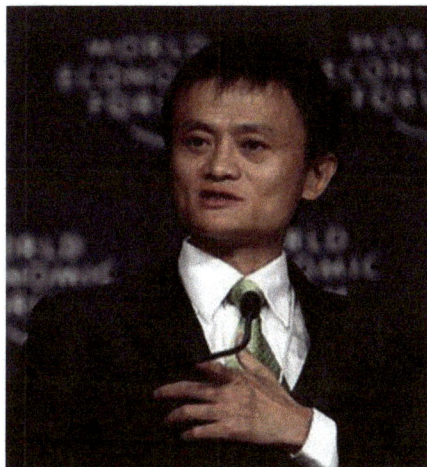

Jack Ma 2008 - Wikimedia commons

In 1999 he founded Alibaba as a business-to-business international marketplace. He and his wife and 17 friends came up with $60,000 to fund it. After that, it was venture capital. Jack is the only person besides Bloomberg that we have discussed who has a big venture capital history, and his is bigger than Bloomberg's, extending over several years. Initially $5 million was raised from angel venture capitalists. Exactly how to do this I'd like to know!

In 2000 $20 million was raised from Softbank. In 2005 $1 billion from Yahoo. In 2011 $1.6 billion from Silverlake Partners. Now he has raised $25 billion in an IPO.

Cell phones are more common and important in less developed countries than in the U.S. and western Europe, because the lack of land line communications and other infrastructure gave a big advantage to wireless communications. In China, the lack of brick and mortar infrastructure was hampering commerce. Alibaba therefore has a similar advantage there. It now accounts for 80% of the country's e-commerce, amounting to $248 billion annually, or twice Amazon's in a recent year.

Jack's outlook on wealth and business and life

Jack has been very candid about his feelings. He is tired and does not like being rich. He feels pressured. Wealth is no picnic for him, but a lot of work. I guess he has to answer to a lot of bosses with all those venture capitalists hanging around. But he also has said he feels like everyone around

him is always asking for money now that he is wealthy. Here are some of his
responses to recent questions. [65]

- **Most important lesson learned in business:** *Always trust your people*

- **Are you happy? What makes you happy?** *This month I'm not happy, I think from too much pressure. I need 5-10 days of sleep. If I'm not happy, everybody's jumping like monkeys. That's not good. Forget tech and utilities. There will only be two industries - health & happiness.*

- **On being the richest man in China:** *Spending money is much more difficult than making money. It's a great pain [being the richest man in China].*

- **What does he want for China's next generation?** *[Not to have] deep pockets but shallow minds. [Looking at culture-based acquisitions, e.g. film studios]*

- **On Alibaba's soaring stock price:** *I'm a bit nervous and I'm humble. Maybe the stock goes so up, maybe people have high expectations on you, maybe I think too much about the future and have too many things to worry about.*

China has always been known for its deep philosophy, for the appreciation of both sides of a thing, light and dark, Yin and Yang. I think Jack would make Confucius proud. And he gives us all something to think about.

What exactly is Alibaba? Looking at Alibaba's website, next page, and inspecting the title of the site, we immediately see that Jack has distilled the essence of Bill Gates' platform strategy, without the goal of going beyond a platform. Jack's clients aren't the end customers. Jack is enabling other merchants. If he is this big and does not yet try to compete with them for direct end user sales, then he is not ever going to. Bill always wanted to sell to end users, and was all the while working on end-user software and strategies while licensing the OS to hardware vendors and enticing application developers with a near-universal platform.

Alibaba, though often compared to Amazon, is nothing like Amazon. Amazon does not provide B2B (business to business) support. It provides a marketplace for some resellers, which is convenient for individuals who want to unload old books that might not attract good prices in a garage sale, but for bookstores or others selling on the web, it merely puts them in a venue where Amazon competes directly with them, with its regional warehouses and automated order fulfillment system.

**"Manufacturers, Suppliers, Exporters & Importers
from the world's biggest B2B marketplace"**
Alibaba website as seen in USA

Instead of putting small businesses out of business like Jeff Bezos (Amazon) or Sam Walton (Wal-Mart), Jack Ma is giving them the tools to expand their product selections and lower costs and be competitive. He is helping create small independent entrepreneurs, the kind of people that Thomas Jefferson thought would form the backbone of America. One of the responses to Jack's candid interview quoted above said that China needs more like Jack Ma. Frankly I think America needs a few Jack Mas. Maybe I can persuade you to become one of them?

My favorite rich person

I did not plan to pick a favorite when I started these two chapters surveying the life patterns of the wealthy. But after doing so, and comparing their characters to my own values in life, it will be obvious to the reader that I would pick Jack Ma, for his philosophical attitude, and because his goal of making a large number of people wealthy is similar to my own. I must in fact support Jack because of this alignment.

What about Warren Buffett and Bill Gates? Each has made a lot of other people millionaires. Most of the early Microsoft employees are millionaires, and so are the early shareholders of Berkshire Hathaway.

Yes, but so are the early shareholders of Wal-Mart. Are we supposed to believe that the only way to become wealthy is to make a lucky guess?

One may as well buy lottery tickets. You can't become a millionaire working at Microsoft now, in fact I hear it is a terrible place to work. It isn't likely Berkshire-Hathaway will continue to beat index funds, especially if Warren retires or dies, and you can sure get more dividends elsewhere. Wal-Mart stock would definitely be a worse bet than an index fund now. Also, and importantly, these are passive roles. They leave decisions about products and values up to some self-declared genius. The people who get wealthy this way have had no say in society. I said I wanted to give you a say, remember? Then my vote has to go with Jack.

Bloomberg, Ellison and the Kochs are okay guys, but they get few points under my criteria.

I did not say I wanted to be any of these people. Most of them lived far too stressful lives for my tastes. Bill has of course retired, so that's fine. Of the bunch, Warren Buffett seems to be the most relaxed. He keeps the former owners to manage companies he acquires, and does not try to run the businesses himself. At least that's what we are told.

Conclusions?

Are there any updates to our previous conclusions? It seems Jack challenges some of our ideas. But his story supports the notion that one starts young. The age of 12 seems to be common to most of the highly successful people, and I believe it applies to success in sports or academics as well. I know that I had chosen my field by about 12.

> *Conclusion #1: Choose your career at 12 and begin to prepare for it outside of school.*

Since Jack was allowed to work the hotel job and pursue studying English, I assume his goals were supported by his parents, or at least not opposed. So Jack is in line with the other biographies on this point. How many stories of slightly less successful people do you know who were opposed by their parents? I know many. This seems to be a factor that differentiates the very top successes from the rest. My mother did not particularly want me to be an engineer (or an inventor I called it then). My dad was neutral. I actually had to beg him to teach me electronics. My mother wanted me to be a doctor or a lawyer. My sister became a lawyer and she is much wealthier than I am. My dad did get me started with investing, which has turned out to be useful.

> *Conclusion #2: Support your child's choice. If you have not been able to influence them before 12, you will not have any luck at 13 when they are no longer children but teenagers.*

A personal analysis of friends and collaborators

It is hard to evaluate brief reports of other people's childhood and school relationships. But I can evaluate those closer to me and draw comparisons. First my sister's, since she was very successful.

There were a lot of lawyers around Greenwood where we grew up, and a lot of mine and my sister's classmates aspired to be and did become lawyers. Some joined local law firms. Many studied together and helped each other. My sister studied in college with her future husband Mike. They went in business together and eventually helped start the states vs. tobacco lawsuits. In the law field, it doesn't get much more successful than that.

By contrast there were only a couple of engineers, and none of my classmates aspired to be such or had dads that were such. Finally, I had a few friends in college at Mississippi State who had similar interests, including Jimmy who came to Rice with me, our mutual friend Bill who with others started a technology company in Jackson, George who wrote one of the early chess playing programs and participated in competitions, and Tim a physicist who could build just about anything.

Jimmy quit Rice even before I did, worked for T.I. in Austin for a while, and went back to Jackson to join his dad in the insurance business.

The author boarding one of Warren's NetJets
(ride courtesy of his lawyer sister)

Bill's company found that venture capitalists in Mississippi were interested only in agriculture so they moved to Austin to get support. Bill long ago quit them and I have lost touch with him.

George went to graduate school at Purdue and then worked for Information Storage, Harris, and HP in the instrumentation group, which was split off into Agilent.

Tim, the most collaborative of the bunch, entered the coop program and was gone every other semester, and then went to Maryland to get his PhD. We have kept in touch somewhat. He confided recently that he doesn't collaborate with me as much as I want because he is still annoyed with me for knocking him out of first place at the state science fair his senior year.

Tim's memory is incorrect. I met him at the state fair in Gulfport in 1967, our junior year. The vacuum chamber on my Thompson mass spectrograph was leaking and the project was not impressive and didn't win anything that year. It just looked intimidating. My research paper, an entirely different competition that Tim didn't enter, won a prize with a nice trip because in it I could relate all the trial and error of trying to find a suitable way to make a vacuum chamber and get the thing to work. It was quite exciting and my dad worked on it with me. For one experiment we tried a meter cover (he was in the electric power business), and being unsure of it, we put it in a wooden box the first time we pumped it down to vacuum. We hid downstairs and flipped a remote power switch. Pump-pump-pump-boom! The inside of the box was covered with a fine glass powder and that was the only trace of the meter cover. If you want to make glass powder, that is the recipe.

The next year, our senior year, my dad had a heart attack and mother forbade me to enter the science fair. I could not possibly have affected Tim's senior year standing. I don't even know where the fair was that year. For some reason he was jealous. I never remotely suspected this. Some of you will wonder about my including such a personal story and exposing Tim's feelings. It wouldn't be effective I don't think if I were too general and vague about it. This book is not about abstractions. My first book was abstract and people read it and nodded and went right back to their old comfortable notions of finance. In this book I want to grab you in the gut and get your attention on the fact that something is different than what you think it is. If it were not so, you would already be in the Forbes Top Ten, or equivalently successful at whatever you are doing. A little self awareness is all it takes, and you will spontaneously figure out the rest. In fact I hope Tim reads this and gets mad enough to go and try to prove his memory is correct, and discover the truth.

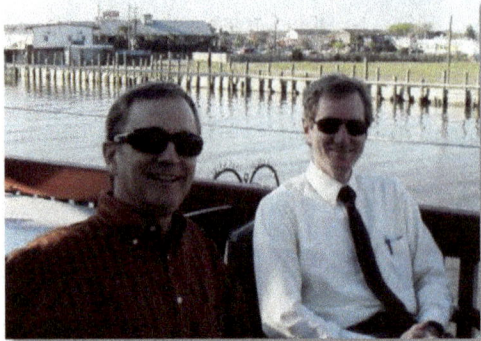

The author (left) and Tim

The takeaway point for you is that you may not even be aware of jealousy and resistance as you become successful in any field, or even just get a lot of attention. Others only see the superficial image, not the details of your problems and disappointments. Tim has a very high character. Most people will not tell you.

If your friends are listening to country music (the losing kind – the kind that if you play it backwards you get your car back, your house back, and your wife back) or rap music and believing they are stuck in those roles, in fact happy with lower middle class life, then that is good for them and you should not bother them with your aspirations. Without dropping or insulting them, you need to find some new friends. Wealthy friends, unless you plan on marrying one, will not make good collaborators either. They are coming from a different place and it is unlikely you will be seen as an equal by them. It is also unlikely you will be able to carry your share in any of their schemes. Where to find the sort of friends you want I cannot tell you, only that you must.

I suspect that most of us spontaneously find these people. If not, then we are driven by something artificial, perhaps our parents' wishes for what types of friends we should have, or our own social envy. Parents, after the age of 6 when your child starts regular school, you are pretty much helpless to pick their friends, sorry.

Conclusion #3: Always keep making new friends and keep close to those whom you find share interests and aspirations and are willing to be collaborative. (i.e. conspiratorial)

By the way, in case you are wondering, Tim has nothing to be jealous of and it is I who should be jealous. While we both had kids late, Tim has two and they are nearly grown. He found his lovely wife long before I found mine (by the way she briefly worked for Microsoft). Tim has the PhD, not me. And he wrote me recently to tell me that he had got a contract with JPL to build an instrument for a future Mars mission. Despite being in the space business my whole career, I've never had a large role in flight hardware development, only in testing as far as flight hardware goes. He is right I suppose in thinking I got a lot of attention in '67 at Gulfport due to my flashy topic and piles of equipment, but the judges asked for a demonstration and I couldn't get it to work due to vacuum leaks after the many assemblies and disassemblies of several fairs.

Earlier I mentioned Rajnish Mehra whom I met at Rice in graduate school. This was a minor collaboration compared to the ones that produced Top 10 list members or "richest person in ..." list members. Rajnish I believe is about as successful as he wants to be. There is a lot still I would like to do.

Three things make it extremely difficult to collaborate with people:

- If you don't trust them, you'll spend most of your time looking over their shoulder to make sure they don't run off with the money. Or you'll be fretting over getting your share. Or whether they will steal the idea and go away to work it on their own (which happens, a lot).

- If either of you is jealous of the other, this will lead to fighting over credit, and irrational behavior. A good example is the tobacco lawyers, who fought with each other over fees and credit. Several went to jail including one Mississippi lawyer and the Texas Attorney General.

- If either of you is over controlling, the other one will eventually resent it. This is another way of saying one person views the collaboration as very unequal. You don't work for each other, you are collaborators. If you can avoid it, never work for anybody. This includes being in a small business where you are a slave to your customers. Remember, Jack Ma never made a sale to a customer himself.

This kind of trust is best developed when nothing is at stake. As you get out of school and get older, it is harder and harder to come by. People who befriended me in my early career mostly wanted me to come to work for them or do them a favor (there were exceptions, of course). In mid-career many people were friendly when I would meet them at conferences and offer to collaborate, but eventually it came to light they expected grant money which I didn't have. As I get close to retirement, the only people interested in collaborating are retired scientists. Some of these collaborations have been very productive, but these people are retired and enjoying themselves, not planning big things.

These three conclusions are supported by all the biographies. If you are older than 12 and you didn't meet these criteria, I can't say you won't make it to the Forbes Top 10, but you will probably be a lot more stressed than Jack Ma. Investing in index funds is a low stress way to make the Top 10, but it takes about 100 years even starting from the 90th percentile. A realistic goal in that case might be to prepare the solid launching platform for your children.

It is not politically correct in America to make a multi-generation plot to increase wealth or anything else. I never said I was writing a politically correct book. One cannot objectively look at any of the three topics: money, wealth or war, and be politically correct. Think about this. One in 200 men in the world (10% of the men in the area corresponding to the former Mongol Empire) carry Genghis Khan's Y chromosome and are direct descendants of him. [66] The modern nation of Russia was assembled from 12 distinct kingdoms by Khan because he found it too bothersome to collect tribute from 12 separate kings. How much of his belligerent disposition is present on that Y chromosome? We do not know. I hope someone dares to ask this politically incorrect question one day and obtain and publish a real answer. Children matter. Period.

Genghis Khan
Wikimedia commons

Humans can spread ideas and culture to their children as easily and naturally as genes. Who would not think that Steve Jobs and Larry Ellison were hugely influenced by their adoptive parents? Your children probably have your genes as well as your culture. If you would not have them be like you, then why have you not already changed who you are?

Another thought to ponder is that the creation of the Russian Empire was essentially a financial decision, an administrative consolidation much like the mergers of giant corporations today. Understanding Russia has always been about understanding how very few people can control an enormous financial empire, whether those people are Mongolian warlords, Tsars, Soviets or Oligarchs.

Wealth vs. Power

By wealth, in this context, I mean control of capital resources, the means of production, independently of government. In no society is this separation perfect. Failure to appreciate the gray area can cause sudden and complete loss of wealth. Exploitation of the connection can lead to rapid wealth gains, but equally rapid losses.

By power I mean governing and political power - the ability to make and enforce laws, either reasonable or arbitrary, to arrest and imprison, and to carry out military action. In the absence of a highly organized state to enforce some separation of wealth and power, then wealth naturally is seized by the powerful, or power seized by the wealthy, depending on various factors.

Transitions of power

There are seven types of transitions of power:

- Most nations provide some traditional means of transferring power from one person or group to another, such as by elections or inheritance or appointment. If this is codified in a document it is usually called a "constitution," and the power transfer is referred to as "constitutional."

- If power is seized by force of arms from outside the government, by persons inside the country (even if they have outside support, which they often do), this is called a revolution.

- If power is seized by force of arms from the government's own military, it is called a coup d'état. Although similar in the use of arms, a coup d'état is usually far less disruptive of social institutions since it comes from within those institutions. This does not necessarily make it preferable, and violence can be disguised as police action.

- If power is seized by an invading force this is called conquest.

- Countries may be created or destroyed by special treaties or actions of the United Nations, as for example the dissolution of the Ottoman Empire and creation of Iraq, Syria, Israel, etc. This could be lumped under conquest, but may not have involved specific military action in the geographic regions affected, and is treated differently by international bodies. There is not a good name for it. I suggest we call it administrative conquest. It is not as new as you might think. Civilizations of the early Iron Age practiced the forced migration of populations and redrawing of the boundaries of their vassal states.

- If power is seized by commercial interests, this is usually termed "corruption," though no term exists for the extreme degree of corruption implied. Another possible term for this is "conspiracy theory" since most such seizures are not overt, and if successful cannot be confirmed.

- An apparently new type of power transition might be termed a "color revolution," although the name of a color is not always used (Cedar revolution in Lebanon, 2005).

Color revolutions
Wikimedia commons

Most of the color revolutions have occurred in former Soviet states (Orange revolution in Ukraine 2004, Rose revolution in Georgia 2003, etc., see [70]). These involve strikes and protests that pressure a government to such an extent that it suspends or accelerates some part of its constitution to speed a change in power. This would be distinct from a change in policy accomplished by similar means, or the influence of strikes and demonstrations on ordinary constitutional processes. While not as bloody as armed revolutions, the track record of these revolutions has not been all that good, and Putin uses fear of instability following such transitions to maintain support for his policies among Russians, who felt betrayed by perestroika due to the economic disruptions that followed the collapse of the Soviet Union.

Ordinary revolutions might be further distinguished between those which overthrow the local government in the geographic region of the revolution (French, Russian and Cuban revolutions), and those which cast off a colonial power (most initial revolutions in the Americas and Africa).

Internal revolutions could theoretically overpower the existing regime by sheer force of numbers. Occasionally this happens. More often the rebels find some means of generating funds to support their efforts, such as through diamonds, oil, kidnapping, or external benefactors.

Later we will see many examples of how economic (or wealth) forces drove power transitions. You will want to understand this to plot how to preserve your wealth as the world changes. But first let's examine how wealth and power interact in a few individual cases we have already looked at.

Will your government protect or seize your assets?

By assets I mean your money, investments, property, business, job, liberty, health, children and anything else you value.

Taxation implies the ability to seize assets. In this respect, investments in stocks, sometimes called equities, have an advantage in that they are not taxed directly, only the income from them.

Property, at least land and buildings, is directly taxed, which may force you to use it for economic activity and not let it sit idle. Many people, including my grandparents, lost property during the Great Depression because they could not pay the taxes on it. Even though property might be rental property, the rents that could be collected were insufficient during this time, as a result of the deflation of salaries and rents relative to the taxes (which didn't decline as fast) and acquisition costs (in the case of mortgage repossessions).

A military draft can seize your children, and we saw earlier how the father of the richest man in the world emigrated to avoid conscription into the Ottoman army.

Corruption, or running afoul of important government policies, can cause precipitous loss in any country. It is not even necessary to actually break the law. Politically incorrect statements ruined the commercial empire of celebrity chef Paula Deen. [71] I can only imagine what would happen if the Koch's or Warren Buffett or Bill Gates made a strong defense of leakers Ed Snowden or Bradley Manning, which they might do out of conscience, but they are smart enough to stay out of that one. What happens when this subtle line is crossed, even by an insider?

The richest man in Russia in 2003

In the months I spent in Russia I was struck by how pleasant it is to live there, even in a two room plus kitchen flat, and how friendly to Americans the people are. In getting to know them and their history, I soon realized it has been pleasant to live there for most people since the end of the Stalin era, whenever the price of oil was high or modest. Much of their economy is oil dependent, and we now know that Fred Koch's innovations were at least partly to thank for that, and of course the big companies who tied Fred up in the courts can be credited with driving Fred overseas to do business.

Boris and Marina Khodorkovsky lived in a two room plus kitchen concrete block flat on the outskirts of Moscow in 1963. Boris was Jewish and Marina Orthodox. They were both engineers who worked in a measurement instruments factory. This meant that they were "well off."

The author leans out the window of a concrete block flat
in Novosibirsk built in the Khrushchev administration

This may sound incongruous to American middle class ears. I have relatives with more closet space than the area of one of those flats (apartments). But I have also spent months in one of them, one built exactly in that era, and I found it amazingly pleasant. I believe I could live there indefinitely. The sounds of children from the "children's garden" across the parking lot wafted up through open windows, even in the winter. Russia has ample energy to heat their icy paradise. I could walk down two flights of steps, keeping me active and healthy, and step out into a city center (not "the" city center, there are many of them), walk under the street (in winter) to convenient shopping, or take a bus or metro to the opera, the circus, the bazaar, or the forest park for biking in the summer and cross country skiing in winter. Virtually all Russian cities are planned with these amenities. And at least as of 2011 doctors still made house *calls*, which helps keep down the contagion of winter flu by avoiding patient waiting rooms.

Boris and Marina had a son that year named Mikhail. They didn't themselves have much confidence in the communist system, but chose not to share this with their son. They thought it was too complex and difficult to teach a youngster to censor his own opinions and learn the art of duplicity and doublespeak. So Mikhail joined the communist youth league and applied his energy and intelligence and ambition and idealism and exactly 40 years later he was the richest man in newly-capitalist Russia. But he was not satisfied with the system. And in a few months he lost 99% of his wealth and the next 10 years of his life. I have checked his biographical details with numerous public sources. He is much more well known than Alisher Usmanov. But the direct quotes from Mikhail and his close associates are taken from an article by one of his associates, author Masha Gessen. [72]

With a Jewish surname Mikhail could not attend Moscow University, so he got a chemical engineering degree from Mendeleev Chemistry and Technology Institute in 1986. In the Young Communist League (Komsomol) he exploited a loophole allowing the conversion of purely administrative currency units to actual cash. By 1988 he had started Bank Menatep. It turned out the parents of a friend in the youth league held top positions in the state bank of the USSR. These and other connections helped him start business activities, some under the guise of the youth league. He engaged in currency trading and the import of sometimes illegal items. After perestroika, he purchased privatization vouchers from citizens who were all too happy to turn over these questionable documents for cash. As Boris Yeltsin's regime unfolded, bankers such as Mikhail lent the Russian government money they knew it could not pay back, with various industries as collateral. This is how Khodorkovsky acquired Yukos Oil for extremely little money.

In the 1998 financial crisis, the Russian Central Bank was requiring banks to hold unrealistically high capital reserves as Russian treasury bills. These defaulted, thus bankrupting Menatep. [73] (I am reminded of various conservative and libertarian calls for high bank reserves in the USA and other western countries, which could eventually have much the same disastrous effects).

In the late 1990's Khodorkovsky appropriated assets and allowed managers to siphon off funds and property like any other oligarch. The price of oil, however, had dropped to $8 a barrel in the late 1990s, and it cost Yukos $12 a barrel to drill and pump oil. Mikhail visited with workers who were fainting from hunger, especially if they had no vegetable gardens, and who said, in effect, "*We never expected anything good. We are just grateful you came here to talk to us. We'll be patient.*" He lost faith in capitalism just as he earlier had lost faith in communism. He and other shareholders of Group Menatep in 2001 paid 15,000 small account holders out of their own funds, an unprecedented move. When the price of oil began to recover in late 2001, he founded Open Russia. He reformed and modernized Yukos. Throughout, he maintained close relations with long time associates such as we have found with other highly successful people.

Due to continued rising oil prices, the increased company transparency, and modernization, Khodorkovsky became by 2003 the richest man in Russia, and the 16th richest man in the world. Because of his Jewish father he was unelectable in Russia, but he determined to reform the country by other means. In February Putin called an unusual conference with wealthy Russian businessmen open to the media. Against all advice, Khodorkovsky confronted Putin over corruption. This was after the media empire of Vladimir Gusinsky had been confiscated by the government for being critical of Putin, and Gusinsky forced to leave the country.

Khodorkovsky in 2001 - source: Press Center of Mikhail Khodorkovsky and Platon Lebedev via Wikimedia commons

In addition to generic comments about corruption costing the Russian economy $30 billion a year, and students preferring civil service and tax collecting careers when factoring in what they could make from bribes, Khodorkovsky made more pointed comments such as criticizing a recent merger of state-owned oil company Rosenft with a smaller private company. He said "*Everyone thinks the deal had, shall we say, a second layer. The president of Rosneft is here - perhaps he'd care to comment.*"

Putin responded with his own not-so-subtle hint at charges of corruption: "*Some companies, including Yukos, have extraordinary reserves. The question is: How did the company get them?*"

Then Putin indirectly accused Khodorkovsky of bribery: "*And your company had its own issues with taxes. To give the Yukos leadership its due, it found a way to settle everything and take care of all its problems with the state. But maybe this is the reason there is such competition to get into the tax academy?"*

The video of this exchange is in the Frontline documentary mentioned earlier, *Putin's Way*. I find it interesting that it is not the glaring calculated threat that you might infer from reading it years later. Putin was looking down and casting about with his eyes, obviously thinking hard to make up his response in real time. He uses the word *problema* several times and stammers, giving more of a repetitive emphasis effect on the idea there is a "problem" here which he is going to figure out how to deal with.

By July long time partner Platon Lebedev had been arrested. His friend Nevzlin was advising him to leave the country. Mikhail did not take the hint, but instead went on a speaking tour urging Russia to quite running its companies like "fiefdoms or prisons" and to build an economy that exported "knowledge and expertise rather than just oil and gas." On October 25th he was arrested at 8 am at the Novosibirsk airport, a place where I have been many times, where I first laid eyes on my future wife. It is eerie to think about.

A tax attorney, Pavel Ivlev, employee of a law firm independent of Yukos, represented Yukos employees when they were called in for questioning over the next month. After the interviews, the lead detective said: *"Now I am going to interrogate you."*

Pavel responded: *"You can't do that, it's against the law."*

"I guess we are going to have to break the law then. Tell me all."

"...You want me to describe how we took sacks of cash out of Yukos and delivered them to Khodorkovsky personally?"

"Yes."

"But nothing like that ever happened."

Then Pavel was threatened with arrest. He left the investigator's office, took a plane out of the country, and did not even call his wife until he landed in Kiev. Today they live in New Jersey, but Pavel cannot leave the United States because Russia issued an international arrest warrant for his detention. I wonder if anyone ever suggested swapping him for Snowden?

I cannot condone Russia's actions. It is especially annoying because I now have relatives there, and to be honest with my readers, had invested quite a bit in Russia which after sanctions and the recent oil declines is now worth very little. I am not sure when I will feel comfortable traveling there again.

However, Mikhail was not very smart in his strategy either. How much good did he really do as a prisoner-activist? Some, yes. He was annoying enough that in December of 2013, along with Pussy Riot, he was released. He lost 99% of his wealth. To be sure, he still has around $170 million, more than you or me, but a long way from $17 billion, and think what he could have done with it had he learned the art of duplicity and doublespeak which his parents declined to teach him?

Aside from the miscalculation of dealing with state political power, Khodorkovsky otherwise conforms well to the patterns we have found extremely wealthy people tend to follow in life, with an early start, support from parents, friends-partners who stay together, changing paradigms, and powerful connections. Taking those powerful connections for granted, even if you have outgrown them in your own mind, may not be the most effective way to proceed. Wealth is not power in and of itself.

The merry-go-round of capital assets

In communist revolutions, "people's revolutionaries" seize property, wealth and control of capital assets - factories and farms, the means of economic production. In the Russian reforms of the 1990s, crony capitalists seized those assets by such tricks as indulgent lending followed by the use of bankruptcy default. Again in the 2000's the state re-seized the assets of media and oil companies. Now the state-owned Rosenft is by far the largest oil company, after acquiring Yukos and others. In Civics Class in the 1960s we learned half of the picture, about how revolutionaries seized private assets. In the Soviet equivalent of Civics Class, people learned how capitalists used tricks and corruption to seize the people's assets. There was apparently some omission and some truth in both schools.

In case you think American capitalists are above such tricks, keep in mind that Paul Elliot Singer of New York, a U. S. citizen, has used exactly the bond default trick to reap 3000% profit against Delphi Automotive on 2008 bond defaults, a division of GM which was itself "bailed out" by the U.S. government (though its shareholders lost all), and is currently repeating the procedure in New York courts to claim Argentina sovereign assets. His firms Elliot management and NML Capital bought Argentine bonds during a 1998-2001 severe recession for $49 million dollars, which now have a face value based on their original terms of $832 million. [74]

Paul Singer hedge fund manager & former lawyer
at the World Economic Forum in Davos, Switzerland
WEF via Wikimedia commons

Approximately 93% of the Argentine bondholders agreed to a restructuring in 2005. Paul Singer is the lead "holdout." The other bondholders, which cannot be paid while this legal battle is ongoing, include citizens of Argentina (25% of bondholders) and Italy, and the government of Venezuela, in addition to the so-called U.S. "vulture" funds. The same strategy has been used against Peru and several African nations. The only invention of the Russian oligarchs was to use this strategy against their own government, which backfired.

The American practitioners have several advantages. The U.S. currency is the world's reserve currency. They are able to induce borrowers to promise to be subject to U.S. laws and courts, much like European lenders similarly conned the Chinese Empire at its end. And they have the U.S. Government in their pockets. Singer's lobbying group American Task Force Argentina spent $7 million lobbying U.S. Congressmen. For several of them it was the top campaign contributor. That gets noticed. Western Hemisphere subcommittee chairman Connie Mack (Republican, Florida) sponsored a bill in 2012 that would force Argentina to pay $2 billion. Fortunately, in the U.S. votes still get noticed, and Connie Mack lost his reelection bid. But with this kind of lobbying pressure, no one in the Congress is in a public outcry that would cost them valuable campaign contributions. Their silence and therefore complicity has been bought.

When I said in the introduction that it matters how you vote, and one of the purposes of this book was to give you a full understanding of the impacts of the policies you vote on when you select representatives, you now see I was serious. I will not tell you how to vote. If you want to make Argentina more of a basket case than it is and destroy any market there for

U.S. goods and services, put Connie Mack back in Congress. But if someone tries to deceive Americans into thinking this is somehow right and good for capitalism and American workers, I'm here to point out otherwise. Lenders take a risk, and the fear of that risk is supposed to keep them from indulging those who would borrow more than they can pay back. This practice is called predatory lending. It led to the financial crisis, and is still prevalent. If you give these American oligarchs the full power of the U.S. to enforce their schemes, then they will make Russian oligarchs look like Good Samaritans.

I guess if we compare Singer to Khodorkovsky, maybe the Russian oligarchs already look like good Samaritans? If Singer's fund goes bust, do you think he will pay shareholders out of his own funds? (He is worth $1.9 billion.)

Singer and Khodorkovsky are both white and have Jewish backgrounds. So my comments are race and culture neutral. Khodorkovsky publicly defends his actions every chance he gets. Singer never speaks other than to exclusive, friendly audiences. Khodorkovsky was idealistic and naive about his relation to his government. Singer cleverly uses his wealth and influence (at least $7 million of it) to secure the support of his government, legally under our system.

Davos Man says "lower your expectations"

Singer represents a new breed of human somewhat farther above us than homo sapiens were above Neanderthals - literally looking down on us from private jets, above the fray of airport security, when they are not busy confiscating resources from our governments. This new breed, "Davos Man," refers to attendees of the annual World Economic Forum in January in ski resort Davos Switzerland. The phrase seems to have been coined in a 1997 article in The Economist, recently researched and reported by Marketplace. [104]

The original editorial closes by defending Davos Man: "*Although 40 or so heads of state will troop to Davos this weekend, the event is paid for by companies, and run in their interests. They do not go to butter up the politicians; it is the other way around ... he does not give a fig for culture ... Sinic, Hindu, Islamic or Orthodox ... If an idea works or a market arises ... an approach more likely to bring peoples together than to force them apart.*"

Apparently the World Economic Forum is intended to gain some leverage in the game of wealth vs. power.

In the more recent review of Davos Man's evolution on Marketplace (a somewhat liberal business news program, just to be clear about biases) a professor of political science from Yale laments, "*the forces that Davos Man represents have also pulled people apart, exacerbating global inequality,*" and a senior editor at Fusion cable channel who has been attending the meeting for several years says, *"Rich people don't change that much."* The Economist was less flattering in 2013 saying:

"Ordinary folk trust Davos Man no more than they would a lobbyist for the Worldwide Federation of Weasels. ... What can be done? Much of the answer lies in giving the little guys better tools to keep Davos Man in check: stricter accountability for government leaders, sounder regulations to curb corporate abuses. ... Most trade occurs within national borders. Nearly all politics is local. ... global leaders need to immerse themselves in local cultures." [106]

Hmm..., those tools sound ineffective to me, just minor irritants that depend on the corruptible integrity of accountants and regulators. Better to simply get rich yourself and put the stamp of your own character and integrity on the world. Only then can you hold the accountants accountable.

Davos, Switzerland [105]

Jeff Greene [108] created a stir in 2015 by saying in an interview with Bloomberg News, *"America's lifestyle expectations are far too high and need to be adjusted so we have less things and a smaller, better existence."* [107]

What caused the stir was the juxtaposition of that comment with the fact that Jeff arrived at Davos in a private jet with wife, children and two nannies, not to mention that he once owned the most expensive home in the U.S. [109]

Unexpected Consequences

The Most Important Duty of a Citizen

If you are a citizen of some country and you have the ability to vote, then you can potentially vote to go to war, like the U.S. Congress has done repeatedly in my lifetime. So you need a user's guide for war, do you not?

Do you think that citizens never vote for war? The Athenians voted to go to war with Sparta. The Athenians lost. Rome voted to start the 2nd Punic war with Carthage. They kept their empire eventually but lost 25 years, an entire generation.

If you are liberal or conservative or libertarian, Tea Party or frat party, Christian or Muslim, then you need to know what you are doing. Otherwise you might kill someone. Not to mention hurt yourself.

Do you let someone else manage your money? A professional? Do you leave your money in a bank? Does every generation in your family have to start over from scratch? Do you think a job is going to save you? Did you graduate with a load of student debt? Are you saving only for retirement? Are you planning to spend all your money before you die? Then you have no right to complain. You are not making the sacrifices that wealthy families make to stay wealthy, and you cannot expect them to have any sympathy for your spendthrift, debt-ridden ways.

This book will help you sort a few things out.

The American Civil War 1861-1865[1]
this is not your most important duty

If you hold a job or open a bank account or even discuss money & politics; if you have money to spend or save or you owe money or have an opinion about gold or your country's central bank, then you need a user's guide for money. By voting, you affect everyone else's money, so it should be a law for you to have and read and pass a test on money. Do you really want your opinionated neighbors choosing a President, whose single most important act will be to appoint a Federal Reserve chairman who will control money, to vote without knowing what they are doing?

But voting intelligently is only your 2nd or 3rd most important duty. In the context of the welfare of society, what do you think is your most important duty?

What does society do? Provide for mutual defense? Provide for general welfare? Regulate the activity of citizens so that they do not harm or infringe the freedom of each other? Sure, all those things.

Who pays for it? Who causes problems society must deal with if they don't carry their own weight? That's right, you do. Surprisingly, the most important thing you can do for society is to take care of yourself. And your family.

We have a creeping notion in some countries, especially in America and Europe, that the government should take care of us. There are three catches to this proposal.

1. Someone has to pay for it.

2. We give up our freedom when we accept someone else taking care of us.

3. Left unchecked, the number of people being taken care of increases, and the number of people paying for it decreases until resentment on both sides builds into class warfare.

Is planning for retirement one of your financial goals? If you are not able to save for retirement, then you are counting on the government to take care of you. But the surprising thing is that if you are saving only for retirement, you are planning for the government to take care of your children, assuming you have any. Why? Because jobs are not a reliable way of providing for future generations.

In primitive hunter-gatherer societies, only about 20% of a person's time was spent in hunting and gathering. The remaining 80% was leisure time. We have learned this partly from observing the few such societies that still exist in remote regions today. The historical way of providing for future generations was to protect and defend the land that did the providing. When primitive people give up their land, or it is taken from them, most of them invariably fall into poverty. Families break up as members go to cities and even other countries to find so-called jobs. Jobs are always temporary.

You may find yourself resisting these ideas. That's okay. You should resist people telling you stuff without presenting very good arguments that you can verify from your own experience. Another one of your important duties as a citizen is to be informed, and that does not just mean choosing which manipulator to listen to. After spending this entire book going through the data, you will be able to analyze and decide things for yourself. Then maybe the next time someone tells you how much you should be saving for retirement, you will wonder not whether they are right about the amount, but whether they are right about retirement being the goal of saving!

If you take a mate, and especially if you have children, you're most important duty as a citizen is to pass on to your children the means for being self-supporting, productive members of society. Certainly that includes the things you usually think of, like education. But more and more we find that some types of education are not of lasting value. Any kind of technology education is fleeting. Often the student loans will not be paid back before the technology is replaced. And even if the skill remains valuable, the source of labor may migrate to other countries.

The day people came out of the forest and began to plant large tracts of land with crops, large and rapid social upheaval began. Storage of the crops allowed wealth to be amassed. Warfare soon followed. People were cast out of their natural inherited environment. Only a few were able to master the abstract new concepts of stored wealth other than control of raw land. The effort to understand and manage these concepts led to mathematics, writing, art, governments, cities, all the things we associate with civilization.

So, what do you know about it? Do you understand what money is? How much of it there should be? If you answer yes, you are claiming vast knowledge. Even professional economists punt on these questions.

Paper Money Enables Wealth & Power

Some form of representational money was invented before writing or war or the accumulation of wealth. It makes all the other things possible. Gold is not money. Gold is, well, simply gold. A shiny soft metal, somewhat scarce, that makes nice jewelry. It has sometimes been used as a trading commodity, but that came after a sort of primitive money, and paper money had to be re-invented because gold was inconvenient to carry around and highly subject to theft.

Paper (or clay or stone) money, with marks on it, evolved into writing. With writing came tablets of laws, justice and by implication injustice, and mostly a lot of propaganda designed to make you want to go to war when it was in someone else's interest. And by all means laws to keep you from taking other people's paper money, and to force you to do things to get it.

Then came wealth. With paper money, you can pile up a lot of it. Have you ever tried to pile up a lot of chickens? And by using identifiable bank notes and bonds and stocks and land deeds and contracts, with the name of the owner, paper money in its general form of "securities" can be harder to steal than chickens or gold.

With wealth came power, nation states, and the ability to wage war on a large scale. Not just raiding the neighboring village for wives or chickens.

Vietnam War 1965-1975 [2]
more serious than raiding the neighboring village

But it turns out people are not stupid and will not go to war if they are happy and have jobs and are getting along. And pretty much if they have jobs they are happy and getting along. Have you ever seen rich people or even middle class people riot in the streets and start a rebellion? No. Unless someone were credibly threatening to take everything away from them. Mostly they don't riot until it is already taken, which can be too late.

Germany started WWII after hitting 40% unemployment. The Arab Spring was preceded by a world economic crisis which produced 90% unemployment in some of the countries affected. If you want to provoke a country into starting a war, simply bring about such conditions. It is not hard to break an economy. What is hard is making a country prosperous. Prosperity requires cooperation and trust and other qualities that are easy to break and hard to fix.

In other words when your neighbors, the ones I mentioned above, vote for a Federal Reserve appointment maker (the President), for all practical purposes they vote whether to go to war. Or at least whether to have a bubble or a depression. Do you want a bubble and a depression (they usually follow one another)? Do you expect your neighbor to be informed if you do not first inform yourself?

Do you know the old saying that you can't have your cake and eat it too? That applies here. At least at first. Until you have a really big pile of money, you can't have your money and spend it too. In fact, most lottery winners lose their money within about five years, and have a slightly higher probability of winding up bankrupt than people who didn't win anything.

Unexpected Outcomes

You are probably wondering about the picture below, "What does that have to do with money and war?"

Montana speed limit sign 1995-9 [3]
safe at any speed?

This speed limit sign is an illustration of unexpected outcomes. There are a lot of very nice, well intentioned people who believe results will always follow in the direction in which you exert effort. Maybe the results will not be as much as you wanted, but just try harder. Learning that results may come back to bite you, that you may be doing more harm than good, flies in the face of the American culture I grew up in. By golly, if you make people slow down, there will be fewer fatal accidents, if for no other reason than that people hit each other at slower speeds!

Guess what. It is not so. After the U.S. nationwide 55 mile per hour speed limit was repealed, for several years Montana reverted to an older law that on most country roads allowed "reasonable and prudent" speeds in the daytime, with no specified limit. Accidents and fatalities went down and kept going down until a real speed limit was enacted, and then they started going back up and within three to four months had doubled. Not only that, accident rates were slightly higher on Federal roads where speed limits were on average slightly lower than the Montana rural limit then enacted of 75 mph.

When I make a claim like that, feel free to go online and check it out for yourself. In most cases I will include a web link either in the text or in an end note, or you can search using the keywords and it will probably come right up. In this case go to http://www.hwysafety.com/hwy_montana.htm, or click on the little [3] under the image. At the end note, you will be able to click [3] and come back to a location near where you were reading (or at least the chapter, depending on your reader).

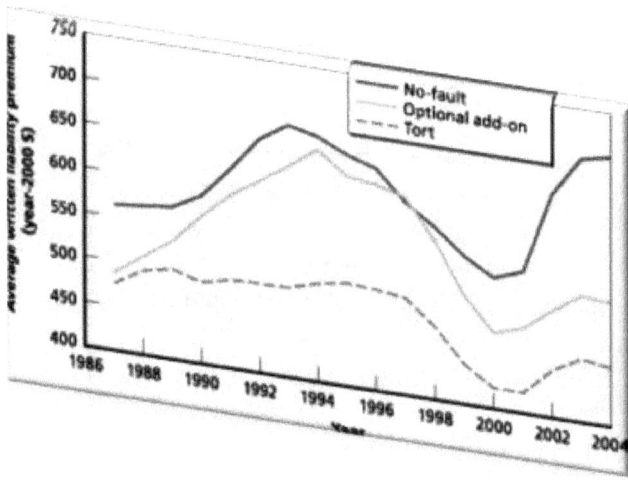

No-fault insurance premiums [4]
why are they higher?

A lot of the cost of automobile wrecks is caused by people suing in court, right? Everyone knows that. For this reason a lot of states passed "no fault" insurance laws. Costs went down, right? Wrong. They went up over 40%, and were still going up when most states hastily backed out of these laws. If you have a wreck in a state like this - I did once - you will understand why. It is hassle free! I clearly was at fault, driving an SUV I wasn't used to, and backed into a guy and totaled his car. I didn't even have to pay his deductible. Now I will not go out and try to have a wreck, of course, but it did cross my mind that if I were going to have another wreck, this was the place to have it. The same kinds of unexpected results are typical of, well, just about everything if you look closely. Especially when it comes to money.

There are a lot of unexpected outcomes when dealing with people. It is the old problem of thinking about what the other person is thinking about what you are thinking about what they are thinking, and on it goes. Animals do not do much of this. Predators do it to one level, probably more by instinct than thinking. A cat may behave as if it is thinking its prey might see it sneaking up. But a cat will also "hide" in plain sight in a clump of grass not big enough to hide in. So they are not thinking very much. But humans will sit around and plot strategy and counter-strategy to five or more levels, even after economists have told them they cannot out think the millions of other market participants.

I'm willing to admit there might be some special circumstances in Montana, like a population that is fiercely independent, self reliant, and used to looking out for themselves. If you have a problem on your ranch out in the middle of nowhere, chances are you will be dead before the sheriff gets there anyhow. However, unregulated speed has been tried and is still in force on some of the busiest expressways in the world, the German Autobahns. See for yourself:

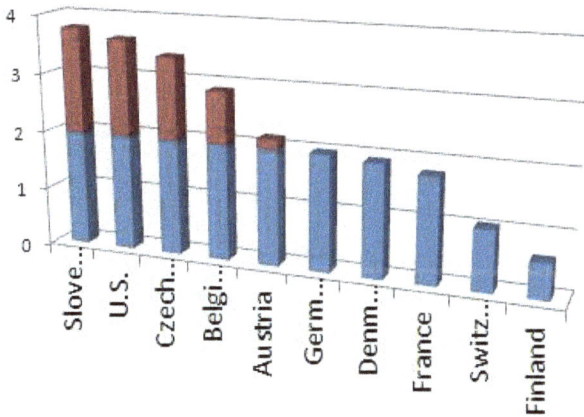

motorways deaths per billion vehicle kilometers [5]

The U.S. with all our safe road construction and air bags and speed traps and what not is second worst in this group, barely, right between Slovenia and the Czech Republic. Germany has about half the death rate per mile or kilometer driven. The only countries notably safer are Switzerland and Finland, which have notably *more dangerous* mountain conditions with terrible weather. It seems that *the more hazardous driving is, the fewer the deaths!*

214 kph = 133 mph
safer than 75?

Finnish Highway [6]
safest in the world?

The Secrets

The First Big Secret

If things are that counter-intuitive with something as "obvious" as how to drive safely, or no fault auto insurance, can you even imagine the unexpected results from healthcare insurance? That gets into big money, and people's attitudes toward risk. Your attitude toward risk. To get something out of this book you will have to get out of your comfort zone a little bit and shed every parochial attitude you have ever had. Because those attitudes that feel good discussing around the dinner table, that give you a shared viewpoint with your family and friends, are superficial and just plain wrong. I don't care what culture, race or political party you identify with, the attitudes are wrong. Unless you are already a billionaire, the culture you are immersed in does not produce billionaires.

what is your family wealth culture?

This is the FIRST BIG SECRET I'm giving you. Your family wealth culture doesn't produce billionaires. You have to change fundamental attitudes and beliefs. Everyone around you will resist this change. They will in the first place misunderstand what you are trying to do. If you announce you are going to learn to accumulate wealth, they will assume that means they will have more money to spend.

We are going to see how the world really works, not how we politely pretend in public that it works so our children can sleep at night and our neighbors won't attack us. If you leave this book lying about on your coffee table, I'm not responsible for the consequences.

The Second Big Secret

It takes *no* brains to accumulate money by investing, and they are positively a liability. A smart person will keep trying to accumulate money faster or think of cool things to use it for, or try to figure out the stock market, or something. Economists have pretty much proven that is not possible, and anyone who tells you otherwise is running a scam. The only thing you can legitimately use your brains for is to remember that most people who try to give or sell you investment advice are running a scam. As soon as you sign up for a broker account you will get on all sorts of junk mail lists and strangers will call you on the phone with hot stock tips. One thing you will learn in this book is how to avoid stock picking.

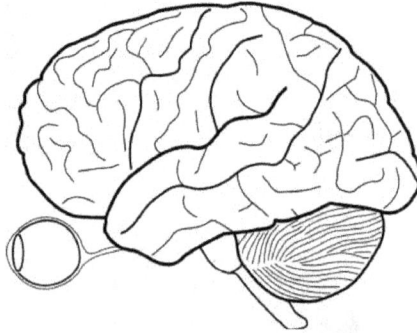

When you apply for a broker account with which to buy investments, you do not have to have any particular degree. You are asked your experience and income, but you can put down anything you want and no one checks. (You might not be approved for option trading if you have no experience or income, but we won't be recommending that anyway.) There is no place on the form to enter race, height, weight, fitness, IQ, family connections, political views, sexual orientation, what your dad did in the war, or any other such thing. You have to give your tax ID for tax reporting, but no one pulls a credit report. No one even asks if you are bankrupt or are a felon.

In every other field of human endeavor, one must either study or practice very hard to perform well, whether it is in sports, a profession, or business. Most of the wealthy people we examined performed well in business to accumulate their money. Acting and sports also provide ways to rapidly accumulate money which depend on a combination of preparation and talent. But here we are talking about accumulating money through investing, which will be a bit slower, but not require our full-time attention. The reason this is true is because of something called "efficient markets." Current prices, and predictions of future prices, already account for known public information. Trying to get beyond that is guesswork and unscientific.

Warren Buffett often comes up in connection with discussions of efficient markets. He presents himself as someone who became wealthy through "investing." That is not true. Warren takes control of entire companies, which from the start he has done using other people's money. It is a full time job for him. And he is persuasive enough to get other people to give him money to use this way, in the beginning his original "partners," and now all the cult-like following that owns shares in Berkshire Hathaway. If he were not making more money by "letting" other people enter his schemes, he would not do it. He dismissed his original partners summarily after he took over Berkshire.

By taking over whole companies, Warren obtains so-called "proprietary returns." These are not available in public markets, and not subject therefore to the efficient market hypothesis. You are free to do as Warren did if you have comparable persuasive ability. Can you persuade a bunch of people to give you millions to invest as you wish? If not, then you cannot do what Warren did. A lot of scam artists, like Bernie Madoff, who have such persuasive skills never even bother with investing, but just take other people's money and build a pyramid scheme (and nearly always go to jail).

The point is that it is easy to show Warren did something that you as an individual investor without full time attention and persuasive abilities cannot do, so he does not completely break the efficient market theory. Even other "professional" money managers do not take over whole companies and cannot match Warren's performance. What he does is more like what a hedge fund does in looking for proprietary, or "private" returns. He should be compared to hedge fund managers, not investors. Warren just found a "loophole" around the statutory requirement that hedge fund investors have a high net worth already, by taking over a long established general purpose stock company. I am not sure he could get a license to set up a company from scratch to operate as an investment vehicle the way he does, without either becoming a Regulated Investment Company (generally required to pay dividends), or a hedge fund (which places wealth requirements on the investors). Of course, before the late 1990s when Berkshire-B shares were introduced, investors did have to be modestly wealthy to afford a single share. Currently, Berkshire-A shares are $225,000. Warren no more intends a stock split than he intends to pay dividends. It has become part of his "cult" persona.

A successful mid-career rocket scientist was telling me the other day about his 401K money that he placed under "professional management." In 2008 and 2009 during the financial crisis, the professional managers kept selling things that had already gone down, and buying things that had not yet gone down, but would. I could definitely relate, because I had done a little of that same thing myself before I discovered what harm it was doing. Not everything went down at once. By switching horses, one can manage to ride the downhill slope over and over, without any lift in between. But when the recovery comes, it goes up only one hill. The people who simply hung on to their index funds did all right in a couple of years.

Notice that it wouldn't have really mattered to the index fund holders if the market had NEVER gone back up. That would indicate that deflation had taken hold, and their smaller net worth would have amounted to the same share of the world they had before the market went down. This reasoning does not apply if they picked particular stocks, only if they owned the whole market via index funds. We will repeat this point again at least once before the book is done, and give charts and examples of how stock picking and fancy strategies by the best professional goes awry.

Efficient market theory

Then my rocket scientist friend began to tell me about a book he was reading, and the strategy he would use next. It was to buy companies that made products one understands, and to research them thoroughly. It sounded like some of the Warren Buffett or Peter Lynch type of advice that sells well in financial books. I asked him if he had heard of efficient market theory? Did he realize thousands of people were studying those same companies, and every piece of information any of them could dig up was already reflected in the stock price? He had not thought of that.

A stock price is like the odds a bookie makes on a sports bet. It may be well known that one team is better than another. But the bookie sets the odds so that given everything known about the teams, it is an even bet. This "evening" out of the bet is also called "equalization."

But that equalization of bets in an efficient market is only for this month or this year. Over the long-term, *groups of stocks* in pro-business economies, like the U.S., do very well, better than things they should have equalized with. Most of us just do not have a 20 year time horizon. If we were thinking more like a family, from generation to generation, we could take advantage of this long-term performance. We could accumulate real wealth - the kind that keeps kings in power, and has produced more governors with the name Rockefeller than any other.

Your social worth as a wealthy person

American middle class culture has a bias against this kind of wealth. People tend to want each person to be rewarded for the work they have done. If you feel this way, it is admirable. But this book will not help you "earn" more. Put it down before it annoys you.

If you become wealthy and your family preserves this wealth, you "earn" your wealth in other ways. You can take care of yourself and are not a burden on the government. In fact the taxes that run our government are paid mostly by the very wealthy. You free up a work-a-day job following orders so that someone else can have it. You provide the capital to finance job creation. Your discretionary consumption of high-end goods, services, entertainment and education creates demand for employment in the most satisfying career fields. You will be the driving force of our civilization.

The Golden Rule

We mentioned investment failure because of over-thinking, professional management, and stock picking. In that connection Warren Buffett came up. Mr. Buffett likes to read company reports and understands them. It surely helps him avoid losers. But much of a company's future performance depends on a combination of external unknowable factors, and internal skill and determination. For that reason, unlike most other takeover artists, Buffett encourages the original company management to stay on.

Did we just say "takeover artist?" Yes, that is what Warren really is. He took over Berkshire-Hathaway and shut down its operations, using it for a holding company to acquire others. He acquires companies that generate a lot of cash.

The "theory" of growth companies is that they reinvest their earnings in expanding the business. Berkshire-Hathaway never pays dividends, something Buffett brags about. But he does not buy a company unless it generates a lot of cash that he can take control of and use for other purposes. And his investments in stock of public companies generally lean toward those that do pay dividends. He is violating the Golden Rule of the Bible:

Do unto others as you would have them do unto you.

Since this has worked so well for Buffett, to get the cash flow of companies, we will modify the general theory of investing in broad indices to include dividends. There is no law of nature that makes corporate planners always better able to invest their earnings just as there is no way to pick stocks. If a company has patents or proprietary designs, they can reinvest for a while. Apple might come to mind in this context. But one glance at Apple's chart and you will see that over the long-term, it is only average among technology stocks.

The black line is the benchmark S&P 500 index. The dark gray line that goes below and crosses over in about 2005 is Apple. By 2012 it had still not caught up with Dell, Microsoft or Intel. It is only if you look at the performance since 2000 that Apple looks impressive.

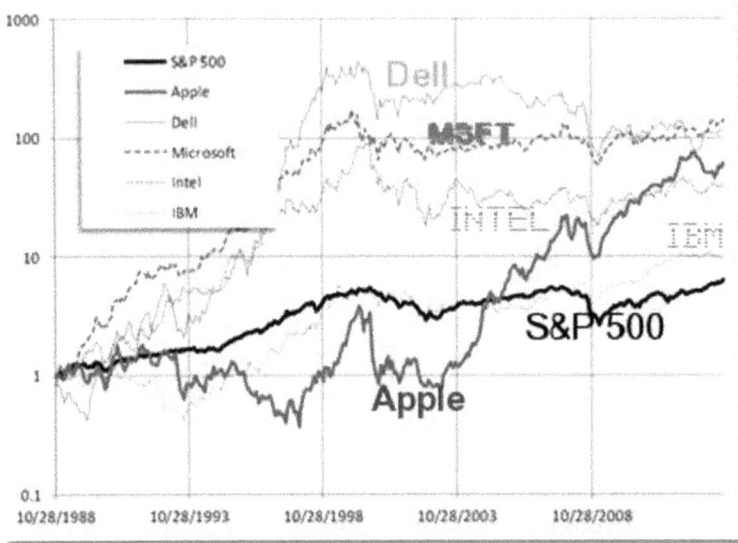

relative performance of tech stocks 1988-2012

And in case you think that tech stocks have overall done better than the S&P 500, guess again. That is only since 1988. Radio and TV stocks did well in their day, but where are they now?

Our golden rule will be to do as Buffett does, not as he says, and capture some cash flow from companies.

Increasing your share

Strategy and tactics will be covered in a later chapter, but a discussion of how the cash or dividend strategy relates to maintaining your "groups of stocks" fits well here, whether you are maintaining your own (long) list of stocks, or just buying an index fund or Exchange Traded Fund (ETF).

From time to time companies go out of business. Eventually they all go out of business. So your list of companies cannot remain static. If you own an index fund, the index maker (an entity such as Standard & Poor's, which uses some objective criteria proved over long periods of time) will periodically make changes, and your index fund will track them. If you manage your own list, even if it is just a supplemental list of dividend paying companies, you have to find money to buy the new companies you need to include. Eventually as your wealth grows, you will not be earning enough to do this out of your salary. Having some dividend generating companies gives you the cash flow to do this.

Also, simply owning a whole market index merely holds your place in line. You should be increasing your share. If you own a whole market index and manage to get some dividends out of it, you can use them to increase your share of the world economic pie.

Before Money

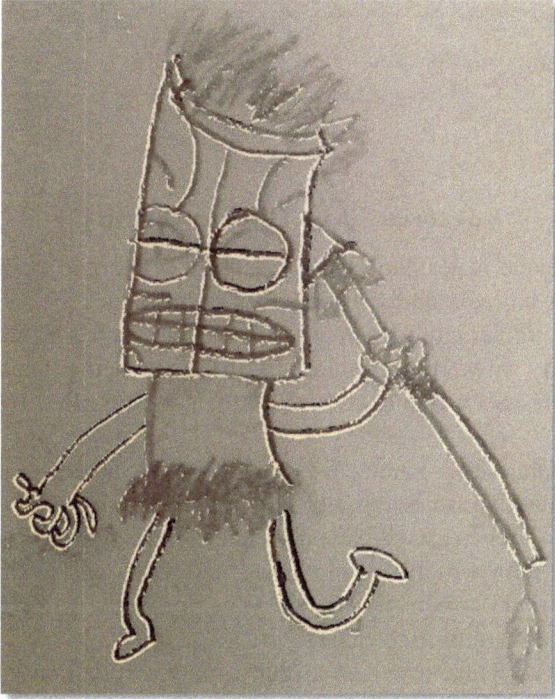

Primitive Spear Thrower
by Talmadge Lewis

A Big Increase in Productivity

When people were hunter-gatherers they lived in small groups. Can you imagine feeding a city of 20,000 (a very small city) by organizing a hunting party into the nearby forest? How long do you think the game would last?

We've been making tools for 2.5 million years, and for most of that time the best thing we could think of to hunt with was a spear. Humans are pretty talented and can throw a spear while running. But to really get it into the hide of an animal reliably, you have to get up close, and so we find a lot of people with broken bones when we dig up fossils from this era.

Neanderthals buried their dead, controlled fire, made tools, and filed heavy wooden shafts to a point to make spears. They had to get up close to use them. Neanderthals were well adapted for cold climates. But they didn't seem to change much with the times. Homo Sapiens invented a spear thrower, kind of a lever to sling shot the spear at a higher velocity, now called an atlatl, shown in the image below. And it was a stone tipped spear, sharpened for penetration.

Advanced Spear Thrower (atlatl) [7]

This device made hunting a lot safer. You could stand farther away from dangerous animals and still deliver a lethal attack. You'd think human lifespan would immediately increase. However, such a device didn't make being human any safer. It particularly didn't make being Neanderthal safe at all. Evidence has been found of Neanderthals being killed by such devices. [8]

Still, there wasn't much evidence of Homo Sapiens vs. Homo Sapiens massed warfare at that time, about 60,000 years ago, only individual assaults. It was probably safer to attack Neanderthals as they didn't have the same long range weapons with which to fight back, and were probably a little slower moving due to body structure. I guess you might say we practiced on them before turning our attention to each other.

What was really invented at that time was productivity itself. More effective hunting meant a slightly larger group could stay together, and thus defend itself better, which became necessary simply because other groups were larger as well. So you see there is the unexpected result again. A clever invention to make hunting safe and allow humans to defend themselves resulted (possibly and among other causes) in the extinction of our closest relatives and in forcing us to huddle in larger groups for self defense.

It is thought that spear thrower technology made encounters between groups very costly and resulted in a strategy of avoidance. This may have even spurred migration out of Africa. Warfare didn't become practical until 14,000 years ago. The first evidence of a massive conflict (lots of bones with evidence of sudden violent death) also includes large quantities of some of the earliest arrowheads. [9] Archers could launch a sudden surprise attack from afar, making warfare more tempting. This of course led to walled cities. The oldest known walled city is Jericho, which had walls about 8,000 BCE.

small super-advanced spear thrower [10]
aka bow & arrow

Why Agriculture was Invented

Within a scant 2000 years of that first war, humans had invented agriculture, multiple times at different places around the world. If you read up on why this came about, you may get the feeling that no one really has a clue. In certain places maybe climate change prompted agriculture, but why did the people not just wander off as they had before? Since agriculture was invented in so many different kinds of places, another theory is that it was due to social factors.

If you think about it, why would humans give up their freedom to roam about wherever the game was plentiful, and devote themselves to the settled life of tedious labor that agriculture inevitably entails? The South American primitive peoples are not tempted by it to this day, and Native Americans appear to have preferred near extinction to taking up Agriculture (although the Cherokee did in Georgia, and were expelled anyway).

The hunting lifestyle is preferable. One of the principle ways rich people spend their resources is on exotic hunting trips to recapture the feel of being wild and dependent on the skill of the next shot. My brother-in-law even hunts with a bow. Farmers are among the biggest hunting fans. A great deal of fantasy fiction entails heroes and heroines surviving in the wild on their wits alone.

Early Egyptian Agriculture [11]

Well I can venture a couple of guesses, as you may also, because I have taken a particular road in this discussion that makes it obvious. The people didn't wander off because there was no longer any unpopulated place to wander to, and it had become very dangerous to wander around. The land was claimed, and the claim could be enforced from a distance by an unexpected volley of arrows. There would have been a necessity to have a large force to defend the territorial claims, and that required more food. Hence agriculture.

With more food, not only humans could be fed but animals as well, so domestication of animals increased for labor, a variety of more interesting foods, guarding the village (dogs), assistance in hunting, and even companionship. The use of animals for labor increased productivity still further. This observation is not meant to imply that domestication of animals depends on agriculture, for the nomadic lifestyle only depended on finding fresh pasture. However, the search for fresh pasture would have even further consumed available land just as it caused the environmental decline of the open range in the U.S. western territories.

Possessions & Accounting Lead to Money & Contracts

Animals are a steady source of food, as long as you don't kill them all. Milk and eggs are regular once you learn how to keep the animals in a reproductive cycle. But this still takes food for the animals, and plants only produce harvests at certain times. So the harvest has to be stored. This is a major upgrade in the necessity for storing and protecting large quantities of stuff, as compared with just sandals, a loincloth, hunting knife and spear.

In a small group, certainly the grain would have been held in common. But as groups got larger for efficiency (basically efficiency and productivity are the same thing) in planting and harvesting and protecting the land and grain, then family and personal connections would not have been strong enough to extend the pure communal life in which warriors shared beer, meat and women as they still do in some isolated South American tribes.

Personal possessions increased. But grain and animals would likely still be stored and herded in common. After a while, memory of who stored how much would not be enough and arguments would ensue. There had to be a record of the count of the sheep, chickens or bushels attributed to a particular member of the society.

There would not have been a willingness to share with less productive group members who were distant and unknown and perhaps unworthy. Only among family are such decisions natural. With strangers, sharing requires *trust* and *accountability* in order to know that each is doing his or her share. That's why it's called *sharing*. The share of the fruits is only half the sharing. The share of the labor is the other half.

Bullae (left) and Tokens [12]

Two systems were devised, both involving tokens. In one holes were punched in them and they were placed on a string or cord, sort of like a charm bracelet. In another, they were sealed inside clay balls. Both methods were intended to make it difficult to add or delete tokens. Loose collections could not be trusted. The clay balls were the most secure. They could be sealed and baked hard, like pottery, and no one could add or remove tokens without breaking the ball, an obvious intrusion.

Of course then no one could see what was inside. This problem was easily solved by molding images on the outside representing what was inside. You can see this on the bullae at the left of the picture above, which represented a contract for a shepherd to take care of 49 sheep. We know this because that particular bullae was from a time period *after* the invention of writing. But we infer that earlier bullae had similar meaning.

Thus we see at an early stage that the precursor of money was a representation of something held by another, or owed to another. We also see that a developed notion of contracts probably predated money.

Writing

Some of the tokens look like jars or animals, but others are completely abstract, like triangles or pyramids. In fact *most* are abstract. Thus abstract symbolism was invented prior to writing, and it seems apparent that writing was suggested by the representation of the hidden content of the bullae.

This is very important. Writing portrays something which is hidden, something that represents economic goods or wealth. The act of writing is associated with creating contracts, contracts that eventually evolved into money. It was perfectly natural to limit the knowledge and function of writing to a few priests and scribes. In effect, they were the first creators of money. The meaning of money was something written, like paper money. Money is not the economic goods themselves, but the representation of them and of a contract to care for or deliver the economic goods.

In other words the first money was paper money, or its prehistoric equivalent, clay. Writing is a very important link in our chain of development from prehistoric money to the modern world, where ideas are currency and money is printed or created with a stroke on a computer keyboard.

Soon it would have become apparent that the tokens and clay balls could be dispensed with. All one needed was a clay or stone tablet which could be engraved or impressed and baked with the appropriate symbols, and which was sufficiently difficult to modify that it was secure. We are one step closer to paper money. But these bullae or tablets or tokens were not money as we know it because they represented specific things like sheep or jars of honey. As a result they were a lot simpler. There were not so many questions about their value. It was a matter of counting.

Facilitating Trade

salt is still sometimes used as a trading commodity

Motives to trade, legitimate and deceptive

Humans have been bartering and trading since prehistoric times. Few geographic regions provide every interesting spice, animal, food, mineral or metal that people might want. Sociologists and economists have the quaint notion that trade evolved because of the need for humans to specialize in order to become more productive. There has from time to time been specialization in specific countries. For a while the Swiss were dominant in watch making. But by and large this notion is nonsense. Anyone can learn to make anything he or she sees another human making. Even technically very complex and miniature devices take only a few months to be reverse engineered and appear at the output docks of factories on the other side of the planet.

Trade is most strongly driven by the uneven distribution of resources and climate. Some countries have oil and others need it. Some countries have fertile plains that grow wheat, and others need it. Some countries have exotic spices, but they won't grow in Northern Europe, and so we must trade.

I want to make something clear. The notion to trade on specialization is spurious and leads to trade based on the cost of labor. Trade based on the cost of labor leads to poverty on both sides of the transaction through the extraction of value due to transportation, theft, tariffs and middlemen. Anything you have heard to the contrary is nonsense.

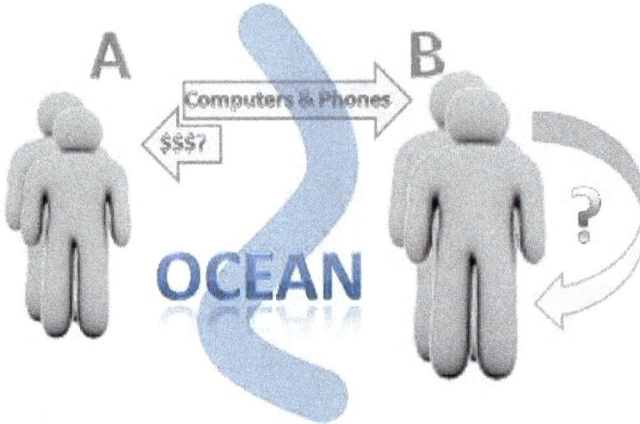

Suppose country A in the figure above has lower labor costs, and exports computers and cell phones to country B. The citizens of A are just as smart, maybe even a few IQ points smarter than those in B. Therefore B cannot make computers and cell phones, or anything which is not specific to a resource advantage, with any less labor hours than A. What is B going to give to A in exchange for the computers and cell phones?

In a world with barter trade, there is no "cost of labor" to confuse the issue, because cost is an artifact of the intermediary "money." There is just the question of how many cell phones or computers a person can make. The productivity, or efficiency, of each side would be at issue only until the other side learned to copy that efficiency (and perhaps even improve on it). There is simply no reason to add the cost of crossing the ocean to a transaction unless there is a different environment with different resources on each side of the ocean.

Of course if country A uses prison and child labor, with no retirement plan or medical care, and does not wish to consume goods from B, then the transaction is favorable to B. But how is it favorable to A? It is not. It can only be favorable to a small minority in A who are owners of the factories.

Even then it is not really favorable to B, because as the goods get cheaper and cheaper, everyone in B finds themselves out of work. This is what economists call equalization, and we'll find it applies not only to labor but to investments, and most anything whose value is expressed in terms of money.

Trade based on labor cost is just a pretext to hire workers not covered by any retirement plan or medical plan or environmental or safety protections, and who don't have to pay such high taxes and insurance out of their wages. In ancient times, contract labor was used for the most hazardous jobs, like mining, for which one would not risk the lives of relatives, or valuable property like slaves. By engaging in trade based on labor cost a country does more than hire poorly treated overseas labor. It imports eventually the same treatment of labor into itself through the process of equalization.

Do you really think that offloading the cost of medical care from employers to the government will make American labor more effective? Not unless the medical care is free, which it is not. It is paid for by taxes on either the workers or corporations or both, or by high premiums for people who do not need medical care, and this shell game does not make anyone more competitive except the uninsured foreign workers.

So legitimate impetus to trade is the uneven distribution of resources. This is like poker. If you cannot find the uneven distribution of resources to justify a trade transaction, then you are the one getting the short end of the deal.

Trading commodities and bank notes

To move beyond barter, and make transactions efficient, at first trading commodities were used. These might be something of essential value like salt, pictured at the beginning of the chapter, or something of esthetic value like gold. But not gold coins, just nuggets or jewelry.

One might also trade the bullae or contracts. Here, you take my contract that lays claim to 49 of those sheep out there, I give it to you, and the shepherd will give you the sheep whenever you want, and you give me some horses. I'm leaving town and I need horses from you.

The owner of the horses might not even want sheep, but knows he can trade the sheep contract for something else. The sheep contract has been used like a trading commodity, except that it is much easier to carry around than salt, and much safer than gold. If a thief steals the sheep contract and presents it to the shepherd, the shepherd may say "I don't know you, where did you get this?" The horse breeder will have a plausible explanation. The thief will try to make one up but a little checking will uncover his lie.

The actual use of gold in the middle ages was not to carry around for trade, but to store in one of the new banks that were being founded. Then a bank note for the gold would be transported which, like the sheep contract, was of questionable value to a thief. In fact, if a similar amount of bank notes were to flow from A to B in the above example, and from B to A, then the banks on each end could just agree to cancel them out and no gold would ever have to be shipped.

The trouble with bank notes is, how do you know the bank is telling the truth? You don't. More about this later.

Oldest known Scottish banknote, 1726 [13]

With a trading commodity, the one item is all you have to carry to market to make trades. Without a trading commodity, you must anticipate what each market participant wants. Maybe Mrs. Jones will have eggs. Perhaps she will need butter and you will take some butter to swap with her. But if you get there and Mrs. Jones already has butter from an earlier customer and now wants salt, you are out of luck.

The solution is everyone agrees to use salt as a trading commodity. You just take salt. It lasts forever and is easy to carry and divide into any quantity. If you don't have any salt, no need to worry. Just bring whatever you have to trade and first exchange it for salt. Then with the salt you can buy whatever you want.

It is easy to see we have discussed three very different types of trading commodities: sheep (or the bullae with tokens that represent them), salt (carried in person) and gold (either carried or more likely represented by a bank note). How are they different?

- **Growing:** The supply of sheep grows entirely on its own, at some biological rate, which you may influence of course by reducing it, but the maximum rate is just natural.

- **Accumulating:** The supply of salt accumulates at the rate people either dig it out of the ground or transport it from the seacoast. It's usually not rare, so the supply of salt will keep up with demand and grow with the economy, according to the cost of digging or transporting.

- **Fixed:** Gold is rare and more than likely there is none on your land. You will have to either trade for it, or go to war and annex a country with a gold mine. Such an annexation was one of the key moves made early in ancient Egypt, and accounts for their lavish use of gold. Otherwise the supply of gold grows very slowly or not at all.

The exchange rate between salt and sheep will not be constant, because it is unlikely the mining or importing rates for salt will exactly match the growth rate of the number of sheep. If sheep reach a maximum population that your land will support, then as more salt is mined the price of sheep will increase. It will take more and more salt to buy them. This is inflation.

If the amount of salt does not double as fast as the sheep population, then we get deflation. The same amount of salt will buy more sheep.

One problem with salt is psychological. If there gets to be much more of it than anyone would ever use, then people may lose faith in salt as a trading commodity. Part of the reason it is trusted is that it has intrinsic value. You can eat it, or use it to cure meat.

There are two ways to deal with this problem of loss of trust in a trading commodity (or a basis for money). The ancient way was to switch to a different trading commodity. The modern way would be to set up an Open Markets Committee to regulate the amount of salt so that it is proportional to the amount of sheep, and there will be neither inflation nor deflation.

With the ancient method, there were two tendencies. One was to go to a more rare commodity like gold or silver or (at the time) copper, which was less likely to increase so much in supply that inflation sets in. However, this means the trading commodity deflates in value as the economy grows and more sheep and salt are produced. People hoard the gold because under this particular circumstance, it is becoming more and more valuable (odd that we should use the word deflation for this). It becomes like an investment.

The motive for war

In fact the gold seems to "grow" in value. But what is actually growing is the amount of other goods and services in the economy, and with a nearly fixed amount of gold divided among these other goods and services, its value seems to grow. Actually, it has no value at all except for jewelry. When people notice the value growth and begin to hoard gold, then much of it is taken out of circulation by the hoarders and its value seems to grow even faster.

Soon this spirals out of control, only a few people have all the gold, and either there is an internal revolution or some foreign power which has more strong fighting men than gold comes in and simply seizes it. In the early days of "ritual" warfare, a strong king just approached a weaker city and demanded tribute. But of course eventually this got out of hand, people got angry, and actual wars ensued.

The sack of Susa [14]

The defeated population would be killed, dispersed or carried off as slaves. Many of the livestock would die, which greatly and immediately reduced the value of the gold, since no one will exchange it for dead livestock or spoiled or burned grain stores. In other words, the motive for war proceeds as follows:

1. A growing or accumulating trading commodity (grain, sheep, salt, etc.) is mismanaged, leading to inflation. We might call this the "liberal" phase.

2. A scarce trading commodity is adopted (gold, silver), leading to deflation. (If the inflation was severe enough to cause unemployment directly, the deflation step may be skipped.) We might call this the "conservative" phase.

3. Deflation leads to unemployment. This is the "collapse" phase.

4. Unemployment leads to economic and military weakness. Either an internal rebellion arises because of the poor conditions, or a foreign power seeing weakness invades and seizes the gold. This is the "war" phase. Factories are destroyed or converted to make weapons. Trade is interrupted. Shortages and rationing are possible.

5. Whether from internal or external adversaries, the economic output and productivity are destroyed resulting in inflation (scarcity). There can also be inflation as a result of tapping the gold reserves, or borrowing gold from an ally, to pay the soldiers for defense. This is the "recovery work" or reconstruction phase, and is a different kind of inflation than the liberal mismanagement phase. Everyone willing can find a job, as much work is needed to rebuild and to correct shortages.

6. With inflation everyone has to work harder and economic output rises. The scarce trading commodity is not perceived to be helping and is abandoned in favor of a more rational trading system. This is the "rational" phase. The last rational phase began in 1971 when gold was abandoned for international trading. The rational phase will last as long as most market participants "remember" the lessons of the cycle.

7. After a while a new generation is born who doesn't have a clue as to what happened before. Increases in the trading commodity are seen as a way to fund humanitarian relief for the citizens and to fund pyramids or other government works. Soon we have excessive inflation and are back at step 1. This is the "new generation forgets" phase.

Together the seven stages form a repeating cycle of currency mismanagement, crisis, war, recovery, forgetting. It has been 43 years since the rational phase was entered and most of the players are now retiring. The currency mismanagement phase began with the adoption of the Euro by Europe. It was not rational because of the differing needs of the member nations. We'll analyze it more later.

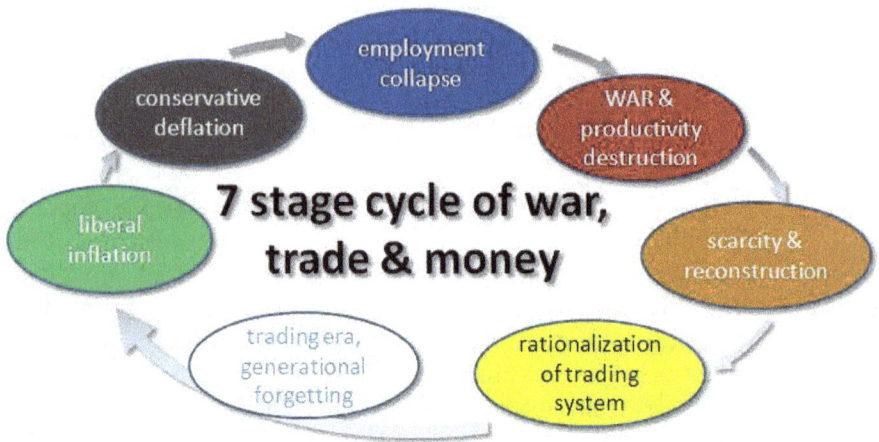

7 stages of trade, war & currency management

There are some variations on this cycle, as for example one can bypass inflation and go directly to deflation. And as we have seen, the lethality of weapon technology, together with whether defense can inflict heavy damages on an attacker, determine the level of war and whether avoidance or tribute may be considered instead.

In the late 1920s, Germany was having difficulty paying war reparations which were due in gold. (Incidentally, the Allies did not invent war reparations. Germany had extracted them from France in 1871, and had seized Alsace-Lorraine in the bargain.) The German supply of gold was thus dwindling, not growing. Had their internal currency been based on gold it would have led to deflation and unemployment. Realizing this they tried to print fiat money without constraining it to the amount by which their economy was growing, which led to high inflation with the same end result of massive unemployment.

In other words, Germany's situation was true deflation disguised as inflation through mismanagement of the currency. Adolf Hitler gained political credibility by joining a coalition seeking to repudiate reparations. In 1933 he came to power and repudiated the reparations by decree, the same year that Roosevelt came to power in the highly deflated U.S. and abolished the internal gold standard. (Much later Germany paid all the old reparations.)

Hitler only liked classic art, but confiscated modern art as a negative example
A stash worth approximately $1 billion recently turned up [15]

The U.S., still recovering from severe deflation, was attacked by Japan. Or was it? The immediate cause from the Japanese point of view was that they were (in their minds) defending themselves against a China backed by Russia when the U.S. sent aircraft to defend China and imposed an oil embargo. Japan had been getting 80% of its oil from the U.S. American public opinion had turned against them after news of the Rape of Nanking and other atrocities. Everywhere Japan looked for replacement oil supplies seemed to be somewhere that would provoke a declaration of war from the U.S. One has to conclude the immediate cause of war was cessation of trade, however justified that might have been.

The German situation qualified as a rebellion and soon their economy had recovered, but the leaders of the rebellion or coup sought to plunder the ailing gold-based economies of Europe, carrying off not only gold but huge quantities of art, much of which is still missing and parts of which turn up from time to time.

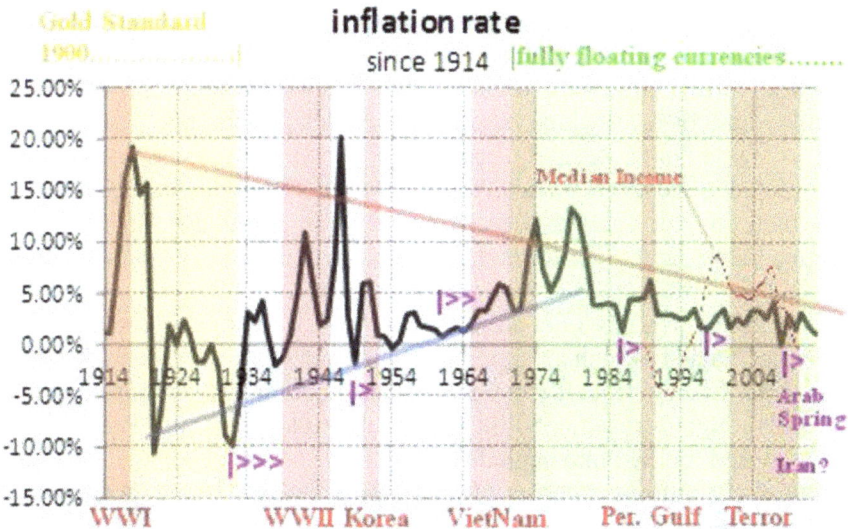

In the inflation rate chart above I have marked the early period of the gold standard in the U.S., and major wars. You can easily see the war and postwar inflation spikes, and the negative inflation rate (i.e. deflation) during non-war periods of the gold standard. The recessions that led to wars are hard to see (|>>> marks recession to war start) except for 1929, largely because this is a U.S. chart and does not reflect other countries. Declining inflation after 1980 and the lack of a big inflation spike for the War on Terror are worrisome in that the expected periods of prosperity might be less than usual.

Postwar inflation brought unprecedented prosperity in western nations. By the time things had begun to fall apart again and inflation ran out of control, Nixon came to power and in 1971 invented a new kind of money, not really tried previously, which has prevented war among the major powers since. We will come back to this after completing the steps by which money came about, because the 1971 changes involved a new kind of money. In fact few economists understand the new money, and almost no citizens, because it simply hasn't been around but a little over 40 years, a mere blink in the history we are covering, and its effects are not present in long-term historical data samples.

Fascism and Communism

A second important variation on the 7-stage cycle is also illustrated by Germany after WWI. If the destruction of productivity is not complete, if a country remains functioning but is unable to recover with a normal government, then either fascism of communism may arise.

In either case, economic activity is "forced" somewhat by central direction, and the citizenry becomes highly motivated by pride in themselves and what they can or will accomplish. In the case of the Nazis it was racial pride. In the case of the Soviets, it was a kind of intellectual-social pride in their ideals. In both cases, problems are blamed on someone else, some particular class or race, which is then systematically persecuted, removed, or killed en masse. In the case of Germany and Japan, both fascist, the pride and overconfidence led to WWI and utter destruction of both countries, which were then rebuilt under the Marshall Plan and not saddled with insurmountable debt. Both then channeled their energy into becoming economic powerhouses.

Communism does not seem to have such a clear cut ending. Perhaps pride is not carried to such an extreme, or the leaders are not as deluded as the population? China eventually did become an economic powerhouse, though it has not thoroughly transitioned into a western style economy. Russia seems to have rushed too fast into capitalism, indulged in crony capitalism, and also seeks to retain a strong measure of government control, but without as much economic success as China.

The cause of revolutions

The event that sparked the **Arab Spring** revolutions was viral on social media, but initially not reported by other media. What was said by the 26 year old man, sole supporter of a family of 8, as he poured gasoline on himself and set it ablaze was not some slogan of hate or ideology or politics or freedom or religion. It was so little reported in the west that I didn't find it in any conventional internet write-up on the revolution. I found it reported by Jim Clifton, CEO of Gallup Polls. The young man, after his vegetable cart and produce were confiscated, not for the first time, after he received no audience when requesting to pay the $7 fine (a day's wages), immolated himself and screamed, "*I just want to work!*"

I just want to work!
(generic image)

As a result of this sentiment, the leaders of four countries were replaced, all of them lifetime dictators with a secure grip on power, some of them replaced more than once when jobs didn't appear, and one entire country is virtually immolating itself (Syria) rather than continue as it was. Several other governments either reorganized, saw violent protests, or the secession of regions followed by warfare.

The **American Revolution** began because colonists thought Britain's new laws giving the East India Company a monopoly on certain trade (via tax exemptions) were a presage to shutting down colonial entrepreneurs and brutally extracting wealth as they had done in India. Most other revolutions in the western hemisphere were initiated because the Spanish had done just that.

The **October (communist) Revolution** in Russia occurred because of massive unemployment, 50% reduction in real wages in about 5 years, 36% decrease in industrial production, as high as 50% closure of all businesses, and continued participation in the unpopular WWI despite a February revolution that toppled the Tsar. It did not occur simply because people were poor. What they had was being rapidly taken away, and they were getting even poorer fast.

For the cause of the **Cuban Revolution**, let's look at the words of an American President: "*I believe that there is no country in the world including any and all the countries under colonial domination, where economic colonization, humiliation and exploitation were worse than in Cuba, in part owing to my country's policies during the Batista regime.*" - John Kennedy, October 24, 1963, less than a month before he was assassinated.

It is possible to find revolutions that were a continuation of the fighting of WWII, for example in Yugoslavia and Vietnam. It is hard to assess whether they had economic causes because their background was an existing conflict. Otherwise, wherever I looked I found that most often revolutions sprung not just from poverty or chronic ill treatment, but because what people had was being taken from them, like the fruit cart of the Tunisian street vendor.

Ending Global War

Trade routes, empires & global war

The relation between trade and war did not go unnoticed by the community of nations. Following the fall of Rome, the European continent was torn by territorial warfare for about half a millennium. Even before its internal boundaries were settled, the Crusades began. While nominally fought at the request of the Catholic Church, the real reason many Europeans willingly participated was because of the possibility of opening or controlling lucrative trade routes to Asia.

OTTOMAN EMPIRE AND VASSAL STATES 16-17 CENTURIES

Ottoman Empire circa 1590 [16]

While various kingdoms and ethnic groups participated in multiple campaigns over several centuries, the Europeans decisively lost when the Ottoman Turks, actually an Asian people related to the Mongols, captured and held Constantinople in 1453. The Hundred Years War between Britain and France concluded in that same year.

By the late 1500's the Ottomans extended their control through Greece and into the Balkans threatening the heartland of Europe, all across the northern coast of Africa, and throughout the cradles of civilization in the Middle East. Their domain was second in extent only to the ancient Roman Empire, and controlled all known trade routes between East and West. This trade made the empire and its ruling family wealthy, and the empire lasted until the end of World War I.

In late fall of 2011 Natasha and I were looking for an interesting location for our second meeting, some place involving old ruins and artifacts which we both love. Egypt was having a revolution. Greece was having rioting in the streets with periodic strikes closing the airport, sort of a revolution without actually changing the government. Both conflicts were about economics. The Muslim Brotherhood managed to commandeer the Egyptian revolution, but when economic conditions didn't improve they were summarily kicked out, so it appears that though the Egyptians changed the government they weren't able to change the facts on the ground any more than the Greeks. Neither was a suitable, safe destination. So we went to Turkey.

Topkai Palace [17]

Among other attractions that had attracted the likes of Alexander the Great and the first Cleopatra (Thais of Athens, who later married Ptolemy), such as walking the streets of Ephesus and wading in the hot springs of Hieropolis, we toured the Topkai Palace with a private guide and got a tutorial on the history of the empire.

I had no idea. I was shocked at the size and longevity and importance of the Ottomans' domain. My mid-20th century American education had barely mentioned them, and had emphasized the role of the Italians in monopolizing the trade routes rather than the Ottomans. But the Italians had been just the empire's front men.

It was no accident then that the Europeans began trying to reach the East by sailing west or south from the 1490s until the outbreak of WWI. This resulted in an endless series of colonial wars of which the American Revolution was but one small part. The American Revolution was symbolized by the Boston Tea Party, which was an economic protest over tea tariffs discriminating against American importers by exempting the East India Company. Pamphlets of the time contained discussions of conditions in colonial India and expressed a fear that America would be next. Another way of phrasing this issue was "taxation without representation." Any way you phrase it, the American Revolution was an economic war.

Sultan Mehmed II [18]
his heirs were the richest people in the world for 500 years

Hundreds of independent German kingdoms were among the last territories to be consolidated in Europe, and Germany missed the era of colonial expansion. Their conflict with France, annexation of French territory and demand for tribute (reparations is just a fancy name for tribute) arose from jealousy of France's highly successful colonial empire. Germany's support of the Austrian Empire's annexation of territory in the Balkans was from the same motive. Thus WWI was effectively an extension of the colonial trade wars, and finally broke the back of the Ottoman Empire. Turkey (the Ottomans) did not have to enter the war, and was somewhat afraid of both sides. In the end they chose the German side because of early German victories and the thought they could opportunistically claim a victory, but it backfired.

In the East, Japan emerged late like Germany and began a colonial expansion to establish a trade empire. When the chaos left by the Allied victors erupted into WWII, again for economic reasons, and as weaponry had evolved to world threatening proportions, the Allied Powers knew something had to be done or the world would be destroyed.

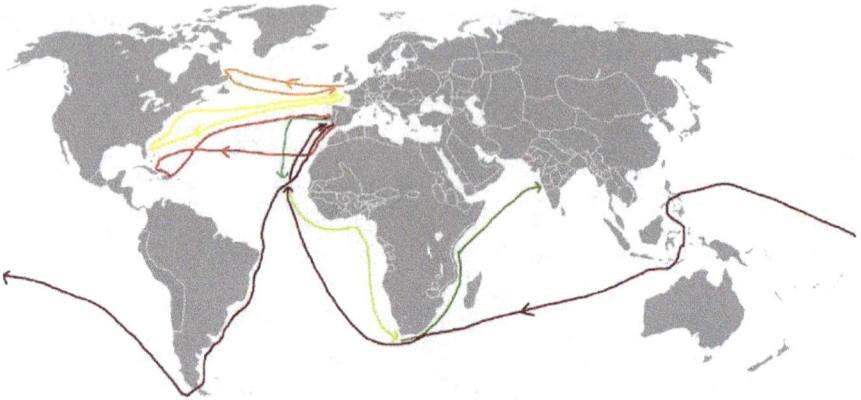

European Explorers Circumvent the Ottoman Empire [19]

The World Trade Organization (WTO)

In 1947 the Bretton Woods Agreement established three organizations: the International Monetary Fund (IMF), World Bank, and International Trade Organization (ITO). The ITO was the organization charged with international trade cooperation, and implementing the General Agreement on Tariffs and Trade (GATT). While American political opinion largely focused on the somewhat impotent United Nations, these other three organizations quietly began the bureaucratic business of organizing and regulating financial, monetary and trade issues around the world. As we have seen, these are the issues that drive people to war, and so these three organizations became almost as powerful (not quite) as a world government.

Periodic negotiations were held and revisions made to the GATT. By the early 1990s, "globalization" was rapidly changing world trade and a major overhaul, GATT 1994, established the World Trade Organization (WTO). The WTO is governed by five principles:

- Every member nation is treated equally (most favored nation status: MFN).

- Every member must reciprocate MFN to others, no free riders.

- Agreements are binding and enforceable and include dispute settlement procedures.

- Member nations must publish their trade regulations and respond to requests for information (transparency).

- In specific circumstances nations are able to restrict trade, for example to protect public health as in the banning of beef from countries with mad cow disease outbreaks.

The transparency principle has been found to be deceptive in practice. It applies to member nations. Development of regulations within the WTO itself as well as the dispute settlement process have often been criticized for secrecy. In general the WTO is set up not only to regulate but to actively promote trade, and not to settle or even address other issues. Thus it does not permit local environmental or labor conditions (child labor for example) to dictate trade decisions. Many have complained that this interferes with national sovereignty. An internet search easily turns up articles on this subject. [20]

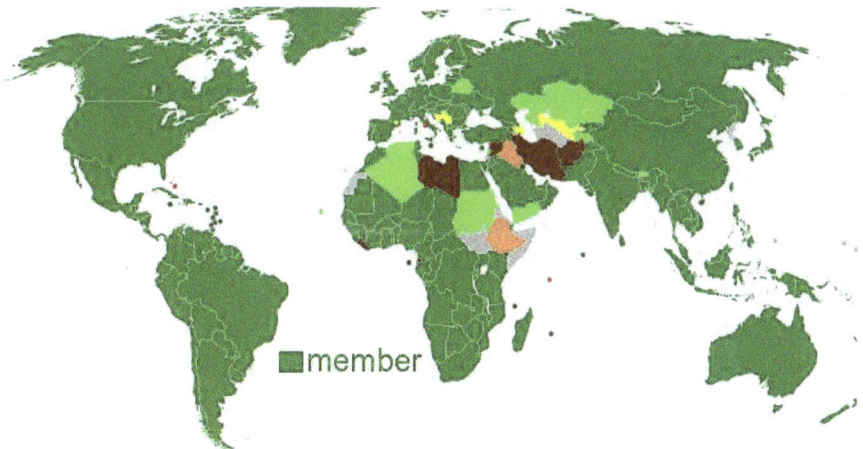

WTO Member Nations [21]

The map above reveals the effect of the pressure to join the WTO. Without membership, nations are cut off from most of the world and can be treated arbitrarily in trade. Turkey is a member and has a strong trading economy, but other parts of the old Ottoman empire which dominated trade for so long constitute the bulk of nations not now full members, including the North African coastal countries except Egypt, several formerly Ottoman Balkan countries where WWI started, and the Middle Eastern trade route countries of Syria, Iraq, Iran and Afghanistan. The world is still divided as it was when Athens fought the Persians.

Many recent and current conflict zones (though not all) are found among the nonmember nations. In addition to those listed above, there are North Korea and Sudan for example. Does this mean the WTO is doing its real job of keeping the peace? More time may be needed to reach such a conclusion, and to evaluate the claimed negative aspects of the WTO.

Trade war vs. plain old shooting war

The term "trade war" means raising tariffs in retaliation for the other country raising tariffs. It can happen when imports from another country undermine a large number of jobs creating a declining internal economy, or undermine an essential industry creating an unwanted dependence on an untrusted out-of-country source. In other words, trade wars are more likely when countries trade for the wrong reasons, for cost of labor reasons.

If there is a problem regarding an essential commodity that only the other country has, a trade war cannot solve the problem. A trade war can only ban items, not force them to be traded. However, if the cost of an actual shooting war is less than the cost of trading for the essential commodity, then a shooting war is extremely likely. The mismanagement of trading commodities which we discussed earlier creates economic weakness within a country, making it hard for them to organize and pay for a defense, thus lowering the cost of a shooting war and tempting their neighbors to raid instead of trade.

Ukraine had been unaligned with any mutual defense pacts since the fall of the Soviet Union, so when trade between Russia and Ukraine was threatened, invasion of Ukraine appeared to be a low cost option to the Russians. I almost wrote "to the Soviets," because that is the way they are behaving. But truthfully, all nations behave this way. Ordinary citizens do not even realize the extent to which war is simple economic calculus. To understand the war with Islamic terror, and in my opinion it is not a generic war on "terror" because all nations use terrorism (U.S. drone strikes for example), one need only look at the WTO map above and understand that the excluded nations are mostly impoverished and facing huge trade barriers. Saudi Arabia is in the WTO and not impoverished as a country, but though its wealthy class may sponsor extremism in other countries, it doesn't show up directly as a conflict with Saudi Arabia.

Recognizing this simple equation, nations have attempted to raise the cost of shooting wars by making mutual defense treaties with allies. Usually these allies are countries with which they have low mutual trade costs. One could call them trading blocs, and in many cases military treaties and trade treaties exist between the same sets of countries. During the late middle 20th century period of so-called Cold War, there was more or less an eastern trading bloc of communist countries, and a western trading bloc of everyone else.

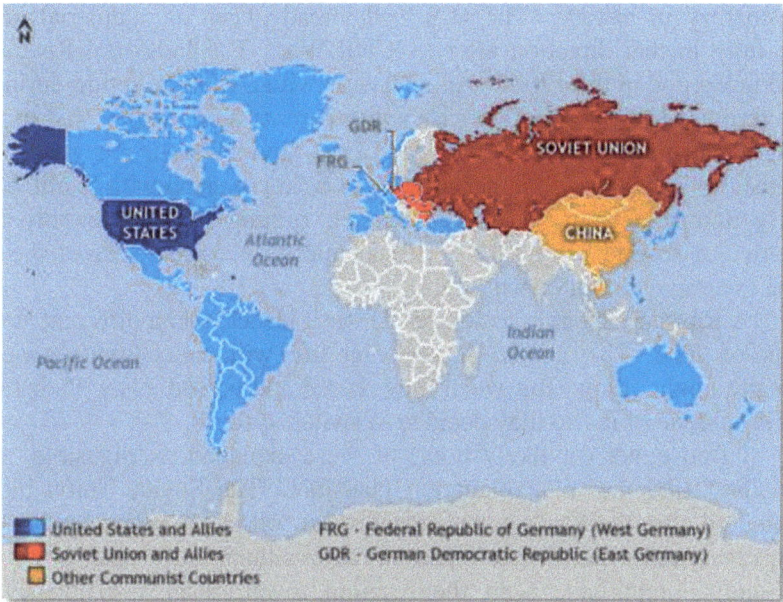

Cold War Trading Blocs 1948-1988 [22]

However, alliances can also cause wars to expand because in a small conflict, many allies are drawn into the fight. Essentially this is how a dispute between Austria and the Serbia became the first "global war" in 1914. We saw earlier that weapon characteristics can make war costly, as for example the spear thrower. Or a weapon such as the bow and arrow gave an advantage to an attacker, at least until walled and fortified cities were developed. Nuclear war, which also was developed during WWII just before GATT, is deemed the costliest of all war yet known, and added to the incentive to solve the problem of trade and war at that time. So far no nuclear war has been fought where both sides have nuclear weapons and let's hope it stays that way. As long as both sides have something to lose and are making rational calculations, it probably will. But if a country is pushed into economic ruin, or if a non-state group obtains a nuclear weapon, then all bets are off.

The Cold War

Americans in the late 1980s felt like they had won the Cold War, proving their hybrid economic system (capitalism with managed-economy patches and safety nets dating from the 1930s depression) was superior. But an interview with someone from Russia or China will give a different answer, depending on who it is. Some of the answers have to do with trade.

Russia is an oil exporting country. It progressed from a rather backward peasant agriculture economy at the time of the 1918 revolution, to a major industrial, space and nuclear power by 1957, a record matched by no other country in history. The U.S. had already been an industrial nation, tilting fully in that direction after its Civil War. The Industrial Revolution started in Europe in the 1700s. An interview with a Russian living during the 1950s through 1980s will report (my wife's parents for example) that life was fine then, much better than after the fall of the Soviet Union. The reason they think the Soviet Union fell is because the U.S. in collusion with Saudi Arabia unfairly dumped cheap oil on the market, ruining their oil export based economy. A second story such a person might tell is that fear of the west caused excessive military spending.

A Russian oligarch, or former political leader, told a different story to a friend of mine. They too had a very nice life, with every luxury a western billionaire might enjoy. But when they retired and passed away, their family could keep none of it. So they decided to switch systems.

I find either (or likely both) of these explanations plausible. Most especially I find the oil explanation plausible. The Soviet Union did not decline until after the Saudi commitment to low oil prices in the early 1980s. Perhaps the Saudis did this for different reasons than the Russian might say. The Saudis might have seen the reaction toward energy efficiency and independence in the west during the 1970s, which saw two oil "embargoes," and decided keeping the west addicted to cheap oil was in their best interest. The Soviet Union might have simply been an accidental casualty.

In either case, we see how trade shapes world empires just as surely as war.

In 1972 Richard Nixon visited the People's Republic of China after opening preliminary ties with them. By 1978 diplomatic relations were normalized. By 1986 imports and exports were approximately equal, but small. China exports to the U.S. grew at a linear pace to $120 billion annually by 2000. There was a year without growth due to the dot com bust or Tian'anmen square or both, but then China exports grew exponentially to over $400 billion in 2012. U.S. exports to China are about $100 billion.

People in America sometimes get very excited about these numbers, but they are dwarfed by our own profligacy. Total federal spending in 2012 was $3.5 trillion, with over $1 trillion of it borrowed. Most of the borrowed amount came from the Federal Reserve (which we'll discuss in the chapter on banks). The Fed's program of Quantitative Easing creates about $90 billion a month to buy U.S. Treasury bills and bonds. That's almost all of the borrowed money. There has not been much new outside investment in U.S. debt since the 2008-9 financial crisis. Compared to the problem we have with ourselves, we have no problem at all with China. However I am not blaming the Fed for this problem. It is doing its job. The problem is very complex as we shall see, and one dimension of it is trade and the relation of trade to wages and benefits.

Nevertheless, from China's viewpoint, the trade is significant. And it is a significant deterrent to war. China also holds $1.2 trillion in U.S. debt which would be worthless to China in the event of war, and the holding of which indicates China is highly confident it foresees essentially no circumstances in which a war with the U.S. is likely. Instead, China has got what it wanted from the U.S. through trade, without war, perhaps in a few cases augmented by espionage. But by and large American Corporations have opened factories in China and trained the Chinese in their technology, and done this of their own free will in hopes of capitalizing on China's intelligent and hard working labor force, at ridiculously low wages, with few benefits.

Chinese manufactured iPhone [23]

The cost to China of acquiring such technology was negative. That is, we paid them to acquire it instead of them paying us. This is capitalism at work. But I am not sure who is the better capitalist. Some companies such as Apple Computer have since regretted their decisions and begun to move manufacturing back to the U.S. This does not necessarily mean a boon to manufacturing in the U.S. because the new plants will be highly automated, but it is an admission that trading based on labor cost had an unexpected downside. Even large corporations run by people we consider brilliant are subject to the law of unexpected outcomes.

Japan acquired similar advantages through war, though the path was circuitous and costly. Japan lost a war with the U.S., a war which subjected them to two nuclear strikes and tremendous costs. But recognizing that chaos would breed only another war eventually, the U.S. rebuilt both Germany and Japan. The Chinese seem to have made a much cooler calculation.

Making war illegal

In the WTO era, trade wars among member nations are illegal. Punishment can include harsh fines on governments, companies and individuals. The only alternative to paying the fine (or complying) is to pull out of the WTO, which as you can see from the WTO member nation map is not very attractive. Any nation who pulls out will experience tremendous disruption to industries that depend on imports or exports while it tediously negotiates separate trade agreements on a case by case basis.

These agreements will be constrained by WTO rules that they can be no more favorable than trade agreements among member states, and they likely will be worse. It's kind of like when you go to the doctor's office and tell them you don't have insurance, and they say well, we have a special price for you. It's 400% higher than the price we give the insurance company who is our most favored customer, and we cannot give you any discounts because of our contract with them.

*So trade wars **are** illegal*, with a high degree of enforceability. The primary deterrent, the thing that makes fines collectable for example, is the motivation of nations not to lose their trade privileges. If nations are able to cooperate sufficiently to take trade privileges away from nations who are already in the WTO in the event that, say, one is the aggressor in a war, then that should have a similar motivational effect. War has become illegal. *(That is the "theory" at least, behind sanctions on Russia for the invasion of Ukraine.)*

Such trade sanctions may not always work on countries not already enjoying trade privileges, but we shall see in the next chapter that in fact the threat of them works quite well on WTO members. While we were watching the not-too-effective U.N., which must after all deal with truly rogue states, the WTO has outlawed war within its borders.

The European Union - a special case

In case you think I'm making this up about the connection between trade and war, or the perception of it by nations, here is a quote from the 2nd paragraph of the official description of the European Union:

The EU Flag - yes, it has a flag like a nation

"The EU was created in the aftermath of the Second World War. The first steps were to foster economic cooperation: the idea being that countries who trade with one another become economically interdependent and so more likely to avoid conflict." [24]

In the next chapter I'll discuss how "equalization" forces countries, perhaps unwittingly, to adopt similar polices and even laws. But the EU embraces this deliberately. The heading of the very next paragraph is *"From economic to political union."* The political aspects of the EU encompass human rights, environmental regulations and numerous other areas.

The next thing you learn from the EU description is that the member nations are not "trading partners" in the sense of the WTO member nations. There are no barriers at all to movement of goods or money, much as between states in the U.S. *"The single or internal market is the EU's main economic engine, enabling most goods, services, money and people to move freely."*

With this piece of information we can decode current news stories relating to the EU, such as a December 2013 dispute between Russia, Ukraine and the EU. The EU was working on a special "association" agreement with Moldova, Georgia and Ukraine. The association agreement is a preparatory stage for nations which will eventually become new "member states" of the EU.

Conflict in eastern Ukraine
Wikimedia commons

Russia in the spring of 2014 persuaded Ukraine to back away from the EU agreement, but that action sparked large protests, especially in European-leaning western Ukraine, and soon a change of government in Kiev. This snowballed into accusations of racism, the nearly bloodless takeover of Crimea by Russia, threats of a renewed Cold War, military invasion of eastern Ukraine by unmarked soldiers of dubious origin, the downing of Malaysian Airlines flight 17 by an apparently Russian made missile, the loss of 5000 or more lives, and sanctions imposed on Russia by the EU and the U.S.

In a mostly unrelated event, world oil supplies exceeded demand causing the price of oil to fall by nearly half.

It strikes me as interesting that during 2014 the Fed tapered its quantitative easing program down to zero, seemingly successfully, but almost coincident with the end of it oil dropped precipitously. The Saudis didn't increase production, they just failed to reduce it. Now not only oil but copper and other commodities have started to decline. Is this the deflationary spiral that the equity premium theory, fully explained in *The Equity Premium Puzzle*, predicts would result from not making the stimulus required by productivity permanent?

The Russian economy was very dependent on oil. In December 2014 there were unusually large amounts of Russian corporate bonds due to be paid in dollars. Sanctions prevented the firms from issuing new bonds, so they issued Ruble bonds, particularly Roseneft the Russian oil company, and bought dollars on the currency markets to pay off the old bonds. Naturally this put pressure on the value of the Ruble.

On Monday December 15th the currency markets discovered the Russian central bank had accepted some Roseneft Ruble bonds as collateral, amounting to the issuance of fiat money, and the Ruble collapsed. Since then it has been stabilized by announcing the central bank will convert Rubles to dollars using its own foreign currency reserves (i.e. it promises not to print fiat money), Russian oligarchs have been urged to bring their money back to Russia (see chapter Beyond America, Alisher Usmanov), and Russian banks have also been urged to sell dollars. The crisis may go on for some time. No one expects Russia to appear to "give in" to the west.

Damaged apartment building in Donetsk
Wikimedia commons

Analysis of the war in Ukraine 2014 - ?

In mid-February 2015 European leaders engaged in an all night negotiating session. Russia moved 50 more tanks into Ukraine during the all night session while rebels shelled Kramatorsk some 20 miles across the line, a city not previously involved in fighting and an apparent escalation. Precisely at midnight intense fighting stopped but rebels said they would not observe the ceasefire in the town of Debaltseve, where they encircled several thousand Ukrainian troops.

Later the troops were able to depart but the town was lost. This is a strategy they attempted earlier in another location. It is also a situation similar to the one which developed in West Berlin after WWII. Though West Berlin was Allied territory, it was 100 miles from the nearest border between Soviet occupied East Germany and Allied occupied West Germany. The Soviet's blocked all access, hoping to take over West Berlin by fiat. The Allies responded with an airlift to resupply West Berlin. Planes landed and took off every 30 seconds in West Berlin making 300,000 flights in all. [120] This should give you a quantitative idea of the scale of effort it takes to get the Soviets to back down. And if they are taking over another country, they are no longer Russians but truly again are Soviets. (The Russian word "COBET," pronounced "soviet," means "advice, council, board, guidance, suggestion or recommendation.") And why do I call the separatists "rebels?" If you are familiar with the rebel flag from the American Civil War, you will see that effectively they have taken that label for themselves. There is some controversy over whether the resemblance is deliberate. [121]

Confederate (L) & Donetsk Republic (R) battle flags

Why have Russian forces not swept over Ukraine already? In view of a payment of $385 million by Ukraine to Russia for natural gas at the first of December, it is not surprising at all. If Russia presses its claim and the Kiev government falls, then Russia would cut off a much needed source of foreign currency! The withdrawal of heavy armor is proceeding. My Russian wife has learned from her relatives that as of December 22nd, Russian news agencies are reporting that the rebuilding of destroyed buildings has commenced. That means the Russians are not planning to provoke Ukraine to blow them up again.

Some people are concerned about a larger scale European war. While it is a possibility, the Russians have preferred small manageable conflicts since WWI, when they got their tail kicked and the Tsar got his whole family killed. They all remember this. They got dragged into WWII by the Germans, and they don't want to repeat that either.

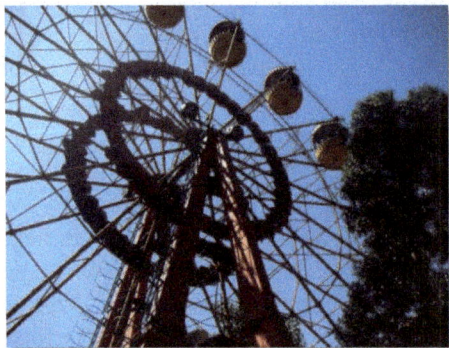

Ferris wheel in Luhgansk in 2011
photo by the author

Putin is the new Tsar. In private they call him that. The main concern of any Russian or Ukrainian leader since 1918 is to avoid jail on leaving office, or worse fates like the Tsar. I have traveled extensively in both eastern and western Ukraine and experienced the pro-European anti-Russian leanings there personally. In western Ukraine I noticed I was being treated somewhat rudely by clerks in stores. My guide informed me it was because I was speaking Russian. I switched to my Texas drawl and was treated much better. It even seemed they understood me better, though more likely they were just paying attention to my gestures and being more sympathetic.

A street in European-leaning Chernivsti in western Ukraine
photo by the author

The people of western Ukraine remember all too well that a few years ago in a bitterly cold winter they had a bit of trouble paying their gas bill and friendly Russia cut off their gas supplies. Without doubt this region of small farmers also remembers that Stalin confiscated the harvest one year to force farmers on to collective farms, and that many died of starvation. Flying over Ukraine, I was astonished that most of the land, especially in western Ukraine, is uncultivated. I had learned in school that Ukraine was the "bread basket of the world." "Why," I asked my guide? "Because they don't believe they will get a fair price at harvest time," she replied. Farmers in the U.S. and Europe can plant with confidence if they sell their crops on futures markets at the time they plant. I hasten to add that people in another country might well resent some European countries for similar aggressions. What we see clearly in the Ukraine-Russia-EU dynamics is that feelings play out where the money is - in trade.

Both sides are capable of, and have committed, atrocities. It is our nature to side with Ukraine because (a) they are the underdog and Americans like underdogs and (b) they at the moment are saying they want to be our friends.

Anna Nemstova writes sensational and anti-Russian articles for The Daily Beast and Newsweek. In a recent article she interviews Kremlin adviser Sergei Markov who says: "*About a month and a half ago, I advised that instead of Novorossia, we should promote integration of the Donbas regions back into Ukraine*," and points out that since November Putin has not used the word "Novorussia" which had been so popular. Earlier Markov was noting certain officials in Kiev who were so against peace that negotiations with them was not really possible.

What the Russians seem to have miscalculated is the democratic election process, which after all they don't truly use and have experience with.   Without eastern Ukraine's participation in Kiev's elections, the government in Kiev became more anti-Russian and moved immediately to join NATO and the EU, the exact opposite of what Russia wanted. So now the problem is to find a graceful way to back down.

Russia will attempt to hold on to their gains, otherwise they would not be rebuilding the captured (aka "rebel") territory. They may engage in military action if Ukraine begins to forcefully retake the territory the Russians would like to rebuild. And the rebels, though the leaders have been rotated by Moscow, may not be fully compliant. They still have weapons and can provoke conflict if they see a deal coming that concedes them too little autonomy. If they see that Moscow plans to reintegrate Donbas into Ukraine, they will not see a future for themselves.

The economic value of Ukraine

The "elected" leader of Donetsk, Alexander Zakharchenko, has said: *"We're like the United Arab Emirates. Our region is very rich. We have coal, metallurgy, natural gas ... The difference between us and the Emirates is they don't have a war there and we do ... [pensioners should have enough money to] travel to Australia at least once a year to shoot a dozen kangaroos on Safari."* [122]

There should be no doubt that Zakharchenko is himself motivated by economic factors, and seeking to motivate the people in his region by the same factors. Ukraine is not presently a significant natural gas producer. Is this just some trumped up war rhetoric?

Hardly.   The gas in Ukraine is in shale deposits which require fracking technology, and not yet developed. It has the 3rd largest deposits of shale gas in Europe. [123] Poland is 1st.

Russia is aggressively seeking to secure its future as an energy exporter, establishing military bases in the arctic. It also uses Ukraine's dependence on Russia to bully and control Ukraine, cutting off supplies in the winters of 2005, 2007 and 2008. On November 5th 2013, a few weeks before the Maidan demonstrations began, Kiev and Chevron signed a 50-year agreement to develop oil and gas in *western* Ukraine, with total investment projected at $10 billion. Then leader Yanukovich said that it *"will let Ukraine satisfy its gas needs completely and, under the optimistic scenario, export energy resources by 2020."* [124]

Is there any doubt the war in Ukraine is driven by economics? Is there any doubt that Poland should be worried that, as a former Soviet republic it should be worried that if Russia is successful in Ukraine it will come after Poland's gas next? Actually NATO is preparing to fend off Russia in the Baltics next. The Baltics and Finland are busy building a terminal to import U.S. gas, which Russia doesn't want. It seems to me that if Russia is not to count its invasion of Ukraine as a success which entices it to continue to further its "development" as Putin euphemistically puts it via war, then its gains in Ukraine will have to be rolled back or come at a stiff cost.

The role of war in economic cycles

The EU has grown from 6 to 28 nations. The advantages of friction-free trade are practically irresistible, so much so that most of these nations adopted a common currency, the Euro, in January of 2002. For many of them that has proven disastrous because it became a gold-like static money basis for them, which they cannot manage. Trading associations do prevent war, but "common" currencies are like the world gold standard in the early 20th century and may undermine the goal of the trading associations.

Destroyed "broken" terminal building at Lugansk airport
the result of a "trade war" - same as any other war (Wikimedia commons)

War, especially large scale war, performs the important step of destroying productivity, bringing the supply of goods down to match the insufficiently expanded money supply, and creating such large demand due to reconstruction needs and scarcity that employment soars. If trade associations are able to suppress this correction, what will replace it? Right now the EU is struggling to find the will to increase its money supply. But even if it does, is this enough without also destroying productivity and creating reconstruction demand? We do not know.

Ukraine is now in the "*war and productivity destruction*" phase of the seven stage cycle. Russia is already planning reconstruction. But Ukraine is not occupying much territory that needs reconstruction, other than that their whole economy needs it, but that really is the following stage "*rationalization of the trading system*" which needs to be put off until after reconstruction is well underway. Russia is not ready to accept an EU-integrated Ukraine, and frankly Ukraine would just become another Greece if they attempted currency union at this time.

Cultural factors

Cultural factors tend to complicate conflict resolutions. For example relative to the EU/US vs. Russia aspect of the Ukraine situation, many expressions are similar between English and Russian culture and language, but sometimes they are different. In America we have a principle that applies either to making war on a country, or letting your child run loose in a department store - *If you break it, you buy it.*

My wife says there is no such notion in Russia. The attitude is that if you break something you are handling in a store, it must have been inferior quality merchandise. So Russia probably feels that if Ukraine is broken, it is because it is an inferior quality country, not because they invaded and broke it. Consistent with this, they will continue to assert that all the damage was done by Ukrainian forces.

Boardwalk at Yalta in Crimea – Wikimedia commons

In a similar vein, there is a difference in trust of government and media. Russians still mostly believe their state run media. They will simply hunker down and carry on under sanctions, like Khodorkovsky's starving Yukos workers.

A third cultural factor complicates any business dealings with Russians. I noticed this with the Canadian company Uranium One in which I once held shares. They allowed a 20% Russian investment to help with a problem in Kazakhstan. Pretty soon the Russians increased their share to 51% because they don't trust anyone and want to be in control. Later after the Fukushima nuclear disaster when the price of uranium tanked, the Russians used their 51% controlling interest to acquire the rest of the company far below what it was really worth.

So this is the Russian idea of democracy. Most of the large companies are once again state controlled, with a 51% or 52% share. They have 51% of the vote and you have 49%. It's perfectly democratic and fair. But nevertheless they have complete control.

There is a fourth cultural factor that often leads to disaster. In "melting pot" countries such as the U.S., we have the idea that everyone can learn to live together. This did not work very well in Iraq where the Sunni's and Shia hated each other for hundreds of years and still do. And it will not work in Ukraine where both sides have been hating each other also for hundreds of years, but especially since the famine of the 1930s when Stalin confiscated crops, and WWII when half the country aligned with the Germans and fought the Russian half. I thought in 2011 after four trips to Ukraine, two each in the east and west, that it might well be better off divided.

The Russians might have acquired half of it without any sanctions had they just been a little more patient. Acquiring Ukraine won't solve their problem with NATO anyway. If Ukraine becomes Russia, then immediately the existing NATO bases near Ukraine will instead be near Russia! What were they thinking? They weren't. They were reacting to a trade war. That is how war starts.

What exactly is the EU and does it hurt or help?

In the next chapter we ask whether or not the WTO was an effective tool in ending or reducing war between member nations, and look at the data. The EU as a currency union, which makes it something in between a unified single country and a loose federation, is not old enough to tell. It seems to be leading to trouble pretty rapidly, between the unrest in the members with high debt, and the conflict over trade with Ukraine and Russia.

How does most-favored nation status apply to nations that trade with the EU anyway? How can EU members trade with each other on more favorable terms than other WTO members? My research was not able to answer this question. But it seems to me that the EU must ultimately undermine the WTO, and that Russia has a legitimate complaint about trade which the EU did not take seriously. When one considers that a currency union implies something of a political union, and that NATO implies a military union, then the NATO-EU empire must look like a rapidly expanding superpower on Russia's doorstep, so the NATO complaint is legitimate also.

Russia made too many mistakes to claim any moral high ground. In the first place, they used a bullying approach with Ukraine back before the Maidan revolution. Then they continued to play the bully with unmarked soldiers who shot everything in sight, even a Malaysian airliner apparently. Every kid who survived the playground knows you must stand up to a bully. But also most of us learned from our youth experiences to admit our contribution to fault. In my view, the EU is headed for a crash even without help from Russia, as it will never be able to manage Greece and Italy with the same currency policies as Germany.

Consequences of Ending War

Did international war end?

Since GATT 1994 and the WTO, there have been no all out shooting wars between full member nations. There is a new conflict that might qualify, but a lot of denial and subterfuge, which we'll discuss.

The closest thing was the Indo-Pakistani War of 1999, which is usually described as "limited" and involved some Pakistani troops infiltrating along with Kashmiri insurgents into the Kargil district. International diplomatic pressure persuaded Pakistan to withdraw and in less than six months the whole thing was over, without there ever being a full scale counter-attack from India.

What sort of international pressure had persuaded Pakistan to back down? Threat of alliances being activated and major powers, possibly the U.S., jumping in on India's side? Hardly. And both countries had nuclear weapons so no nation would risk putting their troops in harm's way. But loss of ability to trade would have been crippling. Pakistan backed down. This was before the 9/11 attacks and the U.S. did not have major military operations in the region.

Tensions flared again after a terrorist attack on the Indian Parliament in 2001, and the 2008 Mumbai attacks, but each time tensions were defused either by the two countries themselves, or by diplomatic efforts. [25]

Numerous provocations between China and the Philippines, Taiwan or Japan have repeatedly failed to produce war.

Indeed, it is easier to look at the exception, namely wars between the WTO nations and non-WTO nations, or wars just between non-WTO nations. [26]

- Iraq is a non-WTO nation.
- Afghanistan is non-WTO.
- Neither Eritrea nor Ethiopia are WTO nations.
- Neither Kosovo nor Yugoslavia were WTO nations at the time.
- Ossetia is not a WTO nation.
- Russia only joined the WTO in 2012, so its previous conflicts were not among members.

War within the borders of a WTO nation is not really addressed by the WTO provisions since it does not control trade within a country's borders, and unless the conflict threatens to spill over it will be treated as an internal dispute or rebellion. This covers Darfur, and the Israel-Palestine conflict since Palestine is not yet fully recognized (explaining Israeli resistance to making it so), and 60-odd insurrections and rebellions and civil wars. So it is not at all that war has ended. But at least for the last 20 years, international war has been more contained than usual.

The conflict between Russia and Ukraine, which is denied and portrayed as an internal Ukraine conflict by the Russian side, is, if you believe Ukraine's version of events, the first military conflict between WTO member nations since 1994. That makes it not only more dangerous to Europe than more remote conflicts. That makes it dangerous to the concept operative since the end of WWII that peace between nations can be maintained by encouraging trade. Ukraine has been a WTO member since 2008, but Russia only since 2012. So one can make an interpretive choice, pending further data. Is it the concept that trade dependency can be used to enforce peace which is failing? Is Russia not yet sufficiently integrated into the WTO to respond to trade pressures (sanctions)? Or is Russia simply a rogue nation who should not therefore have been admitted into the WTO (like North Korea)?

My sentiments lie in the latter two interpretations. Russia is clearly not well integrated. It has persuaded Europe to become dependent on its natural gas, but it is dependent on nothing from Europe. That is partly because it does not intend ever to be dependent on any other nations, which is evidence of its rogue character, deeply embedded not just in its elite but in the governmental bureaucracy which maintains power. The oligarchs do not seem to have gained power, only wealth, as we saw earlier, and may as easily wind up in jail as not. If the world's trading nations - notice that I do not say just the western nations - want to maintain the effectiveness of the WTO system for keeping peace, they will have to quit buying Russian oil and natural gas.

The current time of low oil prices would seem to be a favorable time to do that. American companies are anxious to sell their surplus gas to Russia, and to develop gas resources in Ukraine and Poland. Russia's government would again fall as it did due to low gas prices in the 1980s, and the country would have another chance to sort itself out. The last time Russia "sorted itself out" in the early 1990s, the economic collapse created a negative memory that powers the Putin regime now.

Also at that time, the U.S. reorganized its space program to contract several space station modules to Russia, supporting their technology industry to keep Russian scientists from "leaking" into other countries, taking missile and nuclear technology with them. An external tank upgrade on the Shuttle was required to reach a compatible Russian orbit, and subsequently foam falling from that new tank caused the destruction of the Shuttle Columbia and subsequent cancellation of the Shuttle Program. With a long hiatus in the U.S. manned program, there is no incentive for the Russians to continue cooperating with the U.S.

Prior to the last two decades there were major international wars in 1991, 1980-88, 1973, 1967, 1965-75, 1956, 1950-53, 1948-49 and 1946-54 which takes us back to WWII. All but the last two of those (1991 and 1980-88) involved at least two opposing antagonists who are now both members of the WTO or its predecessors (for example the Arab-Israeli wars involved Egypt and Israel, now both WTO countries). So we can probably extend credit to the trade organizations for preventing international war between members since 1973 (four decades), and note that previously the rate seemed to be at least one or two per decade. It is unlikely that this a statistical coincidence.

It is even tempting to speculate that the ability to end war *between* nations may only be limited by our ability to entice the few remaining nations not already WTO members to join. Some like North Korea sit behind their nuclear weapons and do not seem to care. But one of the major players, Iran, made an unexpected deal in late November 2013, agreeing to restrictions on uranium enrichment to get *trade* sanctions eased.

While we are patting ourselves on the back, I must point out that we learned that trade is also a way of getting something from another country, perhaps something they do not want to give, so is not without its costs. Some of these are indirect and surprising, definitely in the category of *unexpected outcomes*. A 2014 article in Vanity Fair on trade and the rise of China suggests it was a mistake for the U.S. *"to use the short period of its unilateral dominance, between the fall of the Berlin Wall and the fall of Lehman Brothers, to pursue ... the economic interests of its multi-nationals — rather than to create a new, stable world order. The trade regime the U.S. pushed through in 1994 [the WTO] ... was so unbalanced that, five years later, when another trade agreement was in the offing, the prospect led to riots in Seattle. And Washington never fully grasped the consequences of so many of its shortsighted actions— intended to extend and strengthen its dominance but in fact diminishing its long-term position."* [128]

Equalization of wages & benefits

A few years ago IBM closed a major engineering facility in the United States and offered the engineers their same jobs at a new location in India - at the prevailing wage rate for comparable engineers in India. As far as I know, there were no takers.

As I explained at the opening of the trade discussion, trade based on cheap labor will result in lower wages in the country trying to take advantage of the cheap labor. About six years ago I overheard a conversation at my favorite lunch deli. The speaker said he had been head of the information technology department at a major east coast bank. The department did all the data processing, kept all customer account records, and so forth. The bank asked him to outsource the entire operation overseas. He did an analysis and presented it to the bank managers, saying "You know guys, if everyone does this the standard of living in the U.S. will go down and none of us will make any money."

They told him: "We know that. But everyone is not going to do it."

This flaw in thinking not only affects many businessmen, it affects economists too. Many economic models are price models, and are based on changes at a particular company which are assumed to have little effect on the total economy. The trouble is, everyone at every company is reading the same business magazines, using the same consultants, and picking up waves from the same *ether*, and of course they all do the same things. Even macro economists, who consider whole economies, make related mistakes. We can avoid these mistakes if we avoid issues of pricing, which are after all entirely arbitrary. The analysis of the hypothetical economy of "The Land of Zo" in *The Equity Premium Puzzle* does exactly that.

Not only will wages equalize. All costs will equalize. Indirectly, the WTO says this must happen. What it actually says is that we cannot add a tariff to imported goods to cover retirement benefits or healthcare costs. *We must import the goods only based on their quality and price.* Those are the official rules. We are not *permitted* to import. We are *forced*.

Perhaps I need to say that again to make sure it is clear. We cannot favor our own domestic goods and services over foreign goods any more than we can favor one nation over another. We must open our markets to other countries. How did we get in this situation?

The simple fact is that we were the ones who insisted on it. The U.S. easily dominated many technically advanced fields, and also agricultural production in the decades prior to GATT 1994. Many significant economies, at first Japan and later China and the Euro zone, would like to have kept out many U.S. goods, especially agricultural goods and automobiles and aircraft, which were seen as strategically key industries. These countries knew well that if they depended on U.S. goods, they would be unable to differ with the U.S. on matters of foreign policy. They would have to support us in keeping world peace, or at least the U.S. version of it.

1983 First Generation Toyota Camry [27]

Japan came to dominate the automobile industry during the 1980s, with cars that were both cheaper and more reliable. Toyota eventually became the largest automobile manufacturer in the world. The exchange rate between currencies was about ¥250 to the dollar. The Regan administration forced concessions from Japan that resulted in a rapid increase in the value of their currency. After just 3 years, a dollar would buy only half as many yen, about ¥125, making their products twice as expensive here, and ours half as expensive there. The Japanese went crazy in the late 1980s with their new found U.S. purchasing power, snapping up properties first in Hawaii and then on the mainland, then U.S. corporations like CBS. Japan had not managed to take Hawaii by force, but later was simply able to buy it along with much of the rest of the U.S.

Yen per Dollar (i.e. value of dollar in yen)

The U.S. responded with a real estate crash in 1987, sinking the Japanese banks which had funded the U.S. real estate purchases and sending the Japanese economy into a 25 year downhill run. In terms of damage to economies this is clearly war. The only thing it is lacking is body count, but it certainly affects lives. Fresh from this success, the U.S. pushed an open markets agenda in GATT 1994.

After the Japanese yen became over valued (and stayed that way), the Japanese could no longer afford to make cars in Japan and export them to the

U.S., so they built factories here. Their economy as you can see from the chart below, never recovered even though auto sales were fine.

Of course, what goes around comes around eventually, and in this case sooner rather than later. After GATT 1994 American companies wishing to enter foreign markets found they had labor costs too high for most of them, so they aggressively opened factories overseas just as the Japanese had done here. Having established the overseas relationships, they found they could open Information Technology (I.T.) departments and technical support offices as well. In the late 1980s, AT&T's monopoly on telephone service was broken and overseas call rates began to come down. With the internet they came essentially to zero. Even video conferencing now costs nothing. It is free on Skype.

Japanese Stock Market 1990-2013

So our U.S. markets are open to anyone who wants to sell here, *we* cannot impose tariffs on them, and it was done at our own insistence. The situation we have now is that we have a tariff on domestic goods. Domestic wages are subject to a 12.4% social security tax (6.2% worker share and 6.2% employer share, but however you split it up it adds 12.5% to the cost of labor). Add to this any employer sponsored retirement benefit. I call these domestic tariffs because they are added by force of law to the cost of our domestically produced goods and services to pay for benefits U.S. workers have, that foreign workers do not have. And so foreign goods do not have these costs.

From this point of view, offshore labor is simply tax evasion. But under WTO rules insisted upon by the U.S., for the good reason of preventing war, not just to fatten corporate profits, it is legal and mandatory to allow offshore labor and goods. But if wages decline generally in the U.S. then corporate profits must eventually decline also, because the largest component of corporate profits is consumer spending, and this is well known.

Equalization of healthcare benefits?

Of course each employer thinks like the bank managers thought. They think: "We will discontinue our corporate healthcare (GE and Walgreens have already made such announcements) and our workers will get it from the exchanges. That way it will not be in our costs. Even if we have to pay our workers a little more (don't count on it), many of them are already low wage and will qualify for government subsidies. Neither we nor they will have to pay this part of the cost." They are not worried about what will happen if everyone does it, or maybe they are worried everyone except them will do it.

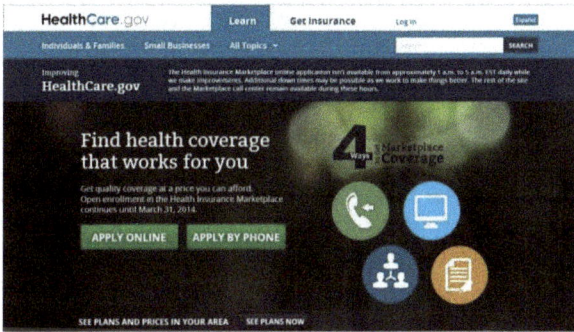

But of course the country collectively pays these costs, through increased premiums on people who don't even need health insurance (young, healthy people), and increased taxes on medical equipment, and increased taxes on the wealthy (3.8% more on dividends and capital gains) who own most of the corporations who are making the decisions to offload these costs. Another unexpected outcome. This is not an argument against healthcare. It is an explanation of the relation between worker benefits here and in other WTO member nations. Which includes just about all of them.

In some of these nations healthcare costs very little, and not just because they don't have healthcare. In Japan MRIs are not regulated and are competitively priced and advertised on billboards. As a result they cost about 10% of what MRIs cost in the U.S. That means less than the co-pay on many insurance plans. It also means that if you don't have insurance and need a $2000 MRI, maybe you should buy a flight and hotel package to Tokyo for $1700, pay $200 for the MRI, enjoy a vacation and come back $100 richer than if you had the MRI in Houston.

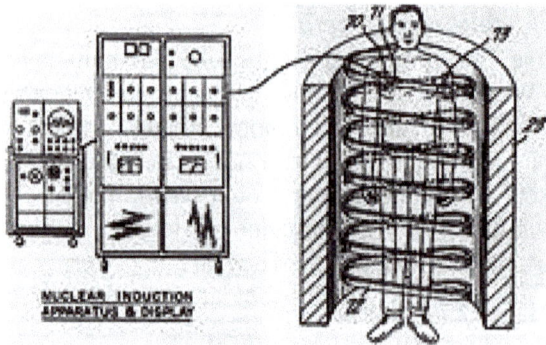

Armenian-American Raymond Damadian's 1971 MRI patent [28]
The first MRI patent was filed in 1960 by Vladislav Ivanov in the Soviet Union.
It appears Americans only lead in "cost."

Do we allow the importation of medical services and drugs? Largely no. It's treated like mad cow disease, with imports labeled inadequate by industry funded "experts." No doubt these industries offshore their I.T., at least some of their manufacturing, and seek to hire foreign researchers using H1-b visas. If the U.S. could have hired Vladislav Ivanov in 1960, we'd have had MRI technology eleven years earlier (see figure caption). In fact it's clear from statistics that U.S. health care is nowhere near the best. It just costs the most. My Russian wife who came here expecting excellent healthcare, was appalled after her first all-nighter in an emergency room. There have been similar disappointments as she worked through her first pregnancy.

The solution to health care costs is obvious:

- *Apply WTO rules to healthcare*, allowing Japanese companies to sell MRI services here and Indians to sell drugs. Of course they will have to meet safety standards. We import food, don't we? Food can easily be lethal, as can automobiles, etc. While we are at it I'd like to import the Russian Lada, a great $10,000 car that doesn't feel cramped or insubstantial.

- *Unbundle services*, like we forced IBM and AT&T to do in the 1980s. Allow a patient to get any test from any lab they want. I already arrange my own cholesterol checks this way, because even without benefit of insurance it is cheaper than a co-payment for a doctor visit to order the test. The test is done by the same company, LabCorp, and is of the same quality. And I have the results already to discuss with my doctor if I want to see him. But if I let my doctor arrange the test under his agreement with LabCorp, my insurance company is billed two or three times as much as I pay for the independently arranged test.

- *Apply modern productivity tools* we use for travel and shopping. Have a smartphone app where one keys in the doctor ordered service code and finds competing providers and insurance adjusted prices and can click to make an appointment, all automatic and no paperwork. Of course, laws will have to be passed to force clinics to allow use of cellphones, which most now don't. And while I'm on the subject of clinic productivity, why do I have to repeat my description of symptoms in detail, along with all the drugs I'm taking and allergies I have, three times to different people who don't seem to talk to one another? It seems right there labor costs could be cut by 67%. *(P.S. Since writing this it turned out that a case of Ebola was missed at a Dallas hospital because information about being from West Africa was not communicated from one of the three interviewers to another. The three interviews are appointment, nurse/triage, and doctor. Sometimes there is a second nurse after the triage.)*

- *Apply market forces.* Require all insurance plans, including government ones, to pass some percentage of costs to consumers so there is an incentive to choose the most effective alternative, like generic drugs and shorter hospital stays, rather than pay a bureaucracy to regulate people's choices. No 100% coverage. The only exceptions are things that serve a greater public good, like flu shots.

- *Apply WTO principles to all healthcare transactions* even internal to this country, as if each entity in the system were a trading partner (they are). Every customer and provider should receive *most favored entity* status and prices, regardless of whether insured or not, or what insurance plan one has. This alone would save billions of dollars in protracted, costly contract negotiation disputes between doctors or hospitals and insurance companies. Instead the competitive market will assure best prices, and consumers will be free to choose. Also this would end the crazy practice of preferred providers, which non-preferred providers called in for consult have learned to work as a scam.

At the time of writing this book, it certainly appears Americans are ready to go to "war" with each other over healthcare. I do not take a position on insurance in this book. I certainly understand points both sides make, and it is my rational conclusion that the two sides will continue to fight and to escalate the conflict until we apply the same principles used to prevent global war.

If the WTO principles are not truly able to resolve and prevent conflict, then we should not be applying them to trade! Precisely because we are applying them to trade, but not to healthcare, we are trying to pay healthcare costs at American monopoly rates from rapidly equalizing international wages in all other industries. Healthcare costs not only should equalize, they will. It is just a matter of time until the finances of the U.S. force it, even if (especially if) no action is taken.

Equalization of military expenditures?

To figure the full impact of equalization of benefits, on top of wages, then in addition to retirement and medical costs you have to add the costs of military, public services, schools, everything which is paid for by taxes on wages. Most government revenue in the U.S. is from taxes based on wages, and for state and local governments the rest is taxes on real estate owned by the workers and sales taxes made on purchases the workers make. Very little is corporate tax, and even it if were this just becomes part of the cost of goods sold, and will come under pressure from trade equalization. Every expense goes into total costs and comes under pressure from trade equalization.

U.S. Military budget is greater than next 10 nations combined [29]

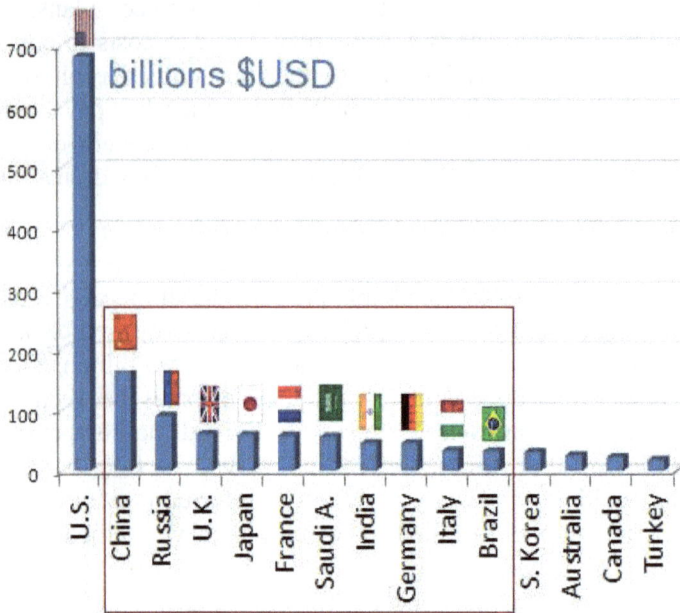

How will the U.S. fund its military when wages and taxes have been equalized by trade?

Naturally, since GATT 1994 went into effect, all American employers who compete with imports have sought to reduce expenses to the levels of their competition. In the short run they can increase automation, which of course lays off workers. But in the long run the foreign competition will automate too if it reduces costs.

Export companies have to reduce costs to compete with foreign companies doing business in the target export countries.

The laid off workers from import and export industries seek other jobs in the economy, putting downward pressure on wages. And so it affects everyone. Not just tomato farmers competing with Mexican tomatoes.

Equalization of STEM education?

Even slogans like *immigration reform* and *education reform* have loaded economic meanings. The former term in this context means more foreign STEM workers (science, technology, engineering and mathematics) from overseas via H1-b visas. Have you heard the President of the U.S. talk about getting more STEM education in American schools? The IEEE (Institute for Electrical and Electronic Engineers) reports a glut of STEM graduates, as many as 50% more than there are jobs available. Increasing STEM graduates and H1-b visa workers (many of whom are treated as indentured servants) serves a useful global business purpose of driving down STEM wages in the U.S. to match global wage scales. Neeraj Gupta, CEO of Systems in Motion, himself a former H1-b worker, said U.S. tech companies are now using the program to hire only average skilled workers, not the best and brightest from around the world as was intended by Congress. [30]

If women's enrollment in STEM programs has declined, it might be they are smarter than men. This problem doesn't just affect old white guys that historically accounted for more STEM majors. Yesterday a young black man at my gym was totally disgusted, saying he'd never work in I.T. (information technology) again. After ten years with a company he was asked to train an offshore team, and then they laid him off. I told him, and I recommend to you, never do this. When you are asked to train anyone offshore, resign immediately and change career fields. You may not be able to stop the company from going to offshore labor sources, but you don't have to lower their transition costs at your own expense. You paid for your education and they are free riding on it. And if you are American your education cost a higher percentage of median income than any country except Mexico. College graduates from other countries are generally debt free. No wonder they can afford to work for less.

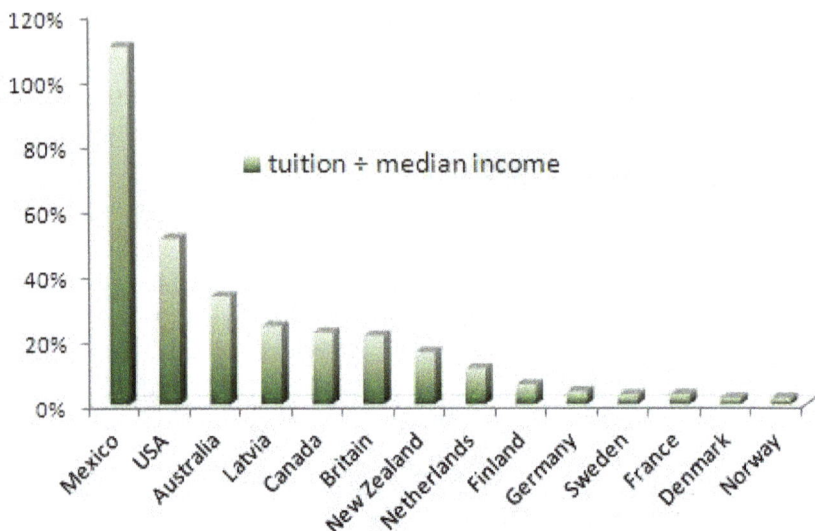

College tuition as percent of median income [31]

Equalization of incarceration rate & laws?

One of the oddest statistics is that the nation which bills itself as the champion of liberty and leader of the "free world" has the highest rate of imprisonment of its citizens of any nation in the world. Here I will comment only that this, too, is a cost borne by society which *the competitors of the U.S. do not bear*. Take a look at just a few countries' rates of incarceration per 100,000: [32]

United States 716	Britain 148	
Russia 484	**China 121** or 170	
Thailand 381	Canada 114	
Iran 284	France 101	
Columbia 243	Egypt 80	
Mexico 209	Syria 58	
Turkey 171	Pakistan 39	
Saudi Arabia 162	**India 30**	
Spain 149		

Incarceration rates per 100,000

Three countries of particular interest as trading partners are highlighted in bold. They have incarceration rates of 29%, 17% and 4% of the U.S. rate. If one assumes prison conditions are not good in these countries then the cost of incarcerations could be far less than the rates.

Presumably the U.S. has a high incarceration rate because of laws which it prefers. Perhaps much of the incarceration is due to drug laws (it is). It is not my concern here whether this is an effective way to discourage drug use or whether drug use in the U.S. is higher or lower. Some countries such as Thailand have a reputation for much harsher sentencing (indeed Thailand's incarceration rate is the third highest, but still only a fraction of the U.S. rate). The point here is that it costs $63 billion annually to implement this preferred policy.

That pays for incarceration of 25% of the world's prisoners (the U.S. has only 5% of the world's population), at costs in some states as high as $60,000 per prisoner. The prison population is over two million, and these people are not working and producing products for export. (In some nations it is alleged that prisoners do produce export products.) The annual prison bill is about 16% of our trade deficit with China, for example, just to put the figure in a trade context to see if it makes any difference. It does.

This puts pressures on U.S. laws to "equalize" with the legal standards and practices of other nations, just as it puts pressure on environmental regulations, wages, education, retirement and healthcare costs.

Columbia spent years fighting back from a state of lawlessness induced by export pressure from the drug trade. Mexico has seemingly succumbed on a much wider scale. It is now reported that iron ore is mined and exported illegally to Asian steel mills, and that sometimes drug precursor chemicals are provided in return. There is no provision in China, apparently, to verify the legality of the point of origin of an iron shipment, and this lack of legal code and procedure gets "exported" to trading partners through a kind of "laws and procedures" equalization pressure. When revenue does not pass through legal channels and legal corporations, it does not benefit legal workers and shareholders or create officially recorded economic growth or tax revenue and in fact benefits very few people. [33]

Open questions

If we want to have retirement, or medical benefits, or housing, or environmental quality, or technical education greater than our trading partners, over the long-term after temporary advantages we might think we have are gone, how do we do that under WTO rules?

And if we change or eliminate the WTO, will we go back to having global war? I did not say the problem was easy. I said I was going to lay it out and give you a guide to money, wealth and war so you will understand them, and understand the sometimes unexpected effects of the policies you vote for, and the career and investment strategies you adopt in your own life.

What we have learned

We have learned there are two reasons for trade: to acquire goods not available in the local environment, and to take advantage of cheaper labor elsewhere. The labor motive backfires in the long run, driving down wages locally.

Awkward barter transactions were facilitated by universal trading commodities, which are of intrinsic value and generally one of three types: growing (animals or plants), accumulating (common minerals), or approximately static (rare gems or metals).

To avoid the cost and risk of transporting trading commodities over long distances, reciprocal banking relationships developed whereby the trader need carry only a bank note representing a deposit of the trading commodity.

Trading commodities, while not exactly money, are similar and have similar problems of inflation and deflation. If the rate of growth of the trading commodity does not match the rate of growth of goods and services in the economy, the resulting chaos and unemployment can and often does lead to war. War usually leads to further changes in the trading commodity which may restart the cycle.

To the extent war involves the taking of tribute, the plunder of goods, or enslavement of labor, it represents a kind of trade carried out by force when mutual trade fails for whatever reason, often because of mismanagement of the trading commodity.

After WWII, a general agreement on trade (GATT) was negotiated, eventually resulting in the WTO which not only regulates trade but actively promotes it, without prioritizing any local issues in the participating countries.

The WTO rules favor trade based only on quality and price, and over the long-term it is difficult to maintain a different set of environmental standards and worker benefits. By default we have moved several steps toward a unified set of world rules and working conditions, which at the moment is trending down for most nations and up only for a few that were at the bottom.

There is an old saying, "If you can't lick 'em, join 'em." While the world works out this problem, that is more or less what I am going to propose in the latter part of this book. At least for those of you who can save enough money to invest. For the rest, choose your career carefully and avoid going into debt to get there.

From Contracts to Money

Origin, measure & risks of personal wealth

If the bullae represent contracts, that puts them more firmly in a commercial category than "neighborly borrowing." Perhaps the theory that money began with reciprocal favors is not entirely wrong, in great antiquity, but it is also likely that from very early there were tasks assigned within groups or clans. Hunter-gatherers tend to have only a few tasks. The men hunt and the women make clothes and beer. With the advent of agriculture, some tasks needed to be looked after for months at a time, like planting and weeding fields, and not everyone in the group needed to be involved. With the addition of domestic animals, more tasks were added. Someone looked after the animals and a few others looked after the fields. The animals in particular required their shepherds to roam away from the group to find pasture.

Shepherd [34]

Just as soon as more than one family was living together in a group, it would have been expedient to have only one or two persons look after grazing animals. The person looking after the animals would not have been related to all the persons who owned the animals, and their interests may not have been aligned in all cases. Some means of accounting for the sheep would have been *used*, *and* some means of compensating the shepherd. An agreement calling for something from each of two parties and providing for compensation meets entirely the modern definition of a contract, and can be legally binding even if it is oral. This may well be the oldest law.

We need not entirely guess about such things from small artifacts we find at ancient sites. We have writing from about 5000 years ago. In fact at least one text which dates at least in part from something over 4000 years ago is common among three of the world's religions, sometimes known as the Old Testament. I don't wish to favor any religion over any other in this book, but since this text is familiar to me, and texts of ancient India or the Far East are not, I will use it. It has several interesting stories about shepherds and accounting for sheep, and these occur before the time of "The Law."

- First the text makes clear that **wealth comes from the multiplication of grain** from planting to harvest, and that the word "grow" is used in connection with wealth. We find in Genesis 26: 12-13 "*Isaac planted crops in that land and the same year reaped a hundredfold, because the LORD blessed him. The man became rich, and his wealth continued to grow until he became very wealthy.*" A hundredfold in a year would be a return of 9900%. Not bad. And no, that's not a misprint.

- Next we find that **wealth is measured in animal flocks/herds and servants** in verse 14, "*He had so many flocks and herds and servants that the Philistines envied him.*" Flocks, like grain, also can multiply.

- The last thing we learn from Isaac is that **he has made a mistake by allowing his wealth to be visible** to others. Of course it is difficult to hide herds in the open country. But here is what happens: "*So all the wells that his father's servants had dug in the time of his father Abraham, the Philistines stopped up, filling them with earth. Then Abimelech said to Isaac, 'Move away from us; you have become too powerful for us.'*"

Well, perhaps there is one more thing. We learn that there is not open empty land available without other humans nearby. The land in 2000 BCE (4000 years ago) is not quite all taken, but it all has neighbors. We also learn a little later that Abimelech concluded a treaty with Isaac, a sort of mutual non-aggression pact. (not a mutual defense pact) The treaty is not enforceable by anything except swearing, and it is not a contract as in fact it calls for no action at all from either party. If Isaac is participating in a treaty, then he is being treated as a ruler, just because he has become wealthy.

A shepherd's contract gone awry

Shortly we learn that Isaac's wife Rebecca is tired of associating with "Hittite women" and finds life not worth living among them. Discovering just who the Hittite women are takes us down an interesting route. In fact a trade route. And there are a lot of Hittite women as it is one of the four great empires of the Bronze Age: Greek, Hittite, Egyptian, and Assyrian.

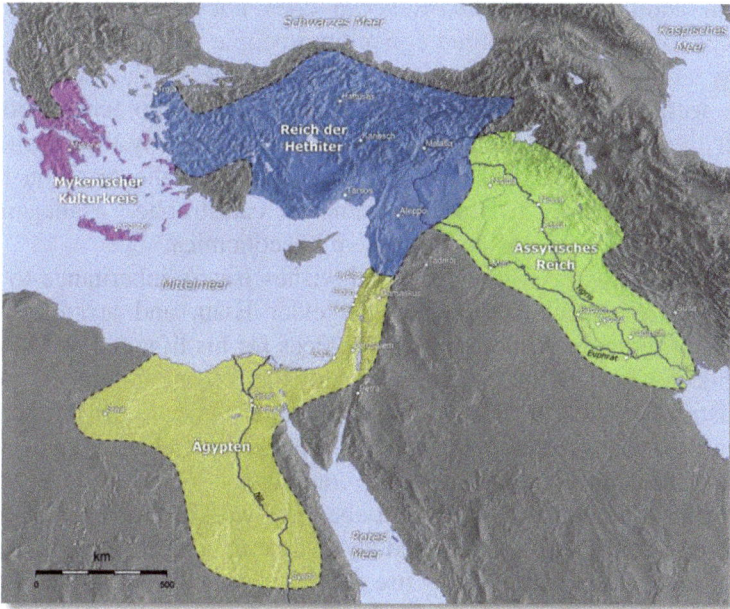

Empires of the Bronze Age [35]

The Hittite Empire from 1600-1180 BCE occupied almost the whole of what is now Turkey (center top in above map) and in addition some territory of the upper middle east in Lebanon, Syria and Iraq. The remainder of Iraq made up the Assyrian Empire. The Egyptian Empire extended up through what is now Palestine and Israel and into southern Lebanon. And the Mycenaean Greek kingdoms occupied the lower regions of Greece and some islands in the Mediterranean.

In other words, the Hittites occupied the key trade corridor later occupied by the western Persian Empire in about 500 BCE, conquered by the Greeks under Alexander, and occupied by the Roman Empire until the fall of Constantinople, whereupon it was taken up by the Ottomans until modern times and was the key locus of world trade *for that entire time*. Trade was either through this region, or by some circuitous route around it, as the region is blocked by desert and ocean on the south, and mountains on the north. The trek around the northern mountains goes through Ukraine, Russia and Mongolia, entering China from the north across the great wall, also severely mountainous, taking years with harsh winters and not commercially feasible. It is not really possible to reach the nearer destination of India this way because of the Himalayas, and of course Southeast Asia by this route lies on the other side of the vast country of China. If China seems to have had an almost separate history from the rest of the world, it is because of these mountain barriers.

In addition to Hittites, Rebecca does not like Canaanite women either. Canaanites were a settled agricultural people with agricultural deities, naturally inimical to pastoral semi-nomadic people in the same way that ranchers were inimical to farmers in the U.S. west who fenced off land. However the open range ended because of overgrazing by the ranchers, not because of the farmers. The maximal exploitation of the common land by each individual rancher led to environmental catastrophe. Management of common resources is an unsolved problem in economics.

Rachael has her own ideas, and wishes Isaac's inheritance to fall on her younger son Jacob rather than the elder Esau, and arranges this by deception. Thereafter Jacob more or less flees for his life, and to find a mate acceptable to his mother travels toward the other empire of Assyria, euphemistically called the "land of eastern peoples," where her brother Laban lives. Jacob encounters some shepherds who know Laban, which is where our story turns solidly to economics and contracts.

After a month of living with Laban and working for him for nothing, like a slave, Laban begins to feel bad about treating a relative in this way and engages Jacob in a contract. They use the term "wages," but in fact it is more like a contract. Jacob will work for Laban for seven years in return for the hand of his younger daughter Rachael in marriage. Some wages.

Jacob is famously cheated by a veil (and you wondered what veils are for?), finds himself married to the elder daughter, and has to work another seven years for Rachael. He takes it in stride. After all it's probably payback for the scam he ran on his elder brother Esau. Karma, the Buddhists might call it. After a detour through the rivalry between the two women for sons, the economics lesson resumes and we find Jacob has been working as a shepherd and doing quite well at it. Except that the livestock all belongs to Laban. After 14 years Jacob is still pretty much stuck.

So, citing the increases in Laban's flocks and herds, he concludes the following deal which seems to cost Laban very little. Jacob asks only for the spotted and speckled animals, the ones that are essentially rejects. This will also make it very easy to tell his flocks apart from Laban's. He takes possession of these animals and puts them in the care of his sons, so at least another decade must have passed.

Jacob continues tending Laban's all white flocks of sheep but engages in a bit of magic involving fresh cut tree branches used when the animals are mating to induce spotted offspring. I have no idea if this has any biological basis. Perhaps the animals would occasionally have spotted offspring anyway. But no animals ever pass from Jacob's herds to Laban's. Only from Laban's to Jacob's whenever they are spotted. Jacob has lived a long life and learned a little about mathematics, apparently. This is the way you need to treat your investment accounts!

The spotted Jacob Sheep
an unimproved breed with less desirable wool [36]

Soon Jacob becomes wealthy, as in Genesis 30 we find "*In this way the man grew exceedingly prosperous and came to own large flocks, and maidservants and menservants, and camels and donkeys.*" Apparently Jacob remembers the lesson Isaac learned about wealth breeding jealousy, and he leaves. His wives are all for it, apparently feeling their father Laban has "sold" them, and Rachael even steals the family's household gods. Sort of like taking the family jewels. The subterfuge almost cost her her life due to an unwitting oath Jacob swore. I suppose an oath was sort of like a verbal contract that had power of life and death. The New Testament advises against them. For another interesting snafu regarding an oath (not particularly relating to economics other than that it is a contract) see Judges 11.

Often tales such as this which are preserved over long periods show a formative stage in culture. This tale shows the need for written contracts, due diligence, and full disclosure at the appropriate time (peeking beneath veils). Had Jacob and Laban held bullae with tokens representing their flocks (abstract tokens were used to count larger numbers of sheep), and a set commission or interest paid to Jacob for tending, then ownership would have been clear when someone needed to know. But on the other hand, with the tokens concealed in the bullae, and the markings on the outside of the bullae known only to a learned priest or scribe, Jacob's wealth would not be very visible and he would avoid the problem Isaac had. He would own some percentage of the commonly tended herds that only he knew.

The bullae are found in the excavation of settlements and cities, where artisans and scribes to make them were available. They have no permanent value and are discarded when concluded like papers from old contracts. While we can't be sure rural people didn't use them, it is a reasonable inference. And the need was greater in cities where relatively few people were close relatives.

End of empires & temple money

There is a gap in what we know ... because there is a gap in history. The gap is deeper than the Dark Ages of Europe, a gap so dark that the Bronze Age civilizations were unremembered and unknown in the time of classical Greece and Rome. The only remnant was the story of the Trojan War, thought to be myth. But even that the gap exists is a lesson.

Bronze Age copper ingot from Crete
in shape of ox hide representing a standard value [43]

We know that the bullae represented something like a contract, and some commodity goods like animals, jars of honey or stores of grain. We know that in ancient Sumer (2000 BCE) money was something like a bank note representing grain stored in a temple. The Bronze Age came somewhat later and we don't know exactly what form money took, i.e. what the receipt or temple note looked like, but we know it was functionally similar. Money represented goods on deposit (in storage).

No one knows exactly why the Bronze Age empires all collapsed in the short space of about 25 years, between 1206 and 1180 BCE, but it did. By now you know that I will be predisposed to a monetary theory before I even look, and I was. Imagine my surprise when I found this list of possible causes, money not among them: [37]

- Climate change
- Volcanoes
- Drought
- Earthquakes

- Migration & raids
- Iron working
- Massed infantry with long swords
- General systems collapse (incl. Jaynes)

None of those are convincing, which is why scholars cannot firmly decide. The last one is more an effect than a cause.

Iron working would have been under the control of the establishment as would massed infantry. Long swords in 1200 BCE were still made by ordinary metalworking, were easily damaged or bent, and were not common until 600 CE when methods of hardening by adding carbon and quenching were invented.

Keuninck's Fire of Troy [37]
Beginning of the end of the Bronze Age?

Massed infantry had to be under someone's control. We do have stories of massed infantry, mainly the tale of Troy illustrated above. But most of the stories from the time of the fall of the Bronze Age involve raiding parties known as "Peoples of the Sea," not massed infantry. However, I would not discount that the fall of Troy, together with the difficulties of travel related thereafter in the wanderings of Odysseus, indicated that the trade routes had been perhaps damaged by an unwise military campaign leaving treaties broken and travel difficult.

Earthquakes, drought and volcanoes are a constant in that part of the world, though if extensive enough drought might be credible. The Minoan civilization, possibly the basis of Plato's Atlantis, was disrupted by a series of such disasters at 100 to 200 year intervals and finally occupied by the Mycenaean Greeks in 1450 BCE, 250 years prior to the end of the Bronze Age. [38]

So the Minoans were rebuilding after each disaster and succumbed to enemies jealous of their wealth only after weakened by repeated episodes. The same enemies who had sacked Troy. Troy was undoubtedly a wealthy trading city, situated as it was on the world's main trading route that has persisted for 5000 years. Mountainous Greece, broken up by the sea, is not a rich agricultural land like the Fertile Crescent, the Nile Valley, Asia Minor (Turkey) or the Levant (Canaan-Israel). The mental attitudes toward the value of grain would not have taken root there, because grain does not do well there.

Even today, Greece is the rogue member of the EU which doesn't seem to "get" investment and capitalism, the modern parlance of growth that grew from agriculture. Their cultural concept is to distribute the stores of grain to the population with one kind or another of public support. Could it be that the ancient Mycenaeans were also a rogue Bronze Age civilization, primarily sea traders, jealous of their trading partners and finally summoning the military skill to disrupt them?

Perhaps the disruptive Peoples of the Sea had roots in a decaying Mycenaean culture, impoverished and scattered beyond recognition through military misadventure which destroyed the trading network on which it depended? Up to 90% of small sites in southern Greece were abandoned at this time. [39] Remains were not found; they went somewhere. Even in the classical period Greeks could not unite and classical Greek civilization destroyed itself with inter-city wars. They were united only later by Philip and Alexander of Macedon, a region which has always and still does have a completely agricultural economy.

Even if "monetary policy" doesn't show up on the list of official causes of the Bronze Age demise (trade does however), a good theory and a little persistence goes a long way. If we search for "bronze age money" we find an article discussing currency (money), written from the perspective of an historical economist, giving a persuasive theory that for some reason has not made the main list, probably because students of ancient history generally are not monetary enthusiasts. First I will reproduce as quotes the key points, and then I will relate it to what we have been discovering about trading commodities and how to manage them: [40]

- *"In [the] first stage of currency, metals were used as symbols to represent value stored in the form of commodities. This formed the basis of trade in the Fertile Crescent for over 1500 years."*

- *"The collapse of the Near Eastern trading system pointed to a flaw: in an era where there was no place that was safe to store value, the value of a circulating medium could only be as sound as the forces that defended that store. Trade could only reach as far as the credibility of that military."*

- *"By the late Bronze Age ... a series of treaties had established safe passage for merchants around the Eastern Mediterranean, spreading from Minoan Crete and Mycenae in the northwest to Elam and Bahrain in the southeast."*

- *"The increase in piracy and raiding associated with the Bronze Age collapse, possibly produced by the Peoples of the Sea, brought this trading system to an end."*

- *"It was only with the recovery of Phoenician trade in the 10th and 9th centuries BC that saw a return to prosperity, and the appearance of real coinage, possibly first in Anatolia with Croesus of Lydia and subsequently with the Greeks and Persians."*

- *"These factors led to the metal itself being the store of value: first silver, then both silver and gold, and at one point also bronze."*

We have learned that using static commodities (like gold) as a money basis is terrible and leads to economic catastrophe and war. The ancient peoples used grain and other "growth" commodities as their money basis for 1500 years. This is longer than the "stable" periods of the post-Alexander Greek empires (about 300 years), Rome (about 500 years) and the modern era (about 500 years) all put together (total only about 1300 years). Why would anyone in their right mind change a system that was working so well into one that is so obviously flawed? And why has humanity clung to it since?

The answer appears to be, because the temples were robbed.

Taboo, technology & coinage

Maybe the temples were robbed because climate change, disaster and dislocation of the Sea Peoples weakened governments? Climate change is slow. People would carry off the grain and go somewhere else, just as the Sumerians came from somewhere else originally (near India, possibly) and just as the Sea Peoples came from somewhere else. Maybe it was because of new weapons? That would just result in a new master of the temple, and we already established that early long swords weren't that common or that good.

Tucked away under the heading of "general systems collapse" is the interesting theory of Julian Jaynes on the bicameral mind. By a greater division between the hemispheres, he supposes, earlier men would talk to themselves, one half of the brain telling the other what to do. Because of the introspective rather than empirical nature of the theory it is not provable, and in any case it is unlikely a psychological change alone occurred simultaneously in four empires and brought them all to an end within 25 years. But some truth may lie nearby.

My own speculation is that perhaps taboos that guarded the temple came to be disregarded. I base this on Freud's account of the power of taboos in Totem and Taboo. In some primitive societies, people will spontaneously die or otherwise develop the symptoms prescribed by a taboo when they have broken it. Since this has been observed, it is empirically supported. Modern humans view such ideas as superstition and show no such reactions. Again there is empirical evidence that some people do not respond to taboo, and that such attitudes are associated with modern times. The presence of two modes of response (one a non-response) and a transition are all empirically supported.

Ark of the covenant used as a weapon at Jericho [41]
Jericho walls fell about 1550 BCE, Middle Bronze Age [42]

That lack of physical taboo reaction is exactly what would allow modern humans to more easily rob temples. Jacob frequently relates conversations and encounters with God, even a wrestling match and a limp resulting from it. Sounds like a taboo effect to me, and quite adequate to scare someone away from robbing a temple. The Ark of the Covenant, an artifact from the very end of the Bronze Age, is credited with military powers and extensive taboo effects on anyone besides an authorized priest who touches it.

One thing is certain. If there were a group of people who knew how to make "long swords" and iron armor, and they were not privy to the temple notes used for trade among four wealthy empires, they would have logically reasoned that they could cut open the temples and get the grain which was the real value. But, would they have been able to figure out that the grain could not be used as a trading commodity unless it was safely stored in the temples?

This is a leap of logic beyond weapon making or military organization. Sword makers are a blend of blacksmith, engineer, chemist and anarchist. It is about the real and the physical. That money would be just a note would make no sense to such a person. Physical possession would be paramount. When the temples were robbed and the notes made worthless, this would only reinforce such a notion. And to such a person, use of an intrinsically valuable commodity (gold) that could be carried on one's person and defended with one's sword would be imminently logical.

People on all sides of the political spectrum are making such mistakes today, endangering civilization and threatening a dark age. That is why I am writing this book. The past is a patient teacher. If the lesson is not learned, it is simply repeated as often as necessary. A gruesome thought.

The political "left" would take the grain out of the temple and feed all the poor and needy. The "right" would trade all their temple notes for gold. Neither would have anything to plant next year.

In a nutshell, the lack of taboo response would have been fertile ground for "rational" minds (yet not far thinking minds) which made superior weapons, employed superior tactics, and acquired wealth through raid rather than trade only to find that the source of it vanished and they were cast into a dark age.

As the darkness resolved and a new age began, money became precious coins instead of temple notes based on grain. It became static instead of growing. And all the classical poets and philosophers lamented the passing of a golden age of prosperity (the Bronze Age historically), replaced by the Iron Age of war and cyclic economic catastrophe leading to war. Isaac's hundred fold return was replaced by deflation and debt. Such productivity today would only wreck the price of grain.

Lydian 1/3rd stater 500s BCE
Athens silver tetradrachm 480 BCE
Roman Denarius 211 BCE

all images from Wikipedia Commons - not to scale
1/3rd slater may be the oldest coin known

King Midas

It would hardly do to write a book about wealth and the Bronze Age without mentioning King Midas, the man with the golden touch. Where and when did he live? How did he come by this touch and what was the result of it?

In the first place, which Midas? There are at least three contenders. They lived at different times, but all of them in Phrygia. I'll bet you can already guess where it is located. Try guessing before you scroll down and look at the map. I'll even give you a clue. Most of the geographic loci in this book seem drawn back to one place.

The short version of the story is that Midas learned the hard way one cannot eat gold, and starved to death. In a version by Nathaniel Hawthorne in the mid-1800s, a hapless Midas turns his daughter into a gold statue. The Midas in Greek Myth was more careful, and we shall see how he made out.

The fact that Midas was in *Greek Myth* gives our first clue as to which of the three had the golden touch. The middle Midas lived in the 700s BCE, and the tomb of his father is thought to have been found. This is probably too late. He would be remembered 200-300 years later in the classical period as a historical figure, not as a myth. In Assyrian texts the middle Midas is called Mita. This period is solidly within the Iron Age, *after* the Greek Dark Ages, when magic had largely gone out of the world along with taboo. So that rules out the 3rd Midas as well, who may not even have ruled as a king.

The first Midas was one of three kings of a particular country during the Heroic Age, the age of the heroes of the Trojan War. These three were:

- **Gordias**, who tied the Gordian Knot later untied by Alexander. The city of Gordium is named after him.

- **Midas**, the king whose touch turned things to gold. The city of Midas is named after him.

- **Mygdon**, who fought with the Amazons.

These kings ruled in Phrygia, squarely within the Bronze Age. Unlike other domains, Phrygia continued to expand during the Greek Dark Age, reaching its peak under the 2nd Midas at the beginning of the Iron Age. It was sacked in 695 BCE. Afterward it became part of Lydia.

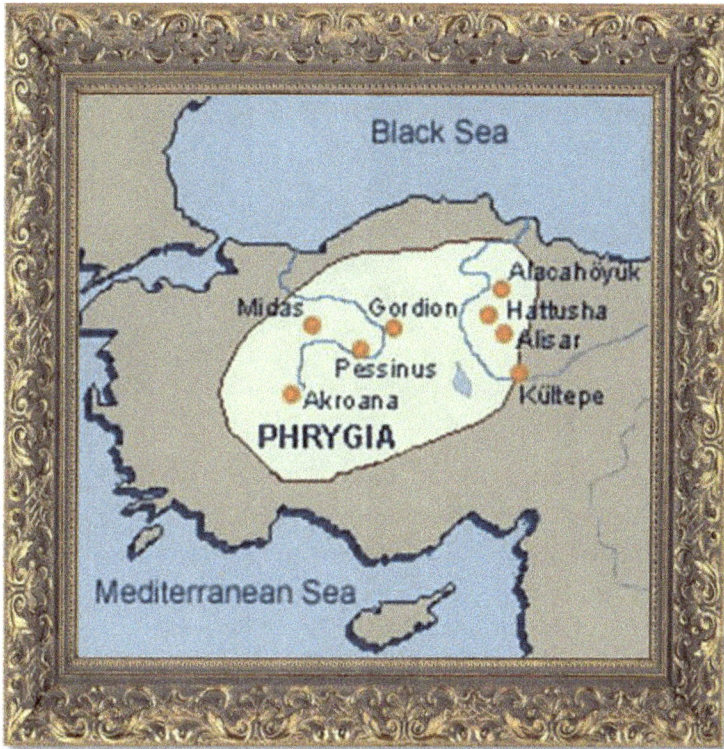

Ancient Phrygia, courtesy Travel Link Turkey [44]

Now you see the map and of course, Phrygia was squarely in the middle of the ancient trade route between Europe and Asia. The region was taken over during the upheavals at the end of the Bronze Age by Sea Peoples from Thrace (just across the Bosporus Strait to the left, in northeast Greece) who spoke a language similar to Greek, further supporting our "guess" about where the Sea People came from and why.

The Phrygians were allies of the Trojans. King Priam was married to a Phrygian. So though the Phrygians were from the region of Greece originally, they were not part of the ruling elite there, of Agamemnon's crowd. That is probably why they left to seek their fortune elsewhere, and find it they did. The most interesting version of the myth from the point of view of money and Bronze Age upheavals, is that after contracting his fatal touch, Midas traveled from Thrace to Asia Minor to bathe in the river Pactolus, where his gift was transferred to the river whose sands were turned to gold.

Golden Sands of the River Pactolus
image courtesy jiga [45]

According to the legend, Midas then encountered the childless King Gordias of Phrygia, who adopted him. What we can read between the lines is that the Thracian Sea Peoples came to Anatolia seeking the wealth of the trading empires, and not recognizing the hidden grain in the far away temples as the true source of it, were entranced by natural objects seemingly turned to gold in the river. The mineral in the river is Electrum, a natural alloy of gold and silver. The fable of Midas - and it is a "fable" with a moral lesson not to seek to turn everything into gold - now seems to become a historical myth of the origins of Phrygia.

Indeed, the Midas legend can be interpreted as the story of the end of the Bronze Age, perhaps the greatest mystery of ancient history. The Midas Touch is a metaphor for the Sea People grasping for gold, and as a result of obtaining it, the trading system was destroyed and then the world was destroyed and plunged into a great dark age. It was also the end of the Age of Myth. Humankind no longer talked with the gods. And with the dawn of the Iron Age, rational intellect and material technology became ascendant.

Croesus

Perhaps the oldest coin known is the 1/3rd stater from Lydia, pictured in the previous chapter. Lydia is also in Asia Minor, or modern Turkey, developed as a new Hittite kingdom after the fall of the Hittite Empire in 1200 BCE. At its greatest extent under Croesus in 547 BCE, it had grown to encompass the western half of Turkey and many famous ancient sites such as Troy, Ephesus, and the former Phrygia.

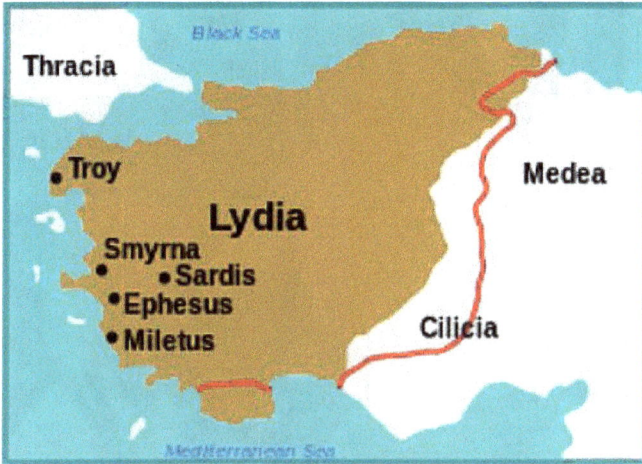

Neo-Hittite Kingdom of Lydia [52]

Perhaps you have heard the expression "rich as Croesus"? This is the man. It seems that even during a dark age the old trade route was prosperous. Croesus is credited with issuing the first gold coin, actually the electrum alloy from the region of the river Pactolus, the 1/3rd stater we saw earlier. He extracted tribute from Greek cities, but was more friendly to them than his father, and provided a buffer against the advancing Persian Empire.

What did the man who issued the world's first gold coin have to say about money?

Croesus was quite satisfied and challenged a visiting Greek wise man, Solon, to name one whose opulence was greater. Solon replied that peacocks were more opulent. Annoyed, Croesus tried to impress Solon with a list of vanquished enemies and claimed territories. Again Solon disagreed, saying the happiest man he ever met was a peasant in Athens.

Soon after Croesus' son was accidentally killed. Croesus asked the Oracle at Delphi for advice on attacking the Persians, and the oracle replied that if he attacked, a great empire would fall. Croesus attacked and the battle was indecisive. But he then disbanded his army for the winter as was customary, and instead of disbanding also, Cyrus the Great counter attacked.

Thereafter versions of the story vary. According to the Persians, Croesus placed himself and his family on a funeral pyre, not wanting to be tortured. But Cyrus was a benevolent conqueror (he was the one who sent the exiled Jews home and authorized rebuilding of their temple), and stopped the fire. He freed Croesus and allowed him to keep his riches and remain king in Lydia. In the Greek version, Cyrus stopped the fire to hear what Croesus was muttering about Solon.

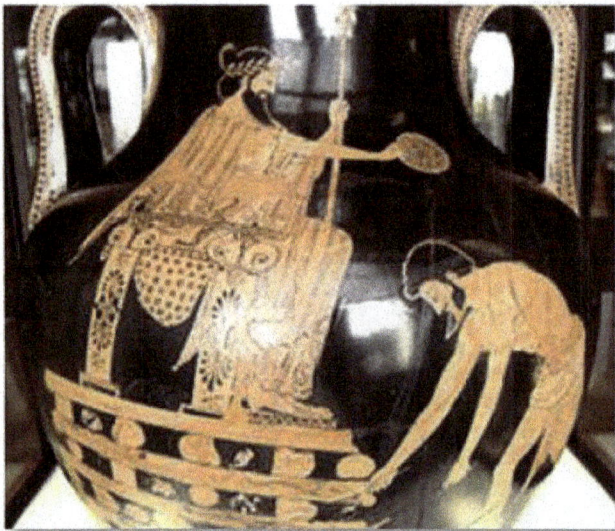

Croesus on the pyre [53]

We have spent so much time leading up to the first coin, I thought you'd want to know this story about the man who minted it. Three lessons may possibly be drawn. First that east-west trade is and has been the economic focus of the world through several dark ages and since the first writing, and it remains true today.

Second is that the new standard of wealth favored by the Greeks and their allies, the gold standard, does not bring happiness even to the likes of Midas and Croesus. Cyrus wisely ignored it and allowed Croesus to keep his gold.

Third, the military way of acquiring wealth after the Bronze Age did not do anyone any good, neither the victors nor the vanquished. The wealth of the world had been agricultural, and war destroys the fields and kills the men who plant and harvest. Gold only represents that wealth, and to carry off gold is to be cheated and carry off nothing. Cyrus also allowed the Jews to retrieve the gold that had been taken from their temple. The empires of the Iron Age before Rome would last 300 years at most, nothing compared to 3000 years of successful Sumerian civilization (5200 BCE to 2200 BCE approximately).

Consider for example the "reasons" given for decline of civilizations and empires. The soil in Sumer (south eastern Iraq) became saline due to irrigation and evaporation. [54] They switched from wheat to barley, but still the food supply dwindled and the people moved northward, strengthening first the region of Akkad where Sargon built a great empire, and then Babylon and Assyria.

While Assyria persisted in one form or another from 2154 to 605 BCE, this is only half the length of the Sumerian period, and the reason for its fall is that it was exhausted militarily. [55] Thereafter the empires of Persia and the Macedonian Greeks each lasted barely 300 years. As for the Romans, we will see later that they wielded an astonishing economic secret weapon.

The Sumerian and Egyptian origins of civilization came when irrigation was used to increase food production. The word *barbarian* means literally "without grain." The Sumerians had a three element economy: farming, fishing and pastoral (herding). But it was the farming element that grew their civilization, and when it waned they waned. The Egyptian civilization has lasted the longest simply because the upper reaches of the Nile do not flow through arid land and do not contain the salt that ruined Sumeria in a Malthusian population collapse.

The universality of money

In the Bronze Age, grain *was* money. A hundred fold increase would not wreck the price of grain, it would make the harvester wealthy! People and animals would magically appear in proportion to the supply of grain. You not only could eat it, it was equated with the ability to live for a certain length of time. With it you could buy servants and livestock by supporting them directly. But you can't carry it to market with you in sufficient quantity to be useful. Coins were superior for that. Ironically, the attempt to instill money with actual value, in the money itself, robbed money of connection to human and spiritual value.

We see this change reflected also in views of religious icons. In the time of Jacob, it was logical for Rachael and Laban to attribute significance to the "household gods" even though such value could not be physically seen. Money had evolved from bullae a few thousand years before to copper bars or something similar (exactly what is still not known, but see example of copper bar earlier) either in a specific shape or with writing on them, whose value was also remote and unseen, though likely Rachael herself did not deal in money as it was something for traders and city folk. But the mentality of money and the household gods, as proxies for an unseen power, was similar.

Much later, actually long after Moses, as local Hebrew household deities persisted right up until the Babylonian exile, the Jewish remnant of the Hebrews disclaimed any value or power of icons and images other than their material composition. Then Islam took the matter to even further extremes, and so a striking feature of the Topkai Palace is that there is elaborate art but no images of people. There are not even landscapes. It is almost entirely abstract patterns. And the Ottoman Empire with this anti-representational mentality is precisely the empire that controlled trade and thus money until 1918.

Unlike temple money backed by belief ("credit" in Latin means "he believes") in the safety of stored grain, coinage was issued by governments and backed by the ruler, whose picture was often on the coins, and the swords of the military. That grain could be a universal trading commodity was obvious. It gave life and was life and life is everything. That coins are worth life has never been entirely obvious. But unless money can be traded for anything, it is not really money. That is its essential characteristic. Today if you lose your health or a limb, your recourse is to sue in court and your compensation is money. Everything is equated with money.

It is fairly obvious to me that money acquired many negative characteristics at this time. It became divorced from life, but still equated with life. The temple tax, if one could call it that, had been paid in expectation of receipt of planting seed the following year. It was to be paid out of the harvest this year. The state tax is due in coin and if a person had no harvest or did not get a fair price, it might be expected anyway. All that follows the next year is hoped for protection from armed marauders other than the ones you paid the tax to. Instead of being a life giving community service, centralized authorities become bully protection rackets. It is the citizens who give service. To preserve the universality of money in the transition to coinage, society is virtually turned on its head.

The return of prosperity & debt

We have another answer hiding in the account of the origin of money. Regardless of the reasons for the Bronze Age collapse, whether there was a monetary or trade factor or not, prosperity did not return until trade returned, with the Phoenicians being the conduit. The Phoenicians also conveyed to the Greeks the new technique of phonetic writing which can be taught in as little as one day and need not be reserved for scribes. And they taught the principles of financial transactions, including borrowing and debt. From the Greeks these concepts were passed to the Romans and to the entire so-called "western world." The Phoenicians were the gatekeepers to the ancient secrets.

In the old Bronze Age empires (except the Mycenaeans) debt was considered useful as it kept everyone productively busy. Interest rates could reach 20-33%. Loans were taken not only for planting, but to pay taxes. If it were a bad year for crops, the debt might not be payable. A person might have to sell himself into slavery to pay the debt. The total productivity of the kingdom would gradually drop in this way, and so occasionally kings declared release from all debts.

In ancient Sumeria the word for debt relief is *amagi*, literally meaning *"return to the mother*," and used to mean *"restoration of persons and property to their original status."* It has been identified as the first written reference to a concept of freedom. [46] A debt contract might specify payment in weights of money-commodities (it is tempting but misleading to use the word "cash") but the debtor was always allowed to pay in produce according to the old law codes. [47]

The smallest currency weight was called a Sheqel, which was 28 milligrams of silver. Other weights included the Korn, Sekel, Mine and Talent, the last of which was 30 kilograms of silver. [48] A partial list of items that in standard weights could be used as currency included: [49]

- barley (grain)
- lead
- copper or bronze
- tin
- silver
- gold

Other sources list special units:

- Cors of wheat
- Baths of wine

Interest rates in Sumeria and the first Babylon (not the later one of Nebuchadnezzar) were 33% for barley loans and 20% for silver loans, but there were several checks on these high rates. First, the law codes provided that if a harvest was bad, a barley loan was postponed until the next year without interest. A creditor was not permitted to confiscate a person's crop leaving them without food, and attempting to do so resulted in a forfeit of the right to ever collect the debt. A debtor might give a wife, child or slave as a hostage while the debt was paid, but for no more than three years.

Even with these restrictions debt would typically grow faster than the economy. An economy will grow very fast for a while, but then the growth of herds or the cultivation of crops runs into geographic or topographic limitations and tapers off in an S-curve. An agricultural economy can grow negatively at times. A common reason to borrow was to get grain during famine. Another reason was to pay the king's levy or taxes, probably also exacerbated when harvests were reduced.

Debt based on interest rates grows exponentially as a mathematical certainty, without regard for climate or taxes. At 10% the doubling rate is 7 years, and at 33% the doubling rate is 2.5 years. Even some modern economists have observed that debt must eventually exceed productive capacity. [50] So at intervals determined by the king, the ancient empires granted universal debt relief, wiping the books and starting over.

By the time of the Phoenicians and the Hebrews of the Old Testament, debt relief was, we are told, ritualized on a schedule. I have not seen an archaeological critique of this, but here are some relevant texts:

Deuteronomy 15:1-3 "At the end of every *seven years* there is to be a general forgiveness of debt. This is how it is to be done: every creditor is to give up his right to whatever he has let his neighbor have; he is not to make his neighbor, his countryman, give it back; because a general forgiveness has been ordered by the Lord. *A man of another nation may be forced* to make payment of his debt, but if your brother has anything of yours, let it go;"

Leviticus 25:10 "And let this *fiftieth* year be kept holy, and say publicly that everyone in the land is free from debt: it is the Jubilee, and *every man may go back to his heritage* and to his family."

Leviticus 25:29-30 "And if a man gives his *house in a walled town* for money, he has the right to get it back for the space of a full year after he has given it up. And if he does not get it back by the end of the year, then the house in the town will become the property of him who gave the money for it, and of his children forever; it will not go from him in the year of Jubilee."

Nehemiah 5:excerpts [after return from exile] "Others were saying, 'We are mortgaging our fields, our vineyards and our homes to get grain during the famine.' Still others were saying, 'We have had to borrow money to pay the king's tax on our fields and vineyards. Although we are of the same flesh and blood as our countrymen [the complaint is against their fellow Jews] and though our sons are as good as theirs, yet we have to subject our sons and daughters to slavery. Some of our daughters have already been enslaved, but we are powerless, because our fields and our vineyards belong to others.' ... [Nehemiah speaking:] 'Give back to them immediately their fields, vineyards, olive groves and houses, and also the usury you are charging them.'"

We see that the schedule of debt relief must have been changing. There must have been great pressure from lenders to lengthen it. Oddly, we see that not only is debt relief granted, but *sales of land outside urban towns are reversed* so that every family gets its ancestral land back. This is a sure sign that all the land was taken, and so without ancestral land, it was difficult to survive.

But the really tricky part is that it did not apply to foreigners. And so the Phoenicians did not tell the Greeks about debt relief, and the western world had no concept of debt relief. Imprisonment for debt was common until about the 1860s in Europe. Debtors often died in prison and their families fell into poverty. It is rather hard to pay off debt while one is imprisoned. In the U.S. particularly, and to some extent in Europe, depending on the circumstances and the debtors ability to pay, there may still be imprisonment for debt. Through the British colony of Hong Kong, China acquired the practice of imprisonment for debt.

In Minnesota there were 60 arrest warrants issued for debt in 2009, for amounts as little as $85, essentially arrests for poverty. The persons were technically not imprisoned for debt, but for failure to respond to the legal system. In modern Greece, imprisonment for unpaid taxes was abolished in 2008, but imprisonment for debt to private banks is still practiced. Greece is at this writing, as almost everyone realizes, deeply in debt as a country and fraudulently so, as they "cooked their books" while selling bonds over the last decade. What is the lesson we should draw? That imprisonment for debt raises the moral character and prevents unwise or fraudulent debt? Hardly.

Notice that the ancient debt relief programs were not just debt relief, especially not the ones in Leviticus. The person relieved of debt had to support himself or herself, and ancestral lands were returned as the means of doing so. If a homeless (landless) person is given debt relief, they will just fall into debt again. One can find a precursor here to the modern adage (based on an 1885 novel by Anne Ritchie) "Give a man a fish and you feed him for a day, teach him to fish and you feed him for a lifetime." (The original text says "do him a good turn.")

I am wondering as I write this section, what happens if you loan a neighbor your land? Or your country house? On the one hand we have Deuteronomy: "every creditor is to give up his right to whatever he has let his neighbor have," implying you must let your neighbor have the land if you have not asked for it back within the seven years. Interestingly, in the U.S. most states have adverse possession laws. A person in possession of land for an amount of time from seven to 20 years without challenge, who fulfills various obligations of ownership such as paying taxes, may sometimes be able to lay claim to the land.

On the other hand, from Leviticus: "it is the Jubilee, and every man may go back to his heritage," implying that though I lent the house, I should get it back in the Jubilee, if it is my ancestral land. Presumably the ancestral claim takes preference, and only non-ancestral land would be forfeit if lent? But if all ancestral land goes back in the Jubilee, one could not really have any non-ancestral land anyway, so all land goes back to the owner-lender in Jubilee, and only debts of money are forgiven?

Note that the doctrine of ancestral land, though still followed in narrow cases as for example the land used by un-contacted tribes [51], is largely a Bronze Age or even earlier concept, and has generally been replaced by the universality of money. Money may buy land and it is an equivalent resource.

Aerial photo of un-contacted tribe [51]

The only thing is, you cannot eat money and you cannot plant it in the ground to grow grain to feed yourself next year. If you spend it you don't have it and have fallen into the necessity of working for wages, a form of labor considered in ancient times lower than slavery. Only dangerous jobs like mining were hired out for wages, as people didn't want to risk their relatives or slaves. If you don't want to be less than a slave then you must learn to grow money like grain, and frankly it is not easy and the returns are not a hundred fold like Isaac experienced.

The deprivation of a permanent means of livelihood in exchange for easily exhaustible money has been the number one problem for indigenous people around the world since the beginning of the Iron Age, and continues to be as mining and lumber and farming consortia promise people "jobs" in exchange for their land and mineral rights. But economic conditions can change in a heartbeat and the jobs are gone. Even the vaunted American middle class has gradually awakened to find their jobs gone. But that is another subject, and those interested can read my previous book on *The Equity Premium Puzzle.*

This section on debt is wrapped up nicely by Proverbs 6:1-5 *"My child, if you co-sign a loan for a friend or guarantee the debt of someone you hardly know - if you have trapped yourself by your agreement and are caught by what you said - quick, get out of it if you possibly can! You have placed yourself at your friend's mercy. Now swallow your pride; go and beg to have your name erased. Don't put it off. Do it now! Don't rest until you do. Save yourself like a deer escaping from a hunter, like a bird fleeing from a net."*

Debt as the default state of citizens

The strangest thing about the new money is that to be without it no longer meant one simply had nothing, but that one was in debt. So it is not possible to wander around and live off the land. The citizens of a country owe somebody something because of the country's use of money backed by the ruler who is backed by the people.

Consider the matter of foreign trade. If you accept a temple note for grain in trade, somewhere there is a temple with the specified amount of grain. No human needs to do anything for the debt to be paid. The value corresponding to that temple note already exists. Usually the grain doesn't even need to be transported. At the end of the year representatives from each country can simply swap temple notes, and you find yourself in possession of a note for grain in the local temple storage.

Lincoln Wheat Penny
a U.S. coin implicitly backed by grain?

Now consider the same transaction with gold or silver coinage. You can't eat the coins, and they don't even make attractive jewelry. They are worthless unless you swap them for something. So a country pays for your economic products with such coins and you have a pile of them. They are like an IOU from that country. They have the image of the leader or the country's deity or some other symbol of the country on them. The country that paid them to you now has a contract of debt. They are obligated to accept their coins back and provide fair value for them. The people in the country who issued them are in debt, and owe labor and products to whomever holds their coins.

The leader whose face is on the coin promises to honor the debt, and to make citizens honor the debt. For example, the leaders whose faces are on U.S. money are...

- **George Washington** (25 cent coin and $1 bill) who led the army which secured the country from England by force and was its first President

- **Thomas Jefferson** ($2 bill) author of the Declaration of Independence, early President who acquired the middle third of the country, the Louisiana Purchase

- **Alexander Hamilton** ($10 bill) founder and early President

- **Benjamin Franklin** ($100 bill) founder and diplomat

- **Andrew Jackson** ($20 bill) who defended the country against a British attack in 1812, secured Georgia from the Cherokee (in the most dastardly maneuver probably in all of U.S. history), and secured the Louisiana purchase

- **Abraham Lincoln** (penny and $5 bill) who held the union together in the Civil War, thus guaranteeing it would meet its money obligations

- **Susan B. Anthony** ($1 coin) who persuaded women to accept full voting citizenship and their own obligation to work and meet the country's money obligations

- **Franklin Roosevelt** (10 cent coin) who rescued the U.S. economy from collapse in the Great Depression and further defended it against Japan and Germany

- **Dwight Eisenhower** ($1 coin, no longer in circulation) military leader in WWII and president during the height of the Cold War.

American money is overdue for a change. It has always been slow compared to other countries. It took 74 years from the founding of the republic in its present form in 1789 for the $1 bill to be issued. Previously we had only coins and bank notes. The $100 bill has been for all practical purposes the largest denomination for 150 years, and with inflation we need a larger denomination.

I forecast that within about 75 years of Martin Luther King Jr.'s death in 1968 we will get a $500 bill with his portrait. That would be 2043. We need it a lot sooner. More than the denomination, we need to recognize that African Americans have been here and paying part of the debt, working in the factories, fighting in the wars. We need a portrait to remind everyone that they too back the money, and are good for the debt we all owe. Eventually, every major new immigrant group needs to step up to its obligation this way.

Recap

And so we have come from contracts for the care of sheep, or neighborly IOUs, to contracts for stored grain carried as copper ingots by trading merchants, through a Dark Age that wiped memory of how the trading system worked to create prosperity. After about 400-500 years of memory-wiping (~1180 BCE to ~680 BCE), precious metal coinage appeared.

The journey took more than 7000 years from the first tokens in 8000 BCE to the appearance of coins. The coin may appear similar to the modern eye, just a disk with some markings instead of a geometric shape possibly with carvings, but its meaning is infinitely more abstract. The tokens contained in bullae or on strings were contracts for the care or storage of specific commodities: sheep, grain, etc.

Later, during the Bronze Age, temple notes of ingots represented tradable stores of grain.

But coins represent the future commitment of the civilization that issued them to provide unspecified goods and services. Money has been taken to a whole new level. Even though nominally the metal in the coins was presumed to have value, in fact the markings on the coins are critical, and foreshadow the coming a mere 2600 years hence of free floating trade currency, sometimes derogatorily known as "fiat money." But in fact the coins were fiat money already. Even if they were gold.

Oh yes, the secret economic weapon of the Romans ... you are wanting to know but at the time we had not fully developed the impact of debt in the western world. The Romans had the lowest interest rates ever heard of before or since, until the 21st century, around 4% in Rome itself. How did they manage such low rates? Was their money backed by gold?

Coins to Central Banks

Where is the gold of Rome?

Have you ever noticed that we do not hear stories of buried Roman treasure, the way we do of other civilizations? Where is the gold of Rome?

Tenney Frank chronicles the economic rise of the Roman Republic, prior to Empire, in his book An Economic History of Rome, available in PDF form on the web. [67] He begins with this dramatic statement:

"Italy's wealth in ancient times as in modern lay in her food-producing soil. Gold was never found in the peninsula, and but little silver. Iron and copper were mined only in a narrow strip of Etruria, too circumscribed to entice many Romans into industries. The commerce of the seas was developed and held by people less well endowed with productive land, races compelled to trade if they were to survive. Agriculture was therefore Italy's industry, in particular the cultivation of the Western littoral composed of the ejecta of the many volcanoes between central Etruria and Naples, and of the deep alluvial deposits of the Po valley. The hardy farmers of the Roman Campagna it was who organized the irresistible legions that united Italy and through the united strength of Italy the Mediterranean world, and it was the submersion of this stock of farmers that hastened the end of ancient civilization."

Roman denarius with Ceres goddess of grain on reverse
Similar to many other Roman coins & reminiscent of the
Lincoln wheat penny - Wikimedia commons

The answer to our question is that there never was any gold. The wealth and power of Rome was wheat. Something you could eat. Just like the money of the ancients before them.

Much of the following is summarized from Frank's book, so I will only list a reference when another source is needed.

Rome managed to do without coins until the 4th century BCE, two centuries after it's neighbors had been minting coins. Gold was too scarce, so Rome somehow provided an adequate currency for a rapidly expanding state and for trade using bronze and silver. Bronze alone was used during nearly a century of Rome's most rapid expansion. Is there a lesson in there somewhere? Bronze is not particularly scarce. Maybe that is the point. A fixed money supply would not allow expansion without crushing deflation. Our modern conservative ideas about money would have removed Rome as an important player in history, much less an empire.

Eventually Rome coined some silver money when it was campaigning near Greece, in order to buy arms and supplies from the Greeks. It might have been better for the Greeks had they not been so eager to trade with the Romans.

About 300 BCE Rome began tapering the weight of certain bronze coins. This never proceeded beyond a devaluation of about half, and may have been due to rising copper prices. The process didn't continue, and Romans never cared for the idea of "fiat" money. Bronze statues captured in war were often melted into coin. By 270 Rome led a confederation that included all of Italy, but the only coinage was the old bronze coin and a Greek silver coin. At that time the coinage was reformed and the denarial system introduced.

Roman bronze coins were quite heavy compared to silver coins of similar value and might have been disfavored by merchant traders for that reason. Frank points out Rome took that risk in order to have a sound currency. I would add that Rome wisely took that risk to have a currency basis (bronze) over which they had some control, rather than a precious metal they could not domestically produce. In other words, it does not appear likely ancient Rome would have consented to join the EU and give up minting its own money.

Rome adopted a system of plantations based on slave labor. A farmer would typically start with 40 slaves and specialize in one crop. The volcanic soil around the city was rapidly over-farmed and eroded, leaving it fit only for pasture and vineyards. This resulted in a system of land grants in remote provinces. Nearby land could only be profitably utilized by a large landholder since pastoral grazing is not intensive production. Displaced farmers either took grants in provinces after serving in the military, or stayed in Rome and competed with slaves and freed slaves for employment in the city. This resulted in Rome's famous welfare problem, and the demand for much more wheat than could be produced locally.

At first Rome simply allowed conquered regions to join their confederation. They learned the practice of extracting tribute from the Carthaginians. It would have been better for Carthage perhaps not to have used this system, because once informed, the Roman Senate voted to start the 2nd Punic War with Carthage in order to acquire Sicily, for Sicily's grain. This resulted in a devastating war, and 25 years lost out of Roman history. But in the long run they prevailed and thereafter did not lack for grain. Finance of the empire had been secured with the acquisition of Sicily.

In the middle of the 2nd century BCE, Rome found itself under pressure from entangling alliances throughout Greece and the east. It had a choice of enduring almost daily insults as a "friend" or assuming some control. The senate disliked the idea of the military power necessary for control. Democratic leaders were afraid of the power that would accumulate in the Senate from direct control of provinces. And Roman demographics were changing due to freed slaves and war captives. There was unrest and the "Gracchan Revolution." The result of these conflicts, from an economic point of view, was an increase in the power and status of the capitalist-merchant class, or "equestrians." Italian lands were closed to colonization, which directed capital into other more far-flung areas. And the acceptance of a welfare state in the city of Rome undermined the future development of industry in the city.

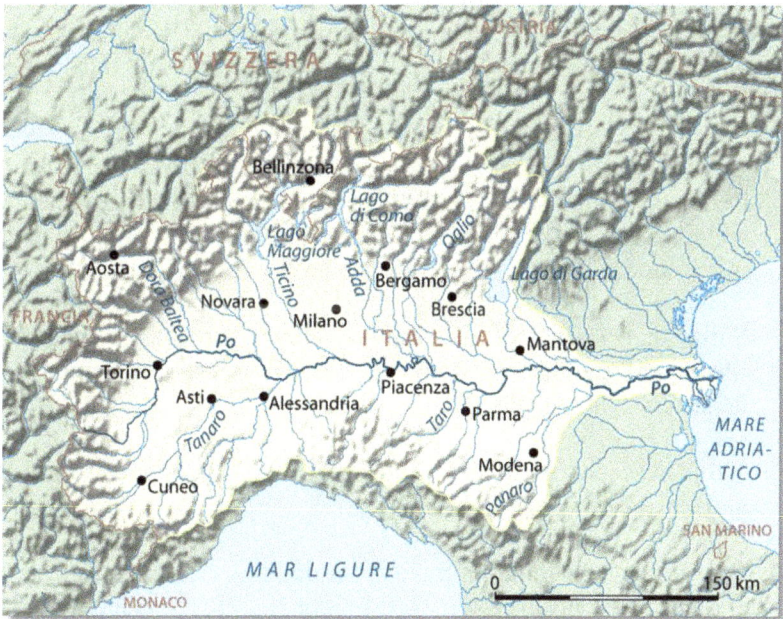

Po River Valley in northern Italy
NordNordWest via Wikimedia commons

Following this period the Senate wished to avoid conflict. It accepted a contract system for provincial administration which greatly empowered the provincial governors, and recognized the extension of the provincial system into Asia. It also accepted the so-called equestrian system of juries. This essentially meant that prominent businessmen decided legal cases. Private ownership of land (in large holdings) was extended, and a tax (probably of a tithe) was levied to support the welfare grants. The status of public mortgages used to finance the 2nd Punic War (i.e. similar to war bonds, with public land as collateral) was upheld.

In 90 BCE certain Italian tribes that had been unable to obtain Roman citizenship set up a competing government. In the Social Wars of 90-89 this was quelled, but the franchise (vote) was extended throughout Italy, all the way to the river Po. The tribes also gained the right to a standing army and courts. However, this seemingly amicable settlement immediately deteriorated, probably due to a lack of trust at root. It only makes sense if the steps are clearly listed:

- The senate grouped the Italians in the city of Rome into 10 wards, kind of like our Congressional districts, effectively removing the influence of their vote. Not that many of the tribes would have bothered traveling to Rome to vote anyway, but to have their right to do so effectively nullified was an issue to them. (Recall that "taxation without representation" was a rallying cry in the American Revolution.)

- A bill to provide equal apportionment of Italian tribesmen and freedmen languished until Marius backed it, in exchange for appointment to be in command of the Mithradatic War, which had just started.

- Sulla, then consul of the army, declared the change in command illegal and marched on Rome "in defense of the constitution." Then he left to fight the war.

- Marius escaped, rallied the Italian tribes to his support, seized Rome and carried out a bloody purge.

- Four years later Sulla returned from the east victorious, seized Rome and carried out his own bloody purge. He conducted a war of pacification in the countryside, seized lands, and established a conservative constitution which lasted until 70 BCE.

- Pompey and Crassius won elections in 71 BCE and restored most of the old democratic constitution. But it was still required to travel to Rome to vote, so Italy was not truly democratic.

Marius amid the ruins of Carthage
painting by John Vanderlyn - Google art project via Wikimedia commons

Sulla's raids left a large class of displaced persons without land. One politician or another used these to stir up trouble repeatedly. Pompey defended the rights of landowners and businessmen. Caesar used this against him to gain popularity. Rome slid into the era of empire.

The painting above shows Marius in the ruins of Carthage. Why? Marius, born in 157, would have only been 8 years old when Carthage fell in 149. Pursuing this riddle leads to the threads of power, war, ascension and finally ruin, a story well summarized in "Roman Leaders at the End of the Republic - Marius." [69]

Marius was a "novo homus," or "new man," without any Senator in his family background, yet he managed to be elected. His parents may have been peasants or businessmen, but they were clients of a rich old patrician Metellus. To increase his prestige he married into an old but impoverished family, the aunt of Julius Cesar. He became second in command under Metellus and so popular with the troops that they wrote to Rome urging he be elected consul, saying he would bring a quick end to certain conflicts ongoing. Metellus did not want Marius to run, knowing this meant Metellus would lose his command position, and this did happen.

Marius needed more troops and instituted a policy that would fundamentally change the army. Previously soldiers had to be landholders, and were supported by their land. Marius recruited poor soldiers who would require a grant of land at the end of their service, and used his position in the army to enforce those grants. Marius was a populist hero to his troops I'm sure, but I'm skeptical. Sounds like it could potentially turn into a move from "citizen defenders" to "thugs."

Gaius Marius
Wikimedia commons

The war they were fighting was in Numidia, in modern Tunisia, and also ancient Carthage. But still the full significance of the painting above is not revealed. Capturing the king, Jugurtha, was harder than Marius thought. He got some help from Sulla, who persuaded Jugurtha's father-in-law to betray him. Sulla thought he should have gotten credit for winning the war.

Marius was elected consul a record seven times. Following the death of 80,000 Romans at the Arausio River in 105, a strong leader was needed to defend against Germanic, Cimbri, Teutoni, Ambrones, and Swiss Tigurini tribes. Marius defeated them in 101. In 100 Marius bribed voters to obtain his 6th term, and with the help of Saturninus got a law passed to effect the land grants to his soldiers.

Following the Social Wars, Marius sought command again to fight the Mithridatic War, as noted above, and was driven out by Sulla. In 87 Cinna was consul and when he attempted to register the 35 tribes to vote as had been provided in the resolution to the Social War, a mob ran him out of the city. Marius had gained military control of North Africa (the Carthage connection in the painting, we see him contemplate what he is planning). He fought north picking up more support, while Cinna gathered troops in the north and fought south to join him, take Rome, and implement the purges.

It seems to me that it was Marius who ended Rome's citizen army, set the tone for bloodbaths, and should be credited with ending Rome's republican form of government.

The gold of Rome was the rich volcanic soil that led to its early rise, and to the class of independent farmers who built it, overthrew their Etruscan masters, ruled it in a democratic fashion, and accepted other peoples as confederates. It was lost through over exploitation, and the society failed to adapt locally to this reality. Instead it reached out to exploit foreign lands, leading to the desertification of parts of North Africa through excessive wheat farming [68], and imposed ideas of conquest and royal governance that sent Europe into a dark age lasting a thousand years.

Even the end of that dark age saw the exporting of Roman ideas of plantation exploitation and colonialism to much of the world, disrupting people's attachment to the land that supported them and setting up future revolutionary conflicts in the style of the Social Wars and their aftermath. In democratic Rome, once "revolution" started it was all downhill to chaos and empire. And that last part of the pattern is certainly repeating like a broken phonograph record or a skipping CD throughout history.

Though much can be learned about wealth and war from the study of Rome, the most striking lesson seems to be to be that of money. Rome used a money that had value, but which they could create plenty of. And the wealth they were willing to fight over was not gold but wheat. Aside from portraits of various rulers, wheat or the goddess of grain was most commonly depicted on money as the indication of its value. Rome was able to increase its money supply to keep pace with its growth and with the productivity of its highly organized system of production, with technology such as roads and aqueducts which the world had never seen, and concrete for construction which even now we have difficulty matching.

Roman aqueduct in Gaul (southern France)
Wikimedia commons

As to the larger question of why Rome rose and why it fell, which surely any book on wealth and war must address, it seems we can come back to Frank's summary with new understanding: "*The hardy farmers of the Roman Campagna it was who organized the irresistible legions that united Italy and through the united strength of Italy the Mediterranean world, and it was the submersion of this stock of farmers that hastened the end of ancient civilization.*"

American small farmers have been under pressure for a century. I consider that small businesses are roughly the urban equivalent of farms, and they are now under pressure from Wal-Mart, Amazon, Microsoft and other giants of the Forbes and Fortune lists. Only Fred Koch of that bunch can be said to have gone against the big corporations. I'm not sure where his sons stand. We need more like Jack Ma. But not like Sulla or Marius.

The banks of Italy

Fast forward 2000 years from the first coin of Croesus, to the banks of Italy. Still we remain affixed to the old trade route. Columbus has not sailed yet, and due to incessant war and a pair of severe dark ages, humans have forgotten that the world is round.

Temples have not been credible places to store wealth since Tulkuti-Ninurta (known in the bible as Nimrod) destroyed the walls of Babylon and stole the statue of Marduk from the temple. After a Babylonian revolt, he made sure they got the message by completely sacking all the temples in the city, a sacrilege not previously seen. This was in about 1200 BCE, just at the time Jaynes claims the bicameral mind was breaking down. The taboos that made the temples safe would never work again. After that, instead of wars that left cities standing and populations intact as had been the case in Sumeria, we have wars in which everything is plundered and the people forced into exile so they will not be a threat again.

In markets and trade, confidence is almost everything. It took 900 years, but by the reign of Ptolemy I (305-254 BCE) there is a clear record of state depositories replacing temples. About the same time Rome began to shift from temples to private banks. Within a century, 35 Greek cities had at least one private bank. [56] The transition was not instant nor universal, and so at the time of Christ there were still moneychangers (and probably lenders) in the Jerusalem temple. First the Macedonian Empire fragmented, and then the Pax Romana provided more stable business and trade conditions than had been seen since the end of the Bronze Age in 1200 BCE. But with the fall of Rome, confidence was gone and banking ended in Europe.

Knights Templar provided money transfer for the Crusades [56]

Banking began to reemerge in the 12th century (1100s) to finance the Crusades. Henry II levied a tax to support the Crusades, and the Templars and Hospitallers acted as his bankers. Funds could be deposited at one Templar location and a note issued which was good for the funds at any other Templar location. Here we see a modern pattern begin to emerge that banking is used not just to finance trade journeys, but also remote military expeditions.

Christianity and Islam put a severe damper on banking by prohibiting interest. The profit in facilitating trade was from the interest on an advance to secure production of grain (yes the primary trade item was still grain), not any kind of price markup strategy. Everyone knew what grain cost and there was only profit in facilitating production. By the 14th century two ways were found to get around this dilemma.

One was the use of Jews to handle financial transactions. Jews were prohibited from owning land in many places, but found they could get rights to sell grain by making production loans to planters. Another variation was that Jews would be employed by nobility to handle financial transactions. The Jews might not be able to charge one another interest, but they were not subject to the Church's dictums, and could charge interest to non-Jews.

Hagia Sophia in Istanbul [author's photo]
Built by Constantine using columns from the Temple of Artemis at Ephesus (one of 7 wonders of ancient world) and later used as a mosque by the Ottoman Turks. Christianity and Islam prohibited charging interest.

A second method that developed later was the use of discounting. A note is sold for cash at a discounted value and redeemed later by paying the full value. This seems just a trick of language to me, but then it had not been long since people thought money was safe in a temple, and apparently the practice of discounting was accepted by the Church.

On the trade route there was still a need for confidence in storage and transactions, and the need to avoid lugging around pirate-attracting gold when going on a journey. And there were grain merchants. But again there was an important extension. In addition to financing the journeys, banking financed production of the grain, and eventually other products. The Medici Bank was established in 1397. In 1472 the Monte dei Paschi di Siena was established, and is still operating, the oldest bank in the world.

U.S. banks & the Era(s) of Free Banking

The U.S. was not on a gold standard until 1900. [83] In addition to various forms of U.S. currency, both gold and silver coinage, Spanish currency was legal tender until 1857. Prior to that the U.S. twice had a central bank, and it was twice abolished. Obviously the experience of doing without a central bank caused some problems, or the 3rd one, the Federal Reserve, would not have been created.

"The Continental," a coin issued by the U.S. during the revolutionary war, was by the 1790s worth only 1% of its face value, at which rate it could be exchanged for treasury bonds issued by the First Bank of the U.S. [84] Benjamin Franklin suggested that its devaluation was a "tax" used to pay for the war.

A controversy arose between advocates of state banks and a central bank. In an atmosphere of general suspicion of banking, the charter of the First Bank of the U.S. was allowed to lapse in 1811. J. K. Galbraith writes of this period: "*State banks, relieved of the burden of forced redemption [imposed by the First Bank], were now chartered with abandon; every location large enough to have 'a church, a tavern, or a blacksmith shop was deemed a suitable place for setting up a bank.' These banks issued notes, and other, more surprising enterprises, imitating the banks, did likewise. 'Even barbers and bartenders competed with banks in this respect.'*" [85] From 1812 to 1815 inflation was 13% per year.

In 1816 the Second Bank of the U.S. was established. It was plagued by bad management and even fraud until 1823 when Nicholas Biddle became its president, but the *opinions* of some were already set, and in 1828 Andrew Jackson was elected president. He thought the bank had too much power and in 1832 vetoed a bill extending the charter, saying it didn't contain enough reforms to suit him. He was not opposed in principle to a central bank, and admitted it was convenient both for the government and for citizens. The charter expired in 1836, initiating a period sometimes called the Era of Free Banking (though it doesn't quite meet the modern definition).

In the Era of Free Banking (or we might call it the 2nd era) things were not quite as open as in 1812-1816. Banks had to have a state charter. These banks issued paper IOUs which could be used in lieu of coinage, and were also called "promissory notes" since it was promised they could be exchanged for coins.

1853 promissory note (IOU) for $5 [86]

The Michigan Act of 1837 allowed anyone who met the requirements for a state charter to set up a bank without actually petitioning for a charter. The average life of these banks was only 5 years. But the reason for failure was not usually fraud, but requirements that the banks hold certain bonds, mostly state-issued, and revalue their notes when the market prices of these bonds fluctuated. Banks would have to call in loans if the bond prices declined. Imagine buying a new car and a few months later getting a call from your banker. You will have to unexpectedly sell your car and pay off the loan. So will everyone else, so you will not get much of a price for your car.

The following table shows that both inflation and deflation were much higher and less predictable then than now. [87]

Inflation volatility in the Era of Free Banking

Period	%Δ Money Supply	%Δ Prices
1834-37	+ 61	+ 28
1837-43	- 58	- 35
1843-48	+ 102	+ 9
1848-49	- 11	0
1849-54	+ 109	+ 32
1854-55	- 12	+ 2
1855-57	+ 18	+ 1
1857-58	- 23	- 16
1858-61	+ 35	- 4

In 1863 without the southern states in Congress, the National Banking Act was passed to reassert federal regulation of banking. During the following period western mining increased the supply of silver, and a national controversy arose between farming and mining interests who benefited from further increase of the money supply, and eastern banking interests who saw themselves as being harmed. This resulted in the famous William Jennings Bryan "Cross of Gold" speech whose imagery made its way into the Wizard of Oz eventually, and in a division in the Democratic Party. There was also pressure from trading interests to follow the Bank of England's lead in adopting a gold standard, for convenience in trade. In 1900 president William McKinley put the U.S. on a gold standard, both internally and for trade.

Following the great radio and automobile technology boom of the 1920s, the gold standard failed to provide for a money supply that could keep up with technology. World trade based on the gold standard also fell apart. We've already seen the effect of trying to make Germany pay war reparations in gold. In 1933 Franklin Roosevelt took the U.S. off the gold standard for internal currency purposes, and in 1971 Nixon took the U.S. off the gold standard for international trade. After a period of inflation in the 1970s, which was related to the international oil trade and possibly some catching up once the gold standard was removed, prices have been much more stable than at any other period in U.S. history. Until recently, that is, when the threat of deflation, the driver of the Great Depression, has showed signs of returning.

A post on a Ron Paul forum states: "*I think that abolishing the fed and the IRS are the most important things that can be done domestically,*" and links to a CPI (consumer price index) graph dating from 1800. [88]

The poster wants you to look at the upswing since the 1950s on the right. When someone calls your attention to financial data, it is almost always a distraction like a shell game at a carnival. They want your attention there so you won't see what is really going on.

Look at the red line at the bottom. The fluctuations of this annual inflation figure are much greater prior to the 1950s. Prices were hardly stable enough to plan anything. Since then they have been relatively smooth, with a slight rise for the 1970s inflation.

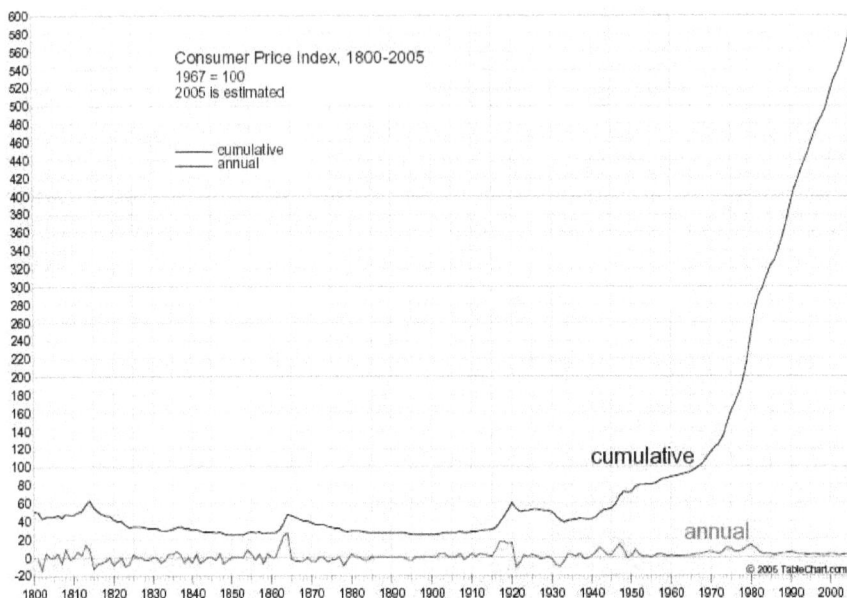

Consumer Price Index, 1800-2005
1967 = 100
2005 is estimated

—— cumulative
—— annual

cumulative

annual

© 2005 TableChart.com

1800 1810 1820 1830 1840 1850 1860 1870 1880 1890 1900 1910 1920 1930 1940 1950 1960 1970 1980 1990 2000

Consumer Price Index since 1800 [89]

The only other smooth period is 1880-1900. This roughly coincides with a stagnant period sometimes known as the Long Depression [90], in which worldwide wealth was concentrated in very few hands and consumers (the word was almost an oxymoron then) or workers had little power. It led thereafter to a quick succession of two world wars, numerous communist revolutions, and the development of nuclear weapons.

The periods of greatest inflation, looking at the red line, are

- The War of 1812
- The Civil War 1861-1865
- During and just after World War I 1916-1920
- World War II and the Korean War 1940-1953
- The Vietnam War mid-1960s to early-1970s (less pronounced)
- The late 1970s, which was a sort of energy war with OPEC

We also see that in most cases, except for the 1950s in fact, periods of deflation followed periods of war and/or inflation. Note that had the chart extended 3 more years it would have captured the deflation of the 2008-2009 financial crisis, which coincided with a wind down in the wars in Iraq and Afghanistan.

Inflation & Deflation

What did a camera cost in 1800?

Since the first photograph was made in 1816, you might think it a trick question. But the truth is if you went into a general store in 1800 to buy groceries, you would likely find nothing that you now buy. I am going out on a limb and say literally, nothing.

Instead of bread you would need to buy flour, or even worse maybe grain and grind your own.

Milk could not be preserved long enough to sell in stores, nor was refrigeration available. So no cold or frozen foods. That means beef would have to be bought from a butcher, not a grocer. All stored meat would have to be preserved by curing.

Consider this astounding statement:

"The Canon EF cost $459 with the 50mm f1.4 lens in the 1976-77 Sears Camera Catalog. (The F-1 with the same lens was $90 more, while the FTb with the same lens was $160 less.) $459 in 1976 equals $1,820.85 in 2011 dollars!" [91]

This is a simple, manual camera with built in light meter and a lever to wind the film after each shot. I had a similar camera, a clone actually, that I bought in 1989 for about $150. So ignoring fantastic claims about what $479 in 1976 equals, the price had gone down over those 13 years, not up. What is one to believe? Did we have inflation or not?

I bought a house in 1975. By the late 1980s it was supposedly worth twice as much and by the late 1990s about 2.7 times as much. It went up and back down and appraises today at about the 1990 value, so the inflation did not on average continue. Again the facts do not seem to agree with the wild claims. We remember the periods that distressed us. It is human nature, a survival adaptation, that crises are burned into our memory. I remember feeling panicked in 1975 that I would not be able to afford a home unless I bought one immediately.

I was just out of college and just married and not ready, and the stress of it broke up that marriage. So instead what got burned into my mind was to not get all worked up about inflation. After all, it affects everyone. It does not affect your relative position on the wealth scale unless your wealth is skewed in an unusual way toward one asset or another. Any such skewing is a focused bet that might win or lose, not a reliable long-term way to build wealth. From the chart below you can see that not all of the rising price of homes is inflation. Some of it is a rise in the median size of homes. Still more of it, not reflected in the chart, is an increase in energy efficiency and convenience. My older home has single pane windows and less attic insulation. Modern homes have double pane windows.

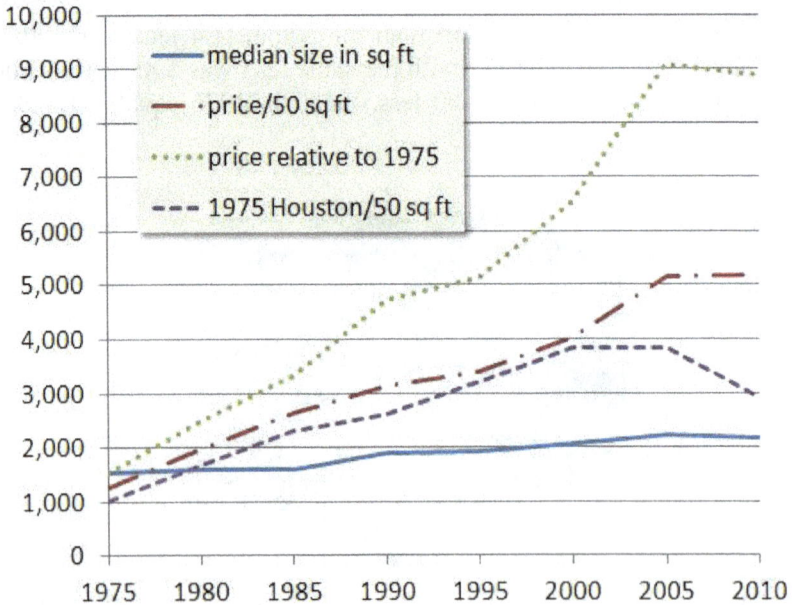

Median size and price of U.S. homes per 50 square feet [91] [92]

If you just looked at median price, ignoring home size or quality, you would think prices had risen by a factor of 6 over 35 years. But if you look at the price of a particular home of a fixed size and quality (there have been a few improvements, such as hurricane film on the windows, larger water heater, better A/C, landscaping) they only rose by 3 times, an annual inflation rate of 3%.

Inflation relative to what?

You can see a problem with any kind of inflation calculation. It measures a price increase relative to something. Relative to what? An obsolete item that you cannot obtain without a time machine and perhaps do not even want? But that is not even the half of it. Suppose I had not bought a house in 1975, and instead invested the money. That was something I was considering. Of course, I did not know then what to invest in. And, someone would loan me the money for the house (at 8.5%, not at today's super low rates). But stocks did not begin to rise rapidly for another 8 years (in 1983), and no mortgage company would finance me to buy stocks. Hindsight is 20-20, but suppose somehow, perhaps a loan from my dad, I had invested in a S&P 500 index fund the paltry $33k that a slightly above median house cost in 1975 in Houston.

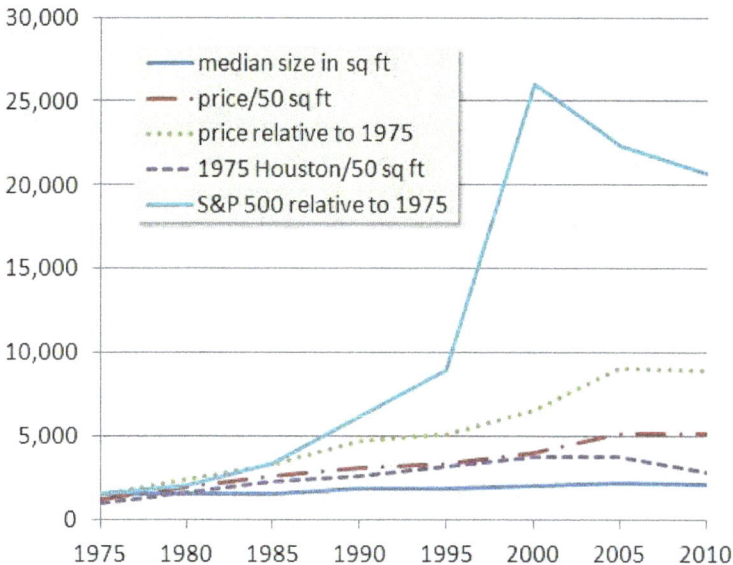

Home prices relative to S&P 500

The equity investment in a broad based index of the largest 500 companies would have increased 13 times, even counting the downtrend after 2001, or more than double the price of new homes, and more than 4 times the price of my home. In retrospect my home investment was stupid. Not unwise or uninformed, but relative to what I know now, stupid. It cost me a marriage and a small fortune and cost me my retirement years also because I am just now getting around to having children.

You might think that there was some tax advantage to the home vs. the investments. No. Within just a few years, mortgage interest payments had dropped below the standard deduction and there was no tax advantage to the house. In fact I was paying real estate and insurance equal to around 5% of the value of the property every year, which if deducted would make the situation look even worse. By contrast if I just left the S&P 500 invested and did not sell it, it would accumulate almost without taxes (there would be tax on dividends, but dividends are not even included in the above chart). There is probably another 1% to 2% annual maintenance for replacing A/C units, painting, roofing, etc. If we assume 7% annual expenditure, the home was a disaster returning a fraction of its purchase price. Of course, I had to have a place to live. That is the only thing that saves it. But having it has made me reluctant to move when perhaps I should have.

Think about this. If I held my wealth in shares of the S&P 500 instead of dollars, then the price of homes, for me, new larger ones with modern features, would have dropped by a factor of two since 1975. Inflation is only annoying for people who hold cash. If you don't like inflation, convert your cash to something else.

Preferences, innovation and standard of living

The manual SLR camera that I bought in 1989 was bulky, especially by the time I bought a large zoom lens, and it cost $6 to $12 a roll to develop and print the photos, most of which were junk in spite of the SLR design. A serious photographer would typically take dozens of rolls on an important shoot. These prints were bulky and still take up several feet of shelf space in my home.

One day while attempting to hike up the Maroon Bells near Aspen, I was struggling to get out my camera on the steep slope and a bunch of guys came by and stopped. One of them pulled a small "point and shoot" out, clicked a photo, and was quickly on his way. That was the last time I took that bulky camera anywhere. I bought 4 or 5 small cameras in the next few years, and when they came out I bought digital cameras, a 2 megapixel tiny one and later a slightly larger 5 megapixel one. They were disappointing because the battery would run down, and in low light I could see a great picture on the LCD screen but the camera wouldn't capture it to memory without blurring, a silly design. Despite the small size, I usually didn't have them with me when I wanted to take a photo.

That's all changed now. Few people use a camera to take photos. It is almost impossible to buy a cell phone without a camera, so basically they are free. The photos take up about one square inch of shelf space for thousands of them, and if you want prints they are 9 cents each at the local Wal-Mart. In 2011 I bought an HTC Android phone, primarily because a review said it had a good 5 megapixel camera. It was $250, and within a year or two I no longer even took my regular camera on vacations. I have a new son and all the baby pictures are on the phone. I am usually around the house when taking them and could pick up either the phone or the camera but - get ready for this - *the phone consistently takes better photos than my Nikon Coolpix 54.*

The phone also takes movies, of course. Even news professionals often rely on video from cell phones. What's more, this phone went through a full washing machine cycle one day in the pocket of my jeans. I pulled it out, took the back off and dried it with a hair dryer, and a few hours later it was working fine and still is. It has a steel case and Gorilla Glass and has been dropped numerous times. (In case you are wondering, HTC didn't pay me anything to say any of this either - but maybe they should?)

So cameras, movie cameras (of modest quality) and sound recording devices suitable for speech are free and everyone has one or more of them. Not to mention that these devices double as a portable stereo and gaming console, and on the larger ones you can stream movies. By the way, you couldn't have bought a cell phone, or any kind of phone, in 1800 at any price. The price was infinite because they didn't exist. But that is not evidence for inflation. Neither is the declining price of the Canon EF-1. Actually, that is called DE-flation. In the case of the phone-camera it was brought about by technology, but my house has also been deflating for most of the last decade.

Let's talk about something mundane like milk. It used to be delivered fresh every morning in the first half of the 20th century by the milkman, because even with refrigeration it would not keep more than about a day or two. In the late 1970s I remember that milk would keep 3 to 5 days in my refrigerator. I would usually have to throw most of it out since there was only one person in my household.

Milk is now practically indestructible. It is sold in boxes, sometimes at room temperature, with an expiration date several months away. I have kept it nearly a year and it is fine. In the refrigerator after opening it generally will last two weeks. How does one compare the cost of indestructible milk with the stuff that was constantly spoiling which I would have to throw out?

Milkman going door to door in 1956
Wikimedia commons

Modern milk is sold in gallon jugs which was impractical in the 1970s. So much milk would not be consumed fast enough and would go sour. About 1/4 of the gallon price is what I was paying for a quart of milk in 1980. Where is the inflation?

The price of dining out has increased. There is no doubt about it. Dining out is entertainment. The price has increased because the demand is high, not because the cost of food is high. A lot of people will laugh at my preference in cell phones and won't have anything other than a $650 iPhone 6, with an $80 a month plan from AT&T. My unlimited plan is only $30 a month. My wife has a flip phone, which she prefers, for $7 a month, but it has a poor camera and won't do any of the other things I mentioned. The price of cell phones has steadily declined and their capabilities have taken amazing leaps. But people spend a lot more than that because of preference. *Preference is not inflation.*

We have two cars. No one had a car in 1800. One of my big budget items is transcontinental air fare, in some years up to half a dozen trips. In 1800 traveling from Texas to the middle of Siberia would have taken months and doubtless would have cost in then-dollars at least as much as today without adjusting for inflation (about $1300 last time I checked). I also have air conditioning, even in the cars, and healthcare including antibiotics, which were unheard of in 1800. I even have indoor plumbing! My standard of living is incomparably different than the living standard of even royalty in past eras. *Standard of living increase is not inflation.*

When I was a kid it was a big deal when the price of Coca Cola went up from a nickel to six cents. All the vending machines had to be modified to accept pennies. The first time I ever paid a dollar for a coke was at a Holiday Inn in Houston Texas in 1972 when I came to visit Rice to see if I wanted to go to graduate school there. I thought that was terribly high for a coke. The price of coke in 2014 is still a dollar out of most motel vending machines, and less than that in convenience stores. The price in the 1950s was for 8 ounces, by the way, and now they are 12 ounces. And what is the grocery store price?

If you have space in your pantry for a 24 can pack, coke is only 32 cents per 12 ounce can, a net inflation rate of 2.1% annually. But coke is a preference. There is no biological necessity to consume soda pop, and it is not even healthy. These indoor pictures of food, by the way, are taken with the free camera on my cell phone. Neither of my digital cameras will take clear pictures reliably indoors, often through frosty freezer glass, but the cell phone usually does.

I was shopping for a car recently. I haven't bought a "new" car since 1989. Instead I have a Mercedes I bought on eBay, and a Jaguar I acquired from a relative. They are 15 to 20 years old. Well it turns out cars are about 10% more expensive than the price I paid in 1989. But that was a terrible car. They are much better now, getting really good gas mileage and having all sorts of electronic goodies. This is progress, or innovation. *Innovation is not inflation.*

HP Stream 2.58 GHz, 2GB, 32GB flash drive $199 (HP/Wal-Mart)
Makes video calls for free with Skype – will be cheaper by the time you read this

Sometimes innovation drives prices down. I saw a laptop the other day for $199 with features that just 5 years ago were about $1400 and which 10 years ago were unobtainable. My wife makes video calls to relatives in Siberia for free. And international calls to any number with any one of a number of services accessible with a WiFi smart phone are about 3 cents a minute or less.

Inflation is natural

What have we learned about money? It is a contract, such as for keeping sheep or storing grain, much older than writing. After some time the sheep die, the shepherd dies, and the grain is eaten by weevils if people don't eat it. If one waits too long, the contract has no value.

Suppose you need some eggs and you tell your neighbor you will help him repair his fence in exchange for two dozen eggs. He says sure and gives you the eggs.

If he comes over the next day or the next week and says "Remember that fence?" you will walk right out with him and repay your debt. If he comes next winter in a blizzard you are liable to put him off again. If he comes next year, you have probably forgotten. If he comes in ten years, your son will say "What?"

A LOW rate of inflation is a reflection of the natural human tendency to devalue old, especially very old, things. It is useful in getting people to call in debts and favors promptly, which keeps economic activity moving along. If people simply hoard their money, their IOUs, then society does not make progress; no one works to make more goods and services.

If prices are falling, hoarding money is exactly what people will do, expecting prices to fall further. And prices will fall further, since no one is buying anything.

However, what if instead of putting money in the mattress, one puts it in a bank which uses it to make loans?

As more people hoard money, the bank has an incentive to loan it out at lower rates, which increases consumption and helps correct the deflation. However, if deflation is too rapid, banks will be afraid to loan money, because whatever is used for collateral will be constantly losing value.

With deflation in place, it makes no sense to invest money in producing more goods and services, because more goods and services will just drive down the already low prices.

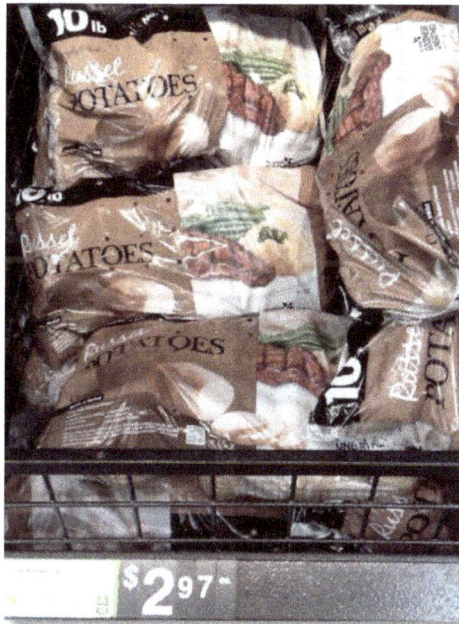

You might not prefer to eat potatoes at every meal, but my Russian wife did just that for several years, if she had anything to eat at all, during "perestroika." With potatoes at 30 cents per pound, you won't starve. If you are willing to work a garden, you can cut up a few of them and have as many potatoes as you want just for digging them. That's why most Russians have country dachas (often very small houses, sometimes just shacks) or a relative in the village, and grow their own vegetables. Sanctions do not scare them. It is just back to normal, like the starving oil workers who told Khodorkovsky that they didn't expect anything more anyway.

I am not actually trying to convince you that inflation isn't happening, though it may seem so. Think about the theme all through this book. I am trying to show you the unexpected, the flip side of everything you take for granted, and how shyster politicians and business people can manipulate you by playing games with carefully selected numbers. If they called it what it is, statistics, you'd know to be leery, but they call it the CPI (Consumer Price Index) and most people suck it right in as gospel.

Of course hyperinflation is bad. So is deflation in almost any amount, because it causes bankruptcies and unemployment and discourages production. So the course of low inflation is not some evil scheme to reduce the value of your savings. It is the natural tendency of old debts to lose value. If you have enough savings that you are worried about their lost value, you should buy something with them. One obvious thing you can buy is businesses. Money is a debt. Business is an equity. So why would you do that? Why would you exchange a nice safe contract for debt for a risky business venture, or several of them, with no contract that guarantees you anything for certain?

From Debt to Equity

The long odds bet

Suppose you have identified 5 businesses you might enter. What are your chances of success with any one of them?

This is actually a controversial statistic, with different answers according to how and whom you ask. If you ask Rand Paul, 9 out of 10 small businesses fail. [93]

If you ask the Small Business Administration, 56% fail after just four years. [94] Most fail because they have insufficient cash and borrow too much money. The top four out of ten reasons listed by Boundless.com [Ibid. 94] involve lack of sufficient cash. If debt is not a viable way to solve this problem, what is?

Information businesses, like Elon Musk's Zip2, have the highest failure rate at 63% after four years. Transportation and retail have over 50% failure rates in that time frame. Insurance, real estate and healthcare have less than 50% failure rates in four years, but only slightly less. [95]

If we look further, it begins to get strange. According to Forbes 65% of new jobs come from small businesses and they employ half of all workers. Half a million new ones are started each month, and half of those are home based businesses. But more fail each month than are started! [96] This is what is called "non-equilibrium." It is not in balance and means that the total percentage of small businesses is changing over time - in this case getting smaller. I have an interesting graphic in *The Equity Premium Puzzle* showing the changing composition of the types of businesses in the economy. In 1900 most people worked on farms but by mid-century that had changed dramatically. Mostly corporations absorbed the workers. Now it is small businesses' turn to yield. It is a slow process though. One can still succeed in small business if you can handle the somewhat low odds.

Chart 3. Survival rates of establishments, by year started
and number of years since starting, 1994–2010

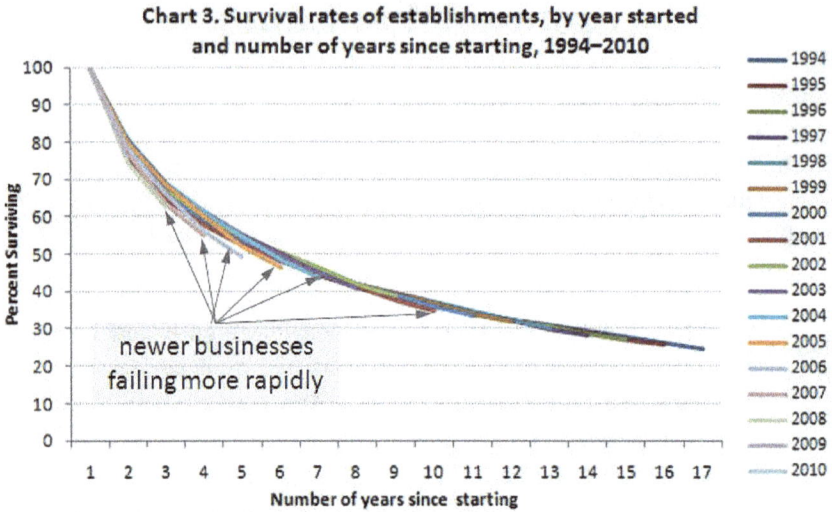

Source: U.S. Bureau of Labor Statistics

The chart above [BLS via Ibid. 93] shows both the survival rates and how these are changing for more recently started businesses. The 50% survival point has decreased from 6.5 to 5 years, a reduction of 23%, between 1994 and 2006. While some of that might be the financial crisis, it is clear that it is a long-term trend and that there has been no particular recovery since the financial crisis.

A working career spans 30 to 40 years. Most jobs now days don't last that long, but a job doesn't take a huge amount of start-up capital, unless you count education. Yet it looks like after 20 years, if we extend the above chart plausibly, only about 1 in 5 small businesses will still be operating. If we extend the curve to cover an entire 40 year career, it seems Rand Paul may be about right. In the 40 years I've been in my present location, there are clearly only about one in ten of the original small businesses remaining, possibly less.

Let's return to our problem of selecting one of 5 businesses, one of which probably will last 20 years. That keeps it within the data we have. It is quite a lottery to pick the right one. You have one chance in 5, and if you start just one we already know from the data your biggest problem is that you won't have enough cash to get over the hump into profitability.

If you could start all 5, and minimize the losses on the four failures, the successful one would probably carry the day. But you don't have cash for all five. No bank is going to lend you that much money with those poor odds.

The origin of corporations

Corporations arose in stages, and were soon specialized to address the problem of the long bet - the high mortality of small businesses. Corporate bodies were recognized at least as early as Roman times as able to "*own property and make contracts, to receive gifts and legacies, to sue and be sued, and, in general, to perform legal acts through representatives."* These included the government itself, towns, religious orders, and businesses. [97] Romans called them "publicani." [98] The class of people who operated businesses, including the publicani, were called "equestrian." Romans even contracted tax collection to the publicani.

Since multiple businessmen shared the cost of the ventures, they could attempt things that had a high level of risk, such as long distance trading. When the risk is not really borne by the owners of the corporation strange things happen. For example, the Senate granted "insurance" to publicani supplying troops in the 2nd Carthaginian War. Derelict ships were loaded with worthless goods and sunk deliberately at sea to collect the insurance. [Ibid. 98] In 1772 a Scottish banker sold short the East India Company. When the stock rose instead of falling he left London owing £550,000, i.e. not bearing the risk himself. The chain reaction from this propagated much like our modern financial crises, and within 3 weeks 30 banks across Europe had failed. [99]

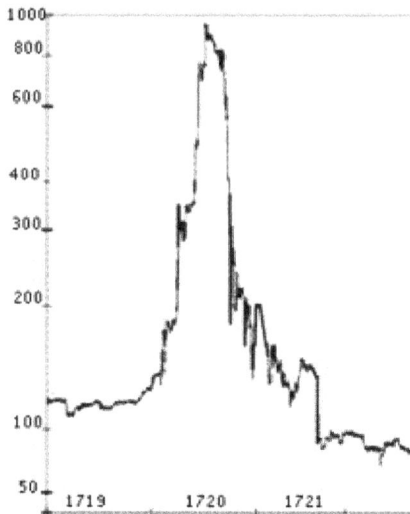

South Sea Company share price

Colonial trading certainly qualified as a risky venture, with pirates, natives and hostile governments standing in the way. In 1711 the South Sea Company was established to take advantage of a treaty with Spain. The Spanish only let one ship a year through, so South Sea Company never really did much business, but promoters managed to hype the company and the stock price soared (see figure above). [Ibid. 97] A 1794 treatise on corporate law by Stewart Kyd gives a nearly-modern definition of a corporation:

"a collection of many individuals united into one body, under a special denomination, having perpetual succession under an artificial form,

and vested, by policy of the law, with the capacity of acting, in several respects, as an individual, particularly of taking and granting property, of contracting obligations, and of suing and being sued, of enjoying privileges and immunities in common, and of exercising a variety of political rights, more or less extensive, according to the design of its institution, or the powers conferred upon it, either at the time of its creation, or at any subsequent period of its existence."

Notice particularly the inclusion of political rights. Corporations in Britain were still closely connected to Parliament, however, and could not be formed without a royal charter or private act (of Parliament). With pressure from the Industrial Revolution to expedite business, in 1844 corporate law was reformed to allow Joint Stock Companies with a streamlined registration process. [Ibid. 97] Even at that initial stage the power that would be wielded by these potentially giant and immortal entities was recognized, as for example in the cartoon below.

1844 - source: Wikimedia commons

So if you can form a corporation and are able to persuade investors to join you, then you might be able to start all five small businesses, giving you a better chance of capturing the one that does spectacularly well. Notice that if you use the capital just to start a large version of one of the businesses, you have only improved the odds a little bit. You have addressed the problem of not having enough cash, but not the problem of which business to choose, and you may have lost control of the business to your partners. There has to have been a reason that when he was finally in control of Berkshire-Hathaway, Warren Buffett dissolved his partnerships in favor of selling stock to smaller investors who would not have as much say.

Or you could buy stock in someone else's diversified business, or in a number of specialized businesses.

Stock is weirdly different from debt. It is not a contract for anything. Many companies never pay dividends (Warren Buffett, for example). There is no concrete promise of anything. There may be some voting rights, but if you buy through a mutual fund or an ETF (Exchange Traded Fund) then you don't even get voting rights. Any one corporation is likely to fail, and none of them last forever. Yet taken as a group the financial returns from stocks wallop the return from debt instruments like bonds. How does this work?

PERMANENT PORTFOLIO SIMULATOR:

Growth Lifetime: 18 years	Run Length: 50 years	Bond Fraction 0 %
Growth Rate: 12 % annually	Starting Capital: $ 100 dollars	Bond Return 0 %
Add New Stock every 6 years		
	Extract Earnings: 0 %	Print first 6 equities
Decay Time: 1 years	Start with 3 stocks	

run

Perpetual Portfolio Simulator
http://mc1soft.com/papers/PerpetualPortfolio.htm

The figure above shows a simulator I have constructed to show how a group of stocks, each of which individually fails after a modest amount of time, can be assembled into a "perpetual portfolio" which grows forever. Basically, the capital is invested equally in all the available companies that pass some test for their reliability, such as membership in a well known index like the S&P 500 or the Russell 2000. Each time a new company is added to the index, a little bit of each of the other companies is sold, and the capital used to buy the new company.

For a number of years I implemented my own perpetual portfolio by buying every stock in the NASDAQ 100 in equal dollar weights (it doesn't have to be equal dollar weights to be a perpetual portfolio). This was a lot of trouble. Now days you can buy an ETF which does this, for nearly any index you can think of. Just get on the internet and search for "ETF" and some description of the kind of stocks you want, the country of the index, or the industry. Check the history of the ETF to see if it really does what it says. Surprisingly many don't.

The value of equities
How do you place a price on a stock?

Dividend based value
Unlike a bond or a contract, nothing specific is promised. If valued only on the dividends paid a stock would be worth about what a comparable bond is worth. But if the dividend is expected to go up or down, it would be worth a bit more or less accordingly

.
Earnings based value
On the other hand even if the stock is paying no dividend, some other company or large investor might buy the whole company. If the stock becomes "undervalued" they almost certainly will. So earnings are more commonly the basis of a stock's value.

Growth based value
Some companies have no earnings, or have heavy losses, but quite high stock prices. Start-up companies are almost always in this category. In this case the value is a prediction of future earnings. In my opinion, these valuations almost always get out of hand. Like the South Sea Company, promoters hype the stock. There may be many companies competing in a field like solar power, or electric cars, or commercial space travel, or some new kind of social media. The founders and backers of each genuinely believe that their company will "win" the expected new market. But in reality most industries have only one or two or at most three long-term winners. For PCs it was Microsoft and Apple. For cell phones it was Samsung and Apple. For automobiles in the U.S. it was GM and Ford with Chrysler now a very distant third. For consumer home pages it was Facebook, and MySpace has lost out. For aerospace companies it was Boeing and Lockheed, with Boeing being the only U.S. company still producing commercial airliners. And so on... All those solar power companies are not going to make it. But some have very high valuations (prices relative to earnings).

Price to Earnings ratio (PE)
The PE is just what it sounds like, stock price divided by earnings per share. If the earnings of a company are $1 per share and the share price is $10, the PE is 10. You might also turn that upside down and state the earnings as 10% of the share price.

The dividends are not necessarily related to the earnings. The above company might pay no dividends, or only half its earnings which would be 5% dividends. Some financial companies manage to pay dividends that exceed earnings. There are two possibilities here. This could reflect arcane accounting and tax regulations. The company might be obligated to deduct depreciation of some asset from its earnings. This is a paper deduction if the asset is already paid for. The actual cash generated by the company is more than the stated earnings. The other possibility is that the company is simply in a going out of business mode, selling off assets and distributing the cash as dividends. By definition a royalty trust is set up to do this. If the stock price is gradually going down over time, this is probably what is happening.

In theory, if the company has additional business prospects it would retain some or all of the earnings to open new branches or develop new products. Warren Buffett retains all of the earnings, but instead of doing one of those things he acquires additional businesses. I suppose he also reinvests in the companies he already owns but he is not obligated to report the details publicly.

Many years ago I read a book by Peter Lynch, former manager of the Fidelity Magellan Fund, who used the following rule of thumb. There is no particular logic to it, and trying to figure out why it might be useful is what started my own investigation into stock valuation and eventually the equity premium back in the late 1990s. Peter thought the company growth rate in percent should about equal the PE multiple. A company growing at 7% should have PE of 7, implying a stock price of about 7 times annual earnings. A company growing at 25% should have a PE of 25.

There are other statistics such as the PEG (PE growth rate) that can be used. But Peter's rule is simple to understand and I suggest you try to apply it. Not because it is a great rule but because it will lead you to great questions.

If you apply it to established companies, the first thing you will notice is that if any estimate of growth rate is available, it is a wild guess. High growth rates predicted in 2007 became negative growth in reality. Pessimistic growth rates predicted in 2009-2010 were easily exceeded.

Peter Lynch interviewed by Louis Rukeyser in 1982
https://www.youtube.com/watch?v=brglcZ-Fuxc

If you apply Peter's rule to companies that have zero or negative earnings because they are starting up, or because they are recovering from disaster, you will see that it completely breaks down. If there are no earnings there is no PE. One would have to look at future earnings and that is a wild guess, especially for individual companies. It might be easier to guess at the earnings of an industry and buy a collection of companies in that industry. But for example, the solar power industry might not realize its expected growth if Saudi Arabia keeps the price of oil down for a long time.

The value of growth

What really, mathematically is the value of growth - not just Peter's rule of thumb?

This is determined by "discounting" the expected value of future earnings to the present time using the interest rate. For example if the interest rate is r, then how much money X would we have to deposit today at that rate of interest to receive a payment of Y next year?

$$Y = X * (1 + r)$$

Suppose I promise to pay you $100 next year, and the interest rate is 2%. Then...

$$\$100 = X * (1.02)$$

$$=> X = \$100 / 1.02 = \$98.39$$

This is a lot like figuring payments on a mortgage. So far at least. Tell me, what is a payment of $100 in 20 years worth today?

Think about it for a minute and determine your answer before reading on.

...

You might have reasoned something like this. It is necessary to divide by 1.02 for each of the 20 years. So for N years we would have:

$$Y = X * (1 + r)^N$$

$$=> X = Y / (1 + r)^N$$

The answer then would be

$$\$100 / (1.02)^{20} = \$100 / 1.49 = \$67.11$$

Except that this doesn't make a lot of sense. No one in their right mind, that I know, would give away $67 expecting to get back only $100 in 20 years - regardless of what the prevailing interest rate is (it's a lot lower than 2% at most banks currently). The problems include:

- How do I know I'll ever see you again or that you'll even be alive in 20 years?

- How do I know the interest rate will remain 2%. In fact it won't.

- How do I know I'll be alive in 20 years, or interested in buying anything if I am?

- Wouldn't I get more enjoyment out of buying something now for $67 than waiting?

- Inflation is likely more than that, so $100 in 20 years won't really be worth $67 today.

I picked 20 years deliberately, because it is the time frame in which equities begin to reliably outperform mortgages and loans and bonds, anything with the fixed determination needed to calculate these kinds of values and backed up by a contract or legal obligation.

You might think stocks would be worth a lot less because they promise nothing. In my opinion, individual stocks are practically worthless over a 20 year period. Since 1970 in the computer field we saw Digital Equipment (DEC) come and go, Compaq come and go, many other forgotten names come and go, Microsoft come and stagnate, Netscape come and go, MySpace come and go, AOL come and go, Apple come and go and come again and who knows from here, and Facebook come and who knows. Are you going to bet on Facebook 20 years from now?

Two things are going on here. Neither one of them are obvious.

1. While individual companies may come and go, the sum of all companies is growing in proportion to all of the following:

- The growth of population (2% to 1% over last century in U.S.)
- The immigration driven growth of population (also 1% to 2%)
- Inflation (since company earnings are ultimately based on the selling price of products and services, currently around 2%)
- Increase in standard of living, evidenced by increased productivity (2.1%)
- Increase in market share (big companies taking business from small companies, approximately 2% estimated)

If you add up the above numbers you get a growth rate for large companies of around 9%. Not all of it is benign. Growth from immigration and from small companies just moves growth around. But since other countries have higher population growth rates, really only the cannibalization of small companies is harmful.

The 9% still does not account for the average 10-12% yield of owning stocks if one combines growth and dividends. That leads to the second thing that is going on:

2. The rate of return or growth of a company is figured only on the basis of the equity, the amount of value of its shares of stock. But that *is not all of the capital a company uses to conduct and grow its business.* Businesses also borrow money by issuing bonds and other debt securities, at rates ranging from a little over 4% for long-term bonds to around 1% for short term borrowing of a year or less.

The equity premium
Would you rather invest in:

- A 20-year bond with a nearly guaranteed return of 4%?

- A stock which makes no promise but typically pays a 2% to 3% dividend and very likely will not last 20 years even if the management is honest?

- A group of stocks representing the entire economy and growing on average at a 10-12% rate while paying 2-3% in dividends, into which new stocks will be taken as old ones die?

The difference between the bond and the 2nd option is (most likely) that the bond performs as promised and the one stock declines out of business. The difference between the bond and the 3rd option is 6-8% in favor of the 3rd option.

It is a no-brainer. If those are really the options, pick #3. If your whole country goes down the tubes, even #1 will be worthless. Otherwise #3 is much better.

There is a catch here. The PRICE of #3 is the SUM of the prices of all the #2's. Even if #3 is worth a lot more than that. If long-term growth becomes over priced in the market, worthless companies will be created by spin-offs or IPOs and the market will crash until good companies are worth more than their growth prices (like Berkshire-Hathaway was when Warren bought it). These two effects enforce the whole-is-the-sum-of-the-parts law, and prevent equalization of the long-term value of whole-market baskets of stocks. Besides, the "worth" of the basket of stocks in #3 is partly based on future companies which don't even exist yet and can't be objectively priced.

Investors cannot "equalize" the returns of a whole basket of companies with the returns of bonds without so over pricing individual companies that short sellers would step in and sell the weaker ones, driving the prices down. Short sellers try to figure out what will happen eventually and accelerate the adjustment. Short sellers and arbitrageurs are normally the force of equalization, but in this case they are equalizing the whole and the parts, the immediate tangible values, not the equity premium. There is this tension between what the stocks are worth individually and in groups, and what the groups are worth long-term.

There is a second catch. The bond has a fixed end date. The group of stocks does not. The bond is priced based on its payment stream ending in 20 years. But the stocks keep going, and in 20 years it will be found that the economy has at least another 20 years of earnings to look forward to, and so forth.

And there is a third catch, the one that forces the equity premium to exist even if some accountants and mathematicians find a way around the first two catches. Growth in productivity will drive prices down, causing deflation. This has caused the worst financial crises in the U.S. of the last 100 years. The central banker will have to step in and increase the money supply to prevent disaster, creating enough money to cover the greater rate of production of goods and services. This will result in a permanent decline in interest rates. These rates will be set by the central banker. The central banker is not an "investor" and has unlimited supplies of money with which to back up its will.

Corporations will then borrow the money at rates lowered by the central bank, and use this as non-equity capital to grow their businesses and create new jobs (as desired by the central banker, at least in the U.S.). Meanwhile this trick also gives them an excess return.

While I have attempted to make this seem simple and intuitive, the subject of the equity premium is complex and controversial. There are literally thousands of academic papers on the subject, and at least hundreds of proposed solutions. There are also academic papers discrediting all of the proposed solutions to the puzzle - except the one I just described to you. For more information on this and many related subjects, naturally I recommend my book on *The Equity Premium Puzzle, Intrinsic Growth and Monetary Policy*.

A century of growth?

     Corporations can live forever. So far at least, you cannot. What will happen if a financial entity can capture a century's worth of growth?

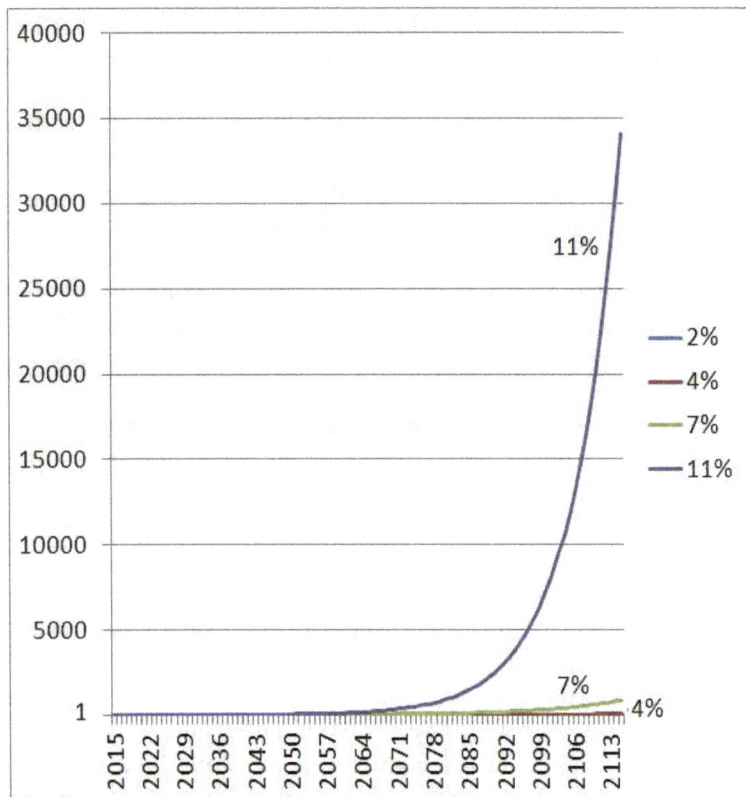

Multiplier effect of a century of growth at 2%, 4%, 7% and 11%

     Suppose a corporation had a mere $1 billion to invest (the larger ones have tens or hundreds of billions). The chart above shows what it would grow to, in billions, after one century at various rates of return. If an after tax return of 11% could be maintained (somewhat hypothetical, but possible), the investment would grow to 35 trillion.

     What the chart makes evident is that long periods of time amplify the difference between growth rates. A respectable 7% growth rate, something you might obtain after taxes if you carefully follow the index investing method, grows to less than one trillion. The other lines are too close to zero to even see. Here is what the numbers will be in 2115:

Century growth effects on $1:

2%	4%	7%	11%
$7	$51	$868	$34,064

The growth wars

This is like a nuclear weapon, only worse. Have you ever been close to someone with a trillion dollars? It could not be pleasant. It would be like being close to a whole room full of 600 pound gorillas. A trillion dollars would squash you without realizing that it had done so.

Even billions have this effect. For example, wealthy Chinese businessman Wang Jing has bought the rights to build a new shipping canal in Central America, without consulting or considering any of the farmers or villagers who would be displaced. The land and rights to build an airport, two ports, a railroad and two commercial free zones have been set aside without any review or authorization. The rights have been granted for in excess of 100 years. Even the Nicaraguan parliament was given only one day to consider and debate the bill. President Ortega admits no studies were done. No tax or other financial liabilities will be granted to Nicaragua. No nation will have jurisdiction over the properties, neither China nor Nicaragua, even if Wang Jing reneges on particulars of the agreement. Even his name was secret until the day of the approval. [100]

Proposed routes for Wang Jing's canal in red
Wikimedia commons

It hasn't been long since the farmers and villagers that will be displaced supported Daniel Ortega in an armed revolution to reclaim their land. It should not be surprising that they are talking about taking up arms again.

Beyond the personal interests of your limited lifespan, there are two important conflicts at issue in *the growth wars*, as I call them. The first is the preservation of your liberty, your personal power, your personal wealth - against incursion by wealthy corporations and individuals. Without wealth, in this kind of environment you will have no power, and without power to defend it you will have no liberty. Many people died fighting to obtain and preserve your liberty. Are you going to throw it away so you can retire to a condo in Miami and leave liberty in tatters for those that survive you? Do you wish to be remembered like the decadent last Romans? My dad and several uncles fought in World War II. It so happens they were not killed but many people were. I suppose I might face my Maker if I abandoned my responsibility, and blame the situation on Him somehow, but I could not face my dad. It is our patriotic duty, those of us who can by any possible means, to acquire the wealth and power to defend our liberty.

The second conflict is one of economies. China has evolved a third principle of central banks, to manage not only prices and employment, but also growth. Either they will figure it out or not (they are doing very well so far), but even if they don't, some national block will. Nations last even longer than corporations. 100 years is nothing to an ancient nation like China, or even Russia, not to mention Europe. Perhaps someday the entire world economy will be regulated in a happy unison. Despite the troubles of Greece and Spain, countries seem in a rush to join the EU. But most likely it will simply be regulated by the winner of the growth wars. We therefore also have a duty both as humans and as citizens to participate in the political process of our country (whatever country you live in), to educate and enlighten our fellow citizens, and select policy makers who will manage the economy based on logical principles, not conservative or liberal ideology. This is a fight for what kind of cultural values will dominate the world. Will it be a culture that values individual liberty and creativity, or one that highly values sacrificing the individual for the good of the many?

There is still a bit of feeling among Americans that it is not good to be really rich, both among liberals and among religious conservatives. I hope I have given you a moral imperative that will ultimately, for some of you anyway, prove stronger than either your longing for retirement or your reticence about wealth, and prompt you to go out there and get as rich as you can, then pass the baton to your offspring or whoever you wish along with the same imperative, so that by 2115 we have an army of people who can stand up for themselves, and stand up to anyone or anything.

The benefits to civilization might be enormous. Think of all the creativity that would be unleashed. This empowered group of people I am thinking of would be able to do things that today cannot be considered because everyone is a slave to making a living.

There is a third reason as well - a third threat beyond corporations and governments. Productivity and technology itself threatens us over the long run, perhaps in the 100-200 year time frame.

Stephen Hawking, gravity guru whose ability to communicate at all depends on Artificial Intelligence (A.I.) software, warned recently that such technology might itself be the greatest threat our species faces, even greater than our own bumbling with the environment. The environment will eventually fix itself after any catastrophe reduces our numbers. But an A.I. that we create, perhaps inadvertently, would not necessarily have an end point. And like a computer virus, it might replicate and grow. It might not have a finite life and could grow for much more than 100 years.

Stephen Hawking at NASA in 1980's
Source: NASA, public domain

Naturally there is disagreement about the capabilities of an A.I. Long before it would have a "mind of its own" an A.I. would be subject to takeover by hackers or enemy states. This is similar to takeover of people's minds using propaganda or coercion, but presumably primitive A.I. which cannot generally comprehend the world, only limited subsets of it, would also not have a moral compass. This simple difficulty has been glossed over by authors like Asimov who postulated the "three laws of robotics" for our entertainment and proceeded to break them in every way imaginable, and to suppose that such robots would voluntarily remove themselves from human society – while still controlling it for the good of humans.

Recently Microsoft's chief researcher Eric Horvitz stated he doesn't feel we will lose control of A.I.'s. [117] However Bill Gates said *"I agree with Elon Musk and some others on this and don't understand why some people are not concerned."* [118]

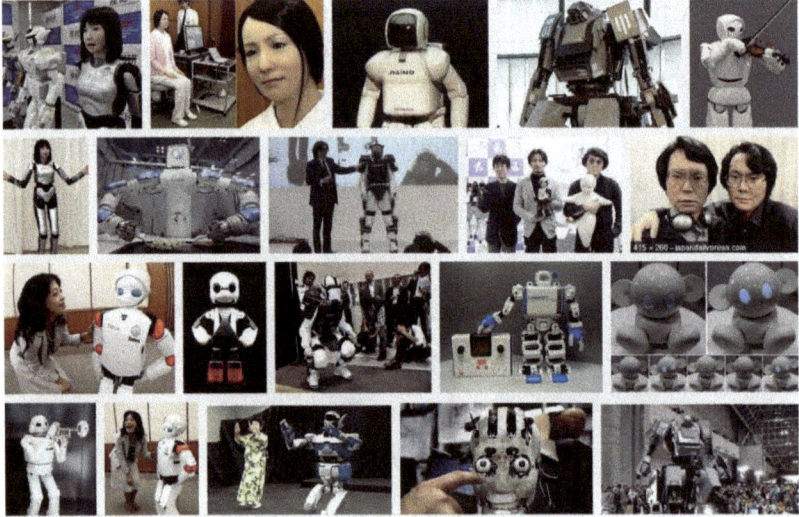

Collage of Japanese robots
source: Google search "Japan robot"
Even the ones with human faces are robots.

It appears the Japanese are not giving up the global contest, and are pinning their hopes on something not quite human. At least as long as we remain in control of A.I., a viable strategy for maintaining personal liberty is to be an owner of industry rather than a worker.

If you are now motivated, that brings us to our last topic, the mundane details of how to protect and grow your share of the world.

Creating Your Wealth

Your strategy

The number one mistake Americans make is thinking only of themselves, and trading away their share of the world economic pie for temporary comfort. This results in a smaller share of the pie. It results in descendants who drop from the upper middle class to the middle middle and eventually the lower middle and eventually poverty. I have seen it. You can hardly keep track of financial news and not read articles on the increasing wealth gap.

If you were intending to obtain wealth using your connections and your hard work and persuasive abilities like the billionaires we studied, you probably aren't reading this book. It's great if you can do that. The Forbes Top Ten list has only, well, only 10 people on it. And only 6 families are represented. That is a clue right there. No one we studied made it with zero help from his or her family.

If you cannot afford to invest, I understand. But you need to read some other book. There are lots of authors who address your needs. There are very few who address people who are actually in "the gap" ... the strange land where one's basic survival needs are met but it is not clear how to cross the gap or whether it is worth it. Oh, sure, there are books on investing or how to get rich, but most of them are just positive thinking or motivational or lists of good sounding advice to sell books, or even worse, sound advice toward what may be the wrong goals, or a scam to relieve you of your wealth. The paradigm of the moment in American financial literature is "*planning for retirement*," and the worship of *education and jobs*. I enjoy my education, but I have always considered it a hobby. Bill Gates, titan of technology and college dropout, along with Larry Ellis, also a dropout, more or less prove that a college education and degree is not the key factor in accumulating wealth.

If you remain dependent on corporate employment, and do not become financially independent (or arrange for your descendants to become financially independent), then you are contributing to the problem of the wealth gap, which eventually must result in unemployment, unrest and war. And when corporate employees vote, they invariably vote their pocket books. Because their pocket books are dependent, their votes are dependent, often without their realizing it.

My recommendation, indeed the main thrust of this book, is to replace planning for retirement with *generational wealth building*. In the process of understanding money and long-term economic processes enough to learn how to do that, it was a byproduct that we also began to understand the economic cycles and conditions that cause war.

I believe you who are near the wealth gap have a moral obligation to cross it to the up side if you are able. If we can just expand the wealth of the top 10% half way to the top 1% (moving the dotted lines on the chart below up closer to the top one), we will have made enormous strides toward a free and democratic civilization that can progress without destroying itself. If wealth and power are less concentrated, and economic decisions more distributed, it is reasonable to suppose those decisions will take better account of the people around us.

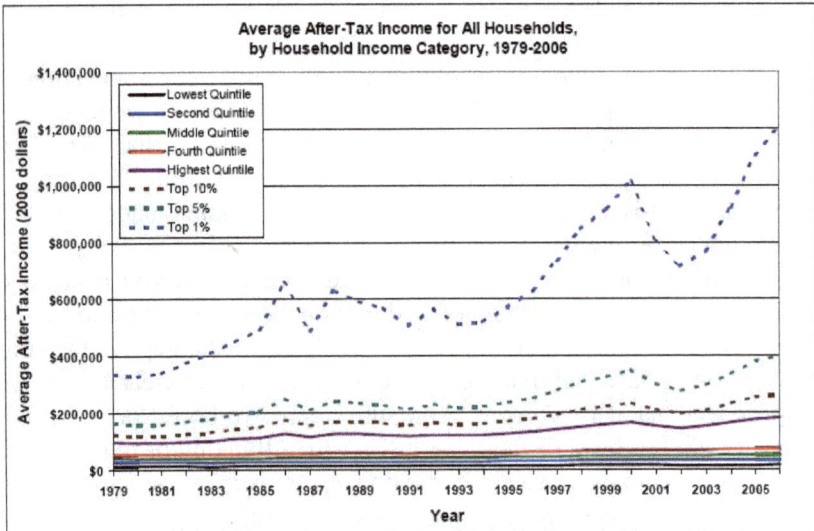

Average After-Tax Income for All Households, by Household Income Category, 1979-2006

source: http://www.exponentialimprovement.com/cms/wealthhappens.shtml
used by permission

If you have decided to invest then you will need to decide on a strategy. If you don't have a lot of experience, this chapter attempts to point you toward some places to go to get information and open accounts, and to highlight some pitfalls to avoid. It also highlights two strategies.

The only wealth accumulation strategy that does not require you to be lucky, a genius, or have access to inside information is to invest in the equity premium, the excess returns that large groups of stocks exhibit over long periods of time, typically 20+ years.

Usually you will have some shorter term concerns, for which we suggest a dividend capture strategy. If you are retired you may need to generate income to meet expenses. This is especially true if the world has entered one of its longer down or sideways cycles like the one that started in 2001. The dividend capture strategy is not by itself a wealth accumulation strategy, but an expense strategy that should be coupled with wealth accumulation, unless you have no heirs and are within 20 years of the end of your life.

The billionaire who comes the closest to what you are trying to do, in that case, is probably Warren Buffett. But I am going to suggest you do some of the things he did, on a smaller scale, and not necessarily do what he advocates. Do as he does, not as he says. For example, Warren says dividends are superfluous, an indication of a failed management, but what he actually does is to buy whole corporations so he can completely capture their cash flow.

Basics

I assume you can find your way around the process of opening brokerage accounts and researching stocks. If not there are some online resources and many books.

To obtain basic information on price history and dividends, a suitable website is http://finance.yahoo.com/. There have been some unfortunate changes recently, and the history data does not go back as far as it used to, but it is still usable. Beware that the new CEO Marissa Meyer has sneakily integrated advertising and promotional articles so they look like news. You can look up stock symbols and see dividends and earnings and charts of price history.

There is a long standing problem with the summary page display of "yield." Yield is the recent cumulative dividend divided by the current stock price. It will fluctuate inversely with price even when the company has not changed the dividend. A price fall will make the yield look high even if a future dividend cut is coming. The problem with Yahoo Finance is that for some stocks the yield will read zero or a small number or "N/A" when actually the company or ETF (Exchange Traded Fund) is paying very high dividends. On the left of a company page you will see a link for price history. You can click that and display only dividends, and see what they really are and whether they are trending up or down. For example, if you look up MORL (technically an ETN, explained later) you will see that the dividend is listed as N/A (not available, or not applicable), but in the history you find nearly a 20% average dividend (with a lot of variability by month).

To look up the company name that goes with a trading symbol like MORL, or to find the symbol from the company name, use the "get quote" box on Yahoo Finance.

MORL dividend history for 2014:

Dec 10, 2014	0.132 Dividend
Nov 7, 2014	0.121 Dividend
Oct 8, 2014	0.992 Dividend

Sep 11, 2014	0.074 Dividend
Aug 8, 2014	0.08 Dividend
Jul 10, 2014	0.964 Dividend
Jun 10, 2014	0.069 Dividend
May 9, 2014	0.072 Dividend
Apr 9, 2014	1.013 Dividend
Mar 11, 2014	0.017 Dividend
Feb 10, 2014	0.062 Dividend
Jan 9, 2014	0.807 Dividend

To get the yield for 2014, we add all those numbers up giving $4.403. Divide that by the share price of $20.27 on January 9th 2015 and you have a yield of 21.7%. In case you are tempted to put all your money in this high paying ETF, don't. It is a 3x leveraged ETF which could have compounded losses. But it seems no more volatile than individual mortgage REITs which comprise it such as AGNC, and less volatile than shipping companies which sometimes also pay high dividends. I have two shipping companies, DCIX which dropped dramatically after canceling its dividend, and NMM which is doing well as of this writing, but goes up and down a lot. We'll discuss MORL more in the next chapter. Relative to other particular investments it might be an improvement or a mistake.

A one page summary of modern widely held beliefs about investing can be found at:

http://money.cnn.com/magazines/moneymag/money101/lesson4/

When I checked, I didn't see any grave errors or misinformation there. You should read that page because I will not discuss all of them in this book. In general you have to really watch out for misinformation and promotion. When you open a brokerage account, and especially if you deposit a sizable sum, you will get on all sorts of mailing lists for investment opportunities and may even get calls from your broker referring you to his friends who want to manage your money. I have never seen anything good come out of any of this, either the mail or the referrals. The mail is often outright fraudulent. Fake money managers may abscond with your money at worst, or at best charge high fees for doing no better than what a market index fund can do. The only money manager who has outperformed the market over a long period that I know of is Warren Buffet, via Berkshire-Hathaway. He keeps saying every year that this year will be the last time he will be able to do that, and someday it will be true - probably about the time I buy some of it.

The luck of the novice, or lack of it

There is another thing that will surprise you. If you are new to investing, you will find that most of the time everything you buy immediately goes down. Academic surveys have proven this is not just an impression, but actually true. There is some kind of underlying reason for it, such as, perhaps you picked up on some idea floating around or some optimism about a particular investment, which you don't even realize led you to buy it. Perhaps you bought it because it has been doing well. But investment performance tends to revert to the mean. If you plan to be a trader, you will have to figure out how to overcome this. If you are a long-term investor, it is a disadvantage but not fatal. Making a series of smaller purchases can help alleviate the problem.

Broker accounts

The most desirable brokers to use vary from time to time. It seems like my main account has changed hands through some sort of merger or acquisition about every 5 years or so. Here is a quick summary of three that have been around for a while:

- TradeKing (formery Zecco) - $4.95 flat rate commission, limitations on cash transfers, best margin rates on large margin amounts

- Scottrade - $7 commissions, offices in many cities which is convenient for novices, and willing to handle such things as trust accounts, best margin on small amounts

- TD Ameritrade (formerly Datek, TD Waterhouse) - $9.95 commission, large fast transfers via ACH, best trading tools, but highest margin rates, but substitute payments only if using margin

A margin account allows you to buy and sell without ever having to wait 3 business days, or paying penalties, even if you never use margin. Don't use margin to buy long-term growth stocks because you cannot know if they are really going to grow. Never use anywhere near your margin limit because if you have to sell to meet a margin call you will be forced to lock in a loss at the worst possible time. You will not be allowed to use fancy 2x and 3x ETFs ("ultra" or "short" or "bear" ETFs) as collateral for margin, and for good reason.

Substitute payments and other tax considerations

If you hold a margin (negative) balance your broker may lend your shares to short sellers. Dividends will be paid to whoever buys them. You will not receive dividends, but instead will get "substitute payments." The trouble is you will pay your full tax rate. They aren't "dividends," either regular or "qualified" for special tax rates. On $1000 in dividends in a 39.6% tax bracket, you'll pay $396 in taxes instead of $200, or about twice as much.

Brokers won't always tell you this, and their policies might not all be the same. A TD Ameritrade representative told me they only lend your shares out if you actually carry a margin balance. A TradeKing representative told me they lend your shares if you have a margin account, even if you are not using margin. I am not sure I trust the representatives to know what the computers are doing, but I'll find out next year when the tax forms come as I have quit using margin in the TD Ameritrade (TDAM) account. Note that TDAM moves cash very quickly, in one day, up to $100k using simple ACH transfers. TradeKing, which gives very low margin rates and advertises their rates are negotiable, uses correspondingly more restrictive policies, allowing only $30k ACH transfers, and taking 3 days to approve even wire transfers. So I maintain the account with TradeKing (recently bought by Ally Financial) for using margin, and the TDAM account for liquidity, when I need money in a hurry, or to trade if I want really fast execution.

Don't worry too much about tax exempt accounts. I've rarely had good luck with these, and as soon as you get in about the top 20% of earners, your income will exclude you from eligibility. If you are going to hold a lot of high paying dividend stocks early in your career, it might be worth it. For stocks which pay small dividends and expect most of their gains from growth, you won't pay tax anyway unless you sell and have capital gains.

Account linking and automatic transfers

You can link your broker account to your checking account at any of the above brokers. At most of them you can set up automatic transfers. During your working years you might want to set up an automatic transfer to invest part of your salary (though you will still need to log on and make the purchases). It makes me nervous to put in after hours orders because some traders will put in artificially low bids which might catch your buy order just as the market opens. If you cannot place your orders during market hours, use a limit order. Otherwise, though, I don't like limit orders because whether they will go through or not is uncertain.

Selecting Assets

You should not take anything in this book as "investment advice" in the legal sense, i.e. a recommendation to buy or sell specific securities, for two reasons. I am not an investment adviser, and I do not know your particular circumstances. I will describe the method by which I recently evaluated a list of ETFs, and you can get ideas from this how to do your own analysis, but I am not recommending you buy any of these particular ETFs.

My goal for this exercise was to identify ETFs which closely followed a major index over long periods, but also paid reasonable dividends. By reasonable we will see that is limited to about 3%, not very high. You would need to have $1 million invested for every $30,000 of annual income. Ouch. What I suggest is to supplement this type of strategy with a variety of higher dividend stocks such as the ones I mentioned above, but every now and then one of them will crater and I cannot predict what they will do in the future. We will cover some of my mistakes, and those of other people including some famous investors, in the next chapter.

The reason for ETFs rather than mutual funds is because they are easy to buy and generally have low fees. The management isn't being paid to "pick stocks" and their holdings are a matter of public record. Traditional mutual funds are bought and sold only at the day's closing price, and may make capital gains distributions for which you will be liable for taxes. I never had an ETF do this to me.

Royalty trusts and limited partnerships

Speaking of unexpected distributions, I want to warn you about royalty trusts like BPT, or partnerships like BBEP. These can declare income for which you are liable for the taxes, without actually paying you the money. Sometimes large amounts. They will send you some type of booklet declaring your share of company expenses and depreciation, with tables you will have to use based on when you bought each lot of your shares to determine how to file deductions on your taxes. Sometimes they will fail to send the booklet and you will have to find it on the internet. Also, they typically make several revisions. Your tax statement from your broker will have several revisions and the last one may even arrive after April 15th.

It can be hard to identify these kinds of companies until you already own them and get the tax statements. For example, there is nothing in the Yahoo Finance summary of Kinder Morgan (KMI) to alert you that it is a limited partnership. One trick I have used is to do an internet search on any energy or pipeline company with the company name followed by the word "partnership." Or you can look on the corporate website. With shipping companies the nomenclature is unfortunately different. For example, Navios Maritime Partners (NMM) is not actually a limited partnership, and pays only ordinary dividends.

Often professional money managers will recommend partnerships. But they will not do your taxes for you and it can be very complicated to fill out the special forms to get fair tax treatment. I have disposed of such assets that make my life too complicated. My friend Nat recommends them, but only for investors who can buy at least $100,000 worth of each company and hold them for a long period, to make doing the tax paperwork worthwhile.

Evaluating a list of large cap dividend ETFs

To start I did a simple web search on "dividend ETF" which produced the website http://etfdb.com/type/investment-style/dividend-etfs/ at which there was a long list. The following from the upper reaches of that list looked interesting for further analysis:

DVY   2.99%   div but 5% less growth than S&P 500
HDV   3.09%   5 year growth almost same as S&P
IDV   4.9%   but way behind S&P since 2012
DEM   4.46%   lots of Russia & some China
DLN   2.26%   Apple, Microsoft
VYM   2.76%   best growth, same as S&P
DGS   3%   emerging small cap, poor growth

The first one, DVY, I have owned in the past. You can see that it gives up too much growth. It looks like to me that HDV or VYM would be a better choice since they have nearly the same dividend.

The ones that pay more than 3% typically give up a lot of growth. You will also find that the very high dividend securities will not grow much. The one exception is HTGC which is a Business Development Company (BDC). BDCs are a bit like REITs (Real Estate Investment Trusts) but invest in businesses rather than real estate, and pay out most of their earnings as dividends in exchange for exemption from most corporate taxes. They are a kind of investment company. They may actually buy stock in smaller start-up companies (HTGC does some of that) so that their investors get some of the benefits of venture capital investing, or they may loan money to start-up or midsized companies, or some of both. It is hard to get information on how much of each they might be doing.

Your voice or your money?

Something you might want to consider when selecting assets is how to make your voice heard, a key theme of this book. To vote the shares you own, you will have to buy them directly, not through any mutual fund or ETF. That is impractical for even the S&P 500, not to mention larger indexes, and the small number of shares of each company you hold will not be significant.

I hope someday this issue is addressed. It is starting to get some attention. There is a website that tracks ETF voting records: http://etfdb.com/2009/etf-proxy-voting-records-in-focus/.

Issuer	% Votes Against Management Proposals	% Votes For Shareholder Proposals (Governance)	% Votes For Shareholder Proposals (Compensation)	% Votes For Shareholder Proposals (Social Issues)
iShares	16.7%	71.4%	0%	0%
State Street	33.3%	57.1%	50%	0%
Vanguard	16.7%	28.6%	0%	0%
PowerShares	66.7%	100.0%	100%	0%
ProFunds	33.3%	100.0%	100%	80%
Rydex	0.0%	14.3%	0%	20%
WisdomTree	40.0%	83.3%	33.3%	0%

source: etfdb.com, Jan 2015

If you wish to vote for shareholder proposals on social issues, ProFunds ETFs is your only effective option. Their funds are listed on their website http://www.profunds.com/. They have an S&P 500 tracking fund which is suitable for equity premium investors, ticker symbol BLPIX. It appears to be an ordinary mutual fund, not an ETF. It trades only at the closing price each day. While BLPIX tracks the S&P in price almost exactly, it issues dividends only rarely and only tiny ones, really insignificant. In other words, the dividends are being used to pay expenses of the fund, and these appear to be much too high for me, so I will not be investing in BLPIX. The ETFs offered by ProFunds are too specialized to be of interest to an equity premium investor, i.e. they are not based on broad indexes.

If you want to vote *against* management 2/3 of the time, and *for* shareholder proposals on governance and executive compensation, PowerShares is a possible choice. They offer a lot of specialized funds, but do not offer a general index tracking ETF. For example, they offer six S&P 500 related funds as shown below.

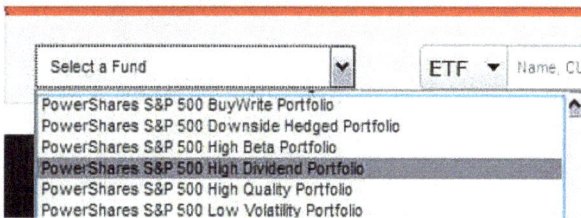

source: invesco.com

Investigating the one labeled "high dividend" we find the following chart:

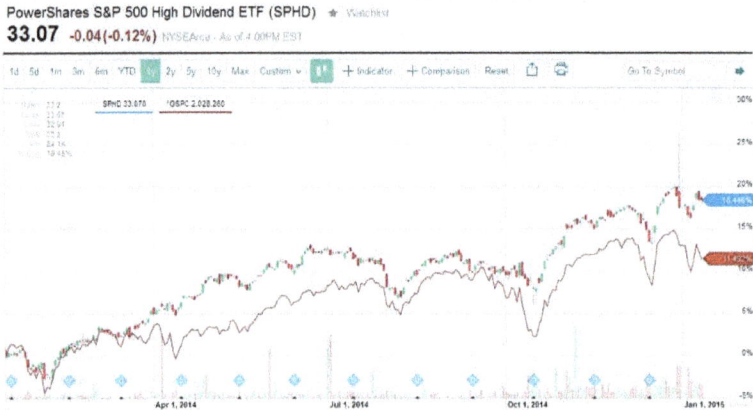

Powershares SHPD vs. S&P 500 index - source: Yahoo Finance charts

The red line, the lower one, is the S&P 500. The candlestick (bar) plot is the PowerShares SPHD ETF. Over the last year this ETF paid a 3.3% dividend, and also performed 7% better than the S&P 500. The dividend ETFs mentioned above, HDV and VYM, paid almost as much and followed the S&P 500 within a tiny fraction of a percent. So you would get the voting you want, but there is no guarantee that return will continue, in fact looking at 2 years the S&P 500 performance is better.

I tried the PowerShares "high quality" version of the S&P 500 and found it split the difference between SPHD and the S&P 500, but paid only 1.66% in dividends. I tried all six of the PowerShares S&P 500 related ETFs, six different ways of slicing the index, all created by professional money managers. Some of them were terrible. See for yourself:

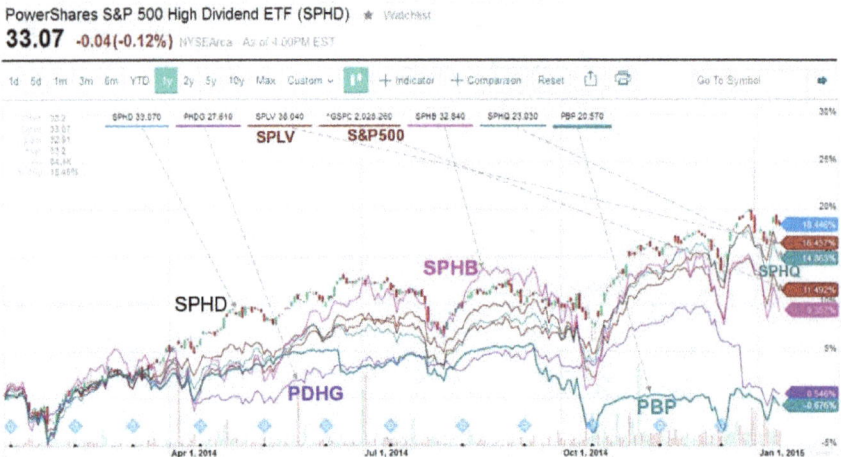

Powershares S&P 500 related vs. actual S&P 500 index

It looks like SPLV (low volatility) did second best, just under the leading SPHD, and had a yield of 2.21%. Overall it outperformed my two previous picks (HDV and VYM), at least over this time period.

The worst was PBP, the "BuyWrite" portfolio. This is supposed to be a conservative strategy but it only works in sideways or down markets. The idea is to buy stocks and then write call options on them. If the stocks go up, the calls get exercised and one loses the profit. PBP lost a lot of profit. Hopefully it would do better in a down market, but, if one gives up the big gains, why invest at all?

Almost as bad was PHDG which is downside hedged, i.e. uses some options or derivatives to protect against loss. Obviously it protects against gains, but look near the end of the year. When the rest of them are going down, it goes down nearly as much, and then when the rest of them rapidly recover, PHDG falls off a near vertical cliff.

What you DON'T get with any of the three PowerShares "slices" of only part of the market is assurance that the analysts that select the membership will capture the equity premium returns over a 20+ year period. In a way, it is back to stock picking again. They could be in a period of good luck like the Magellan fund, which after about 20 years of outperforming the market turned to less than market performance (see next chapter). The stocks are supposedly selected by some objective criteria, not just by following the fund manager's daughters through the shopping mall, but PowerShares (Invesco) does not have the 70-year reputation of Standard & Poors. So you are taking some risk in exchange for the voting performance. It might be helpful to read the prospectus of each ETF and see what the criteria are. Maybe one of them is more committed to following a whole market strategy. But it is not obvious from their names.

What the SPHD prospectus says about stock selection

So how are the stocks in SPHD chosen? This information can be found in the prospectus. You can find the prospectus on the Invesco website, or your broker will probably send you a link to it after you buy the fund. A web search on "PowerShares SPHD prospectus" gives:

http://www.invescopowershares.com/pdf/P-SPHD-PRO-1.pdf

On the first page we learn that total expenses and fees are 0.3%, or about $31 per $10,000 invested per year. This is low compared to the 1% or higher fees for mutual funds, and one of the reasons I like ETFs. The fees of 0.3% do not include transaction costs, but these days transaction costs are very low.

On the next page under "Principal Investment Strategies" we learn the fund invests in just 50 of the S&P 500 stocks. These are selected by a mechanical strategy which is summarized there. First comes a selection of 75 stocks which have the highest dividends, but no one industry may contribute more than 10 stocks to this selection. Then the 50 stocks with lowest volatility over the past year (roughly least magnitude of price fluctuations) are selected from the list of 75.

In the next section under "Principal Risks" we learn that dividend stocks might fall "out of favor" with the market, and that companies might discontinue their dividends. Then there is verbiage about the risks of stocks generally.

Advantages of full S&P 500 tracking ETFs

While you can preserve some of your voice by choosing an ETF with a voting record that approximately matches your preferences, all of the PowerShares offerings are new and unproven and over a two year period they lag the S&P 500. There are three well known **S&P 500 tracking ETFs:**

- SPY yielding 1.92% currently,
- VOO at 1.91%, and
- IVV at 1.88%.

Below is their performance vs. the real S&P 500 and SPHD over the last 2 years.

SPHD vs. regular S&P tracking ETFs 2 year performance

Alternatives to the S&P dividend ETFs

With SPHD you give up a lot of performance for the voting. What about other dividend oriented ETFs, HDV and VYM? Looking as far back as the creation of most of these ETFs, 4.5 years, we see that the trend toward VYM giving up as much in growth as it gains in dividends persisted since late 2010, including the minor downturn in 2011. HDV does not make a favorable comparison. But we just do not have data on the financial crisis.

Vanguard High Dividend Yield ETF (VYM) ★ Watchlist
70.01 +0.21(+0.30%) NYSEArca As of 4:00PM EST   4.5 year performance

VYM & HDV vs. S&P trackers VOO,SPY,IVV 4.5 yrs.

If you held MORL as only 5% of your portfolio, that would produce the 1%. MORL would have to decline at 20% per year continuously for this combined portfolio to give up as much as VYM, which has not happened and does not seem likely.

Small cap, financial and energy dividends

From mid 2014 through February of 2016, all kinds of high dividend stocks took a nose dive, typically around 50%. Most of them are recovering as of April, but it was extremely scary.

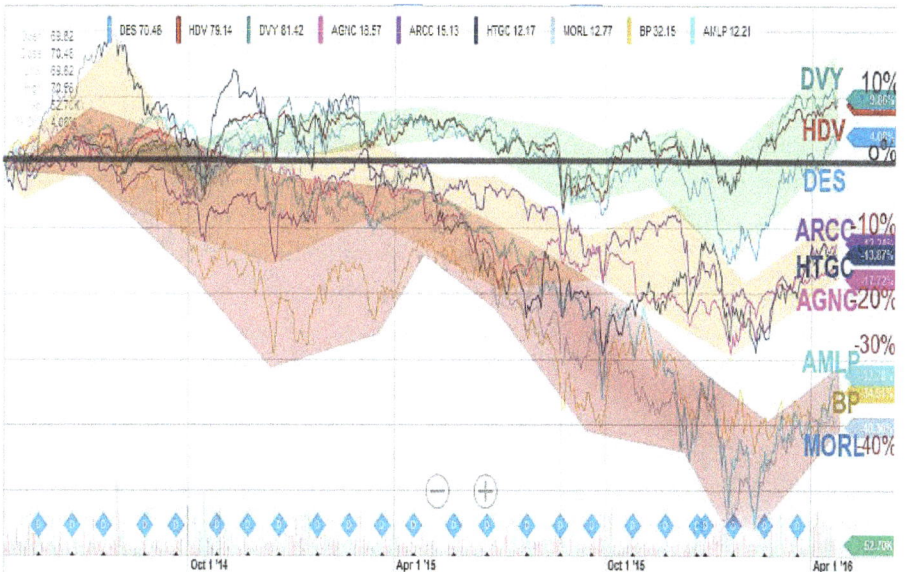

The chart above compares some of the ones we have discussed with the lower yield HDV and DVY, an interesting small cap dividend ETF from Wisdom Tree with the symbol DES in the top band shaded green. These mostly escaped the vicious downturn.

Next in the middle orange shaded band we have three financial stocks that during this period were yielding in the 10-12% range. ARCC and AGNC are well known mortgage related financials, and HTGC is a lender to venture startup technology companies. If you are looking at the value of your portfolio, and not reinvesting the dividends, it looks like these were going down. But add in 24% in dividends over this period and they are doing at as well as the "green" stocks. And if you were reinvesting those dividends, you got a good kick up as they began to recover.

Last in the red shaded region at the bottom we have an energy-related ETF called Alerian MPL (AMLP) which yields 11-12%, the oil giant BP which during this period was yielding a very high 7% of real dividends which qualify for the lower tax rate, and the 3x leveraged mortgage ETN MORL discussed above, yielding 30-35% during this period. Though it appears MORL did the worst, add back two years of dividends and it did the best. If you are in a high tax bracket, subtract again 39% of those dividends and it breaks about even on the period, but should do all right if it continues to recover.

If you held an oil ETF such as OIL or USO, it pretty much tracked the third group, but didn't pay any dividends. On the other hand, the master limited partnership ETF, AMLP, which largely avoids the tax headaches we mentioned for MLPs earlier, yielded 11-12%, while approximately tracking the volatility of oil. If you switched some capital into this ETF during the oil downturn, you will get excellent yields regardless of what happens with oil, and if it does recover then probably AMLP will go up also. It might go up anyway.

While BP doesn't look so good superficially, with only a 7% yield, consider that it is only taxed at a 20% rate. It is worth nearly 9% if you are in the 39% tax bracket.

Figuring the statistical loss from discontinuing dividends

When hand picking my own dividend stocks I find that out of ten stocks, one will discontinue the dividend about every two to three years, and fall in price by about half. That is a continuing loss rate of about 2.5% (1/10 companies times 1/2 years times 1/2 loss = 1/40 = 2.5%). The average dividend from the very high dividend stocks I was selecting is around 10%.

This loss rate reduces the yield to 7.5%. Income tax takes up to another 1.5% (20% dividend tax rate times 7.5%). Such high dividend payers rarely grow. So the after tax dividend rate on these handpicked high yield stocks is more like 6%, roughly equivalent to junk bonds, and an example of equalization.

Can you automate your investing life?

There is nothing more tedious and annoying to me than having to give my attention monthly to managing deposits and bills. I think culturally we have all gotten away from the monthly sit-down mindset due to pressure from companies to automate our bills and cut out paper and mail fees from their expenses, sometimes passing the expenses on to us if we don't.

As mentioned above, most brokerages allow the setup of automatic transfers to and from your bank or credit union account. You can set a percentage of your salary to go into the brokerage account. This will not automatically be invested, however. You will have to log on to do that.

Many types of retirement accounts will funnel the money all the way into your selected investment, usually in very broad categories like S&P 500, small cap, foreign or bonds. I have one such account that I grew tired of managing many years ago. I left it set to 100% small cap and it has done better than any of my other accounts, probably for two reasons. I'm not trying to beat the market, and I'm not losing money by switching between funds at the worst possible time which is what most of us tend to do. If you already know you can pick the fastest lane on the freeway or in the grocery store, maybe you are a born switcher, but the rest of us are not good at it.

What about going the other way - funding expenses from an investment account? You won't be able to fund very much with bank interest. With another family member I set up a joint account to fund utilities at our mother's house and attempted to use high dividend stocks. We set up automatic transfers to a bank account and automatic bill paying to actually pay the bills. The bank account keeps enough balance to cover about two months of bills in case something goes wrong. We attempted to extract 10% annually from the investment account. The average dividend using Mortgage REITs, shipping companies, and business development companies was well over 10%. It worked for a couple of years while the market was going straight up, recovering from the financial crisis, then it quit. A figure of 10% is just too high to extract reliably and gives up all growth. Then whenever there is a downturn or a loss of one of the stocks (DCIX canceled its dividend, for example), there is negative growth in the portfolio.

Recently the extraction rate had risen to 13% because of the accumulation of these effects. Obviously we have to make some adjustments. I suspect that the maximum long-term withdrawal that does not liquidate an account is closer to 6% or 7%. That is a "no growth" number. One problem is that while long-term returns are higher than that, if the market is down 30%

or 40% for a few years, as it was recently, the withdrawal rate nearly doubles during that time, drawing down the account.

How much investment capital do you need?

As we saw above with the analysis of dividend growth ETFs, the most you can get from something that roughly tracks the S&P 500 is around 3%, and that is right at the cutting edge. You will give up a percent of growth or supplement with something like MORL or HTGC or KBWD. It is a slight risk because not all of the S&P 500 index stocks are included. Someone's magic formula selects as few as 50 to optimize the dividend. To meet an average $200 a month in expenses one would have to have an $80,000 account balance at a 3% extraction rate ($200 x 12 / .03). Now you can see that to live off your investments and still grow them, you have to have a large nest egg, basically about $1 million for every $30,000 of annual expenses. According to the investor rank statistics we examined earlier, everyone in the top ten percent has that much. The top 10% of those entering retirement (age 60-70) have around $2 million and if that's all invested (i.e. none of it tied up in real estate) they could sustain $60,000 annual expenses. Probably such a person has retired from an annual salary of around $130,000 or more and will want a lifestyle above that level. If other retirement income is available, then the $2 million might be enough. If not, then a draw-down plan can be used, like an annuity. This withdraws more than a sustainable amount, but not so much that you are likely to run out of money before you die.

You can buy an annuity from a life insurance company, and they will manage this for you, but they will also take their profit. If you manage it yourself, be wary of two problems:

- A specialized portfolio, for example focused holdings in the company you worked for all your life, can lose value unexpectedly.

- If you have a draw-down rate of , say, $60,000 annually from a $0.5 million portfolio, a nominal rate of 12%, in a market growing at an average 10% rate, this should last you 18 years. But if at year 4 the market takes a 20% dive before resuming its former growth rate, you lose 4 years off the end of your withdrawals.

In either case of course, you have left your children nothing unless you die much earlier than expected. Is there any alternative? There is not one that is proven and established by long historical data. Is there an ETF that is able to finance the $60,000 a year without any draw-down, preserving some market growth? This is like trying to have your cake (your gift to your heirs, insuring your family success) and eat it too (gobbling up funds during your own retirement).

Should you draw-down during retirement?

Virtually all retirement planners assume you will engage in a planned draw-down, annuity style, liquidating your investment capital. At an interest rate of 4%, which you can get with good grade corporate bonds, a half million dollars will last 10 years at a draw-down of $60,000 a year.

If you are assuming a bond return, say 6% which is pretty much a junk bond rate, you can start with half a million and draw $60k a year and it will last 11 years, if the junk bond market does not liquidate it for you before then. I used to invest in high yield debt ETFs that generate high rates like that, but they tended to lose value over time. They are liquidating to pay the yield. For all the risk, you only got one more year. Unless you have a terminal disease, you could run out of money before you die.

If you retire at 65 and have a life expectancy of 85, which is typical for males, you need 20 years and you'd still have a 50% probability of outliving your funds. If you stretch it out until you are 90, i.e. for 25 years, even at the 6% junk bond rate you'll have to reduce your draw-down to $40,000. This will be impossible to live with unless you have another source of income.

If you reduce your draw one more notch to $30,000, then at the 6% junk bond rate, ignoring the likelihood your bond fund may be self liquidating, you will still have half a million when you are 90. Some long lost relative will get a very pleasant surprise. Possibly you are not interested in long lost relatives, but if you have closer relatives or children to carry on a tradition of family wealth building, a generational wealth building plan, then for a sacrifice of only $10,000 a year, or 25% of your investment income, you pass your nest egg to them undiminished.

Well we haven't exactly been recommending bonds, have we? If you invest in stock index funds which have long-term growth rates around 10%, you can typically withdraw $50,000 a year from the same half a million nest egg. But there is a catch. During years when the market is down you'll need to reduce your withdrawal in proportion to the amount the market is down. Otherwise you will liquidate your portfolio. If the market is down 20%, only take out $40,000.

The "hump"

If you want to maintain your share of the market, not just the dollar value of your portfolio, of course you can only take out the dividends which as we have seen are hard to get above 3% in a portfolio that keeps pace with the S&P 500 index. So a good rule of thumb is that you need about twice as much money to keep your share of the world while living off your investments as you do to simply maintain a fixed dollar account balance. This is why so few people do it. However, if you are able to climb into even the bottom rung of the top 10% bracket in your lifetime, then you have it and you are "over the hump." Your family can climb from there with less effort.

It is no accident that so much discussion about the wealthy and the non-wealthy focuses on the top 10% figure. That is pretty much where the hump begins. People, or families, tend to slide down the hill on either side of 10% and 1% toward either greater or lesser wealth.

Where do you think the dividing line is between the 10% and the 1% for people in the 60-70 age bracket, near retirement?

It is at $12 million dollars net worth. Let's suppose $2 million of that is in real estate. The remaining $10 million, even at the 3% dividend rate, produces an income of $300,000 a year. This represents a second milestone, the other side of the hump. At that level, a person will only have about $70,000 in taxes due to the favorable rate on dividends. Of the remaining $230,000, it is easy to imagine reinvesting $100,000 to increase one's share of the market and move up, while still having a nice lifestyle, able to travel and hire a maid and drive nice cars. So really the hump is somewhat broad. Between $2 million and $10 million, there is the ability to stay in place. Above $10 million there is the ability to rise rapidly.

Using investments as an annuity

The table below summarizes this discussion in a form you can use for back of the envelop calculations of your own. "Initial draw" refers to the yearly withdrawal as a percent of the initial capital. For example, 6% corresponds to $30,000 if initial capital is $500,000, or $60,000 if initial capital is a million. If you only have half a million and want to withdraw $60,000, use the 12% line. To withdraw $90,000 annually use the 18% line. The word "growing" refers to the dollar balance of your account, not to your share of the market. To preserve that you have to hold withdrawals to 3% or less. Shown below is a table of **years of drawdown:**

		Interest or average returns:			
		4%	6%	8%	10%
initial draw:	6%	28	forever	growing	growing
	12%	11	10	14	18
	18%	6	7	7	8

One can visualize this in graphic form below. If you are handy with a spreadsheet, it is easy to set up your own calculation for exactly your situation. Beware of assuming that the numbers will come out exactly as you plan them, since all sorts of market factors are in play. Even with conservative bonds, deflation can cause them to default, and inflation can cause them to lose value. If there is one thing you take away from this book, it should be the importance of a stable money supply with a consistent 1% to

2% inflation to encourage economic growth. Without stable money we have varying degrees of disaster until in the end, war breaks out.

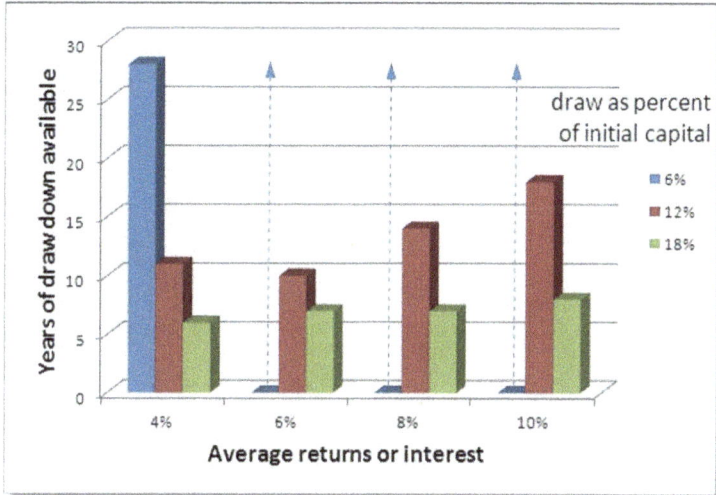

Length of annuity-like draw-down from a fixed initial investment

I continue to look for ways to enjoy a higher living standard while holding growth stocks, but I have not found one yet that allows meeting $60,000 of expenses without $2,000,000 in investment capital, or else giving up growth and taking a risk of loss or draw-down. That is why I recommended at the outset that your target be to enter the top 10%. If you are in the top 10% of your own age bracket at retirement, at the time of this writing you will have about $2 million or more. You can pass $1 million to each of two children and cross your fingers that they won't blow it. Most likely they will do whatever they have seen you do.

The plot below provides another way of looking at this. The 3% yield line (green) refers to the 3% dividend case we have just mentioned. The principal (initial capital) for this plot is $1 million. So the $30,000 annual payout on the extreme left where the 3% payout length goes off chart to infinity represents holding an index-like basket of stocks without liquidating any of them. Other points of the 3% curve with a finite payout length represent increasing rates of liquidation. For amounts over $70,000, the effect of the yield is hardly noticeable. It is almost as if the principal were just divided by the number of years. At $45,000 the curve turns up giving a nice advantage from the yield, and a 37-year payout. Most likely that will cover your lifetime. At less than 37 years you are running some risk of outliving your money.

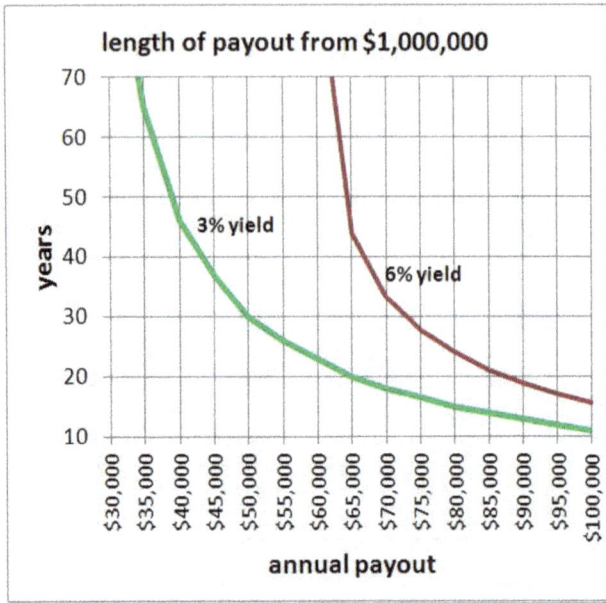

length of payout from $1,000,000

On the other hand, once you have provided realistically for your lifetime, you only have to cut expenses by 1/3rd to leave your principal investment untouched and growing at the rate of the index.

> *The sacrifice needed to extend a <u>retirement plan</u> into a <u>generational wealth building plan</u> is not huge. It is only an expense reduction of one third.*

If you invest in higher dividend stocks (or junk bonds) to achieve the 6% yield, you can meet the $60,000 annual expenses (not counting taxes) from $1 million instead of $2 million. What you give up is growth of your principal. Your descendants will lose their share at an average rate of 8% to 9% a year based on historical market performance, and both you and they will lose purchasing power at whatever the inflation rate is.

If you are determined to liquidate your investments within your lifetime, at least go to the following link and figure out how long you might live:

http://gosset.wharton.upenn.edu/mortality/perl/CalcForm.html

Don't use the average answer, either. You have a 50% chance of living longer than that. Use at least the upper quartile figure. There is a 25% chance you will live longer even than that. If your life expectancy is 86, your upper quartile might be something like 93. These are numbers for a typical male who is healthy. Numbers for a female might be more like 94 and 102. Once you get to retirement age you have already passed a lot of the high risk periods and you should expect to live longer than the averages for your country.

The impact of reproduction on wealth builders

Each child then must double that capital over their working life of 40 years, plus inflation, to maintain the same standard of living for future descendents. That is not an unreasonable goal. Chances are good for beating that goal. Actually, they have to beat it if they want to maintain or increase their share of the world, because market growth generally exceeds inflation.

I know this is not exactly what you wanted to hear. You wanted to make the Forbes list in your lifetime. Maybe you will, or your kids will. A few of them came from middle class backgrounds at about the top 10% level. Once you switch to a generational wealth building plan, you have an enormous advantage. Most of the other top 10% are not even in the game. They are merely planning for retirement and their kids' college.

Having only one child is at best a stop gap measure, as eventually this declining birth rate will liquidate your family. The old fashioned method was to assure that a spouse had approximately as much wealth as oneself before marriage. This allowed two children without the need for the magic doubling, as it had already been accomplished through marriage. But such considerations in marriage have become culturally unpopular. It is also true that a compatible pairing which does not end in divorce, or a partner who has complementary business skills, or both, are worth much more than a wealthy partner where the wealth is squandered in divorce or rich living.

This same problem affected traditional American farm families. Most often the land was inherited jointly by several children. Often for one or two generations beyond, one of them continued to farm and shared the income with other heirs. Or a farm might be divided in half once with each half continuing to be profitable. But continuing to divide the farm is not economically practical. If the family grows, they either have to grow their share of the world, be it land or equities, or resign themselves to falling in rank until they become employment dependent, and their loyalty and voting preferences and social status will be dictated by some corporation.

The advantage of reproduction for the not wealthy

If you don't want to implement a wealth building plan, and are just reading this book for information or entertainment, the impact of children is not so great. The poorer you are, the less the impact is, as long as you can feed and clothe them, and provide an environment where they will stay in school and possibly go to college. Most of your children will share your views in life, and when they vote, your view will be multiplied. Each child is also a bit like a lottery ticket. As long as you meet the minimums of providing a safe environment and living in a decent school district, then the public schools are free through high school. One of your children may become wealthy - who knows, maybe all of them. The biggest risk to this plan is that they will be like you. If you have no aspirations, probably they won't either.

Americans have traditionally used a combination of methods to get ahead. Each wave of immigrants has begun by working at low wage jobs while providing a stable home environment and raising children. As they became successful the reproduction rates declined, but they reached large enough numbers to have a political voice and changed focus to accumulating wealth. The following table shows number of American presidents by ethnicity: [110]

Ethnicity of American Presidents:

27 English
2 English/Scottish
2 English/Welsh
4 Scottish
1 Scottish/Irish
2 Irish
3 Dutch
1 German
1 African

There are more English presidents because Britain colonized the geographic area which became the U.S., and Native Americans were not included in the colonial governing process or initially given U.S. citizenship. They have citizenship now and numerous members of Congress have been Native Americans. Most of those of African descent did not come as voluntary immigrants and were excluded from the political process until the Civil War and partly after that, but they now account for a great number of politicians and one president. I would soon expect to see a Latin American president, which likely would be a person of mixed European and Native American heritage.

Some of these waves of immigrants, such as the Irish who largely came to flee a famine, were quite poor initially and were subject to all kinds of prejudice. But they had generational wealth building plans, and the association with poverty or being in a lower class has been erased.

If you and those you identify with do NOT choose generational wealth building, then you will remain where you are at best.

We have seen that if a family does not adopt a wealth building strategy, then it very likely will slide downward as personal or global crises cause losses.

I warned you this book could not be both truthful and politically correct. There is an idealistic notion in America that every child should have the same identical opportunities in life. Same as who? Same as Bill Gates' children? There is not enough money in the country even if all of it were taxed. This idea is equivalent to simply confiscating all investment capital, and redistributing it, an idea which has been tried and abandoned by a variety of countries and cultures.

Time preference and the equity premium

Over the last couple hundred years, the period that produced the data that suggests the existence of the equity premium, whole market collections of stocks have performed better in 20+ year periods. It can be extremely difficult to take this on faith if one begins investing at the beginning of a 15-year down or choppy market cycle as I did in high school. From 1965 to 1982 the market went exactly nowhere.

I had very little money when I was young, and a lot of immediate needs - school, car, house, food, clothes. Yet I had a long time yet to live. Later in life I find I already have most of those material things. All I really need to buy is food, and my salary is much higher. But my expected life span is much shorter. So our needs and our lifespan are very poorly matched, confusing our time preferences. This problem is recognized among economists, and my friend Mehra has written papers about the difficulty that the young have in borrowing money. In fact, that is one of his suggestions as to the cause of the equity premium - time preferences stemming from the inability of young people to borrow in order to invest.

Country factors

Since the 2008-2009 financial crisis, until the completion of this book in early 2015, U.S. markets have outperformed most others. Whether this will continue I do not know, but there are some concrete reasons for it:

- **The U.S.** has the most proven currency management system via the Federal Reserve, which considers both price stability and employment (implying at least some growth of the economy). Since the U.S. dollar is a world reserve currency, the U.S. never gets in a position of having to pay a debt in someone else's currency. Therefore, unless a default is deliberately engineered by Congress, the U.S. cannot default. If the dollar declines, this actually improves our export situation. The dollar is currently strong because all other currencies except one or two are weak.

- **The EU** central bank is chartered with only considering price stability. The EU members are too mixed in their social goals to share a currency, and it is not clear they have the political will or wisdom to sort this out. This is dragging down all the EU economies as they over-apply austerity and lack the necessary stimulus. This has a history in the German experience in the 1930s and an overabundance of caution on inflation, as we discussed in an earlier chapter. As I write this, the EU is starting to worry about growth, but it has come about five years later than it should have.

- **Japan** has for 25 years been under-stimulating by a factor of at least two. I analyze this in detail in *The Equity Premium Puzzle*. This deficit was produced by their great increases in productivity which led to deflation. They have not created enough money to cover their productivity increases.

- **The Russian** economy is limited by the state thinking it should own 51% of everything, too much corruption, political fighting with the rest of the world, and of course is dependent on the price of oil. I am stuck at the moment with some bad Russian investments as a result of my "irrational exuberance" after visiting there many times and marrying a Russian. Despite my current negativity, the Russian nation is a lot like America in the 1950s, its attitude, dress, tastes and standard of living. Russians are brilliant and creative and want more out of life. Their government may resort to media tricks to win elections, but it does not truly govern by force, and Russians in many ways have more freedom than Americans. There are certainly fewer regulations telling them what to do. Most of them want to be more like Europeans. They have had a taste of the good life, and pretty soon they will figure out they are only holding back themselves.

- **The Chinese** economy is not honest. They will fabricate growth figures and fudge the ingredient list of foods or chemicals. So I invest very little in it. However, I recognize that it uses a managed growth policy that is the most advanced economic strategy in the world. They may have already become the number one economy. [126] Their central bank is the only one that considers THREE factors: price stability, employment, AND growth. They have successfully targeted 7% to 10% growth while the U.S. settles for 2%. Over time, a differential growth rate determines who owns the world. We are in an unrecognized economic war and we are losing at the rate of about 5% a year. China also *"is building airstrips on disputed islands in the South China Sea, moving oil rigs into disputed waters and redefining its airspace,"* [127] possibly leading to future conflict.

- **Most of the rest** of the regions or countries are either government dominated, or too unstable. Islam is taking over Africa, and Islam is unfriendly to business investment and all forms of finance. Some Central and South American countries, like Brazil, have done well in the past but also poorly at times and have critical social issues.

- **Currency fluctuations** are reflected in relative market values. When any country introduces "stimulus" to correct a downturn, this is taken by currency markets to mean lowering interest rates and/or creating money, all of which lower the value of that country's money relative to other countries. This does not continue indefinitely because the affected country becomes less able to buy imports and its exports become cheaper, which eventually stimulates its economy. Its central bank then reverses policy and the fluctuation goes back the other way. At the moment of this writing, the U.S. is about to raise interest rates and the EU to implement quantitative easing. But eventually the export/import headwind will blow the U.S. off course.

At some point you should have global investments, I just don't have a firm recommendation. To an extent, by investing in groups of larger U.S. companies you are indirectly invested in their global operations.

In January of 2001 I was day trading FXI, a tracking ETF for the China 50, a group of large cap stocks that trade on the Hong Kong exchange. It is volatile enough for day trading without any leverage, and there is high enough volume to absorb large trades. At the time the market was going down and I was unwilling to hold it long-term. However, it meets our criteria of being a large index (though country specific) that pays dividends - about 2.5% based on current prices. As you can see from the chart below, in the last 5 years it has not done that well. It has not represented China's 7% annual growth in that short period.

5 year performance of FXI (China 50, Hong Kong) vs. S&P 500
source: Yahoo Finance

The so-called China A-shares do not pay any dividends, and foreign ownership is very, very limited. I'm not sure if I would really own anything if I bought them. It is a lot like buying shares in a Russian company that is 51%

owned by the government, which may decide to confiscate your shares at any time, but at least Russian companies pay respectable dividends. Hong Kong is part of China now, and the large banks and other companies in the China 50 should participate in China's growth. But not if it's fake or restricted.

I would not hold a large percentage of my portfolio in China, certainly not more than 10%, which is about what I allocate to Russia at the moment, but if you look at the 10 year performance below, FXI is actually beating the S&P 500. It also appears that it might soon break above its long-term resistance level (the horizontal blue line). One needs to be cautious about buying anything when it has had a dramatic run up. Imagine having bought FXI at the sharp peak in 2008. It is still more than 50% below that level, whereas the stodgy S&P 500 is above its peak considerably - not that there is any guarantee it will stay there, which is why we like to have at least some dividends.

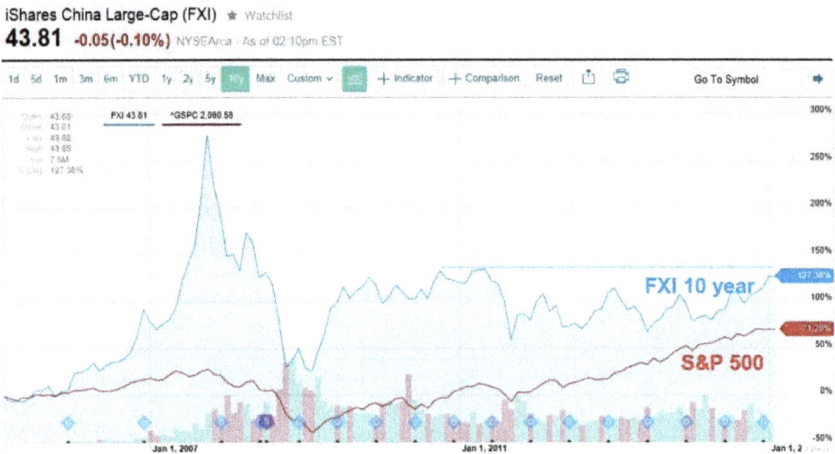

10 year performance of FXI (China 50, Hong Kong)
source: Yahoo Finance

Natural and political disruptions

The retirement ambition of many people near where I live, in a big city in Texas, has long been to retire to the central Texas hill country, and perhaps acquire a small ranch and raise some cattle. It is for them a pleasant quality of life. But I hope they weren't counting on income from those cattle, or from any business related to any of the lakes or waterways. There has been a severe drought for more than four years, with wildfires and large scale losses of trees and livestock.

A branch of Lake Travis near Austin
source: Wikimedia commons

A great many retired people who were friends of my mother had their nest eggs invested in certificates of deposit (CDs) because of high interest rates, often over 5%, in the 2006-2008 time frame. Those banks apparently loaned the money to people who did not have financial reserves. When the price of energy shot up and they began to have trouble paying for their commutes, and even keeping their jobs, they began to default. This of course meant less consumer spending, more job losses, and more defaults.

As the larger banks such as Salomon Brothers began to default, others which had loaned money to these big banks were in danger of default. Even money market funds were disrupted. Losses from bank failure are permanent. While some companies cut dividends, and some mortgage companies disappeared, the bulk of the stock market continued as normal and continued to pay dividends. Within a year stock prices recovered. But my mother's friends curtailed their spending for restaurants and housemaids and cars and it has remained curtailed. Several restaurants went out of business. The variation in income from CDs falling from 5% to less than 1% was much larger than the variation in dividends from a broad index fund holding.

Interest rates were lowered not by the financial crisis itself (which actually tended to raise them) but by central bank policy. Without this policy it is likely we'd have entered a long depression. The standard of living of CD holders was sacrificed for the "greater good." The three most common ways government has of regulating the economy - either to stimulate or to dampen bubbles - all have side effects. For example:

- TAXES - Raising taxes liquidates investment holdings unless investors reduce their expenditure, just as a dividend cut would. Lowering taxes gives investors the intended stimulus money to spend at their discretion. Low investment taxes encourages them to spend it on more investments, which is considered very effective stimulus.

- INTEREST RATES - Raising interest rates is supposed to have a damping effect. However, it gives increased income to banks and CD investors, so direct control of interest rates is often not as effective as it should be.

- QUANTITATIVE EASING (central bank buys bonds) - This method gives discretion over the stimulus to the party selling the bonds, usually the government but sometimes corporations or mortgage companies. How the stimulus is used depends on politics. During the stimulus period following 2009 research and development funding was cut, undermining the long-term future of the country in favor of quick construction projects such as converting a flood control basin near where I live into a rather decorative but useless park.

Notice that two of the three stimulus methods increase debt. We'll discuss the effects of this in the next chapter and explain quantitative easing in more detail.

A tax policy which liquidates the investment capital of investors (either because the market declines directly in response to the tax increase, or because investors must make greater withdrawals to maintain a fixed income) decreases the future tax base and seems counterproductive. If we are concerned about too much inequality, raise taxes on people with annual incomes over half a million dollars. These people exercise a lot of power, but there are not enough of them to constitute much of the tax base.

While half a million a year might sound rich to you, consider that a professional working couple may make two $150,000 salaries for a total of $300,000 and they are probably not getting very far ahead on that income. We should want them to get ahead so they will retire, freeing up their jobs, and invest to create more jobs for the rest of us. People in this category are like us. They don't fly around in private jets nor have several vacation homes. This amount should be indexed to inflation as well.

The complexity and injustice of the tax code itself, as well as changes that are made, qualifies as a *disruption* to any investing strategy. Whenever the dividend tax is increased, careful 40 year plans, which from our above discussion you now understand, are disrupted and income no longer lasts that long.

To make markets efficient, which means making the country productive and competitive and having jobs here rather than overseas, investors need to be able to reallocate their funds to the best industries and companies without suffering losses. Right now when an investor reallocates there are three kinds of deterrents in the tax code:

- The limitation of $3000 a year deductible for capital losses causes investors to hold bad investments hoping they will recover, instead of quickly reallocating to more productive companies. Holding on to bad investments has kept Japanese banks down and affected their whole economy for 15 years. It should not be encouraged by the tax code.

- The capital gains tax has to be paid even if the money is immediately reinvested, also discouraging reallocation.

- The requirement to hold investments for six or more months for favorable tax treatment discourages reallocation.

In business tax accounting, for example an automobile trader, tax is only paid on the net gain for the year. Transaction times are irrelevant. Investing is a business. Why should it be any different than other businesses?

After tax dividend calculations

We did the draw-down (annuity) calculations above without regard to taxes. How much impact do taxes have?

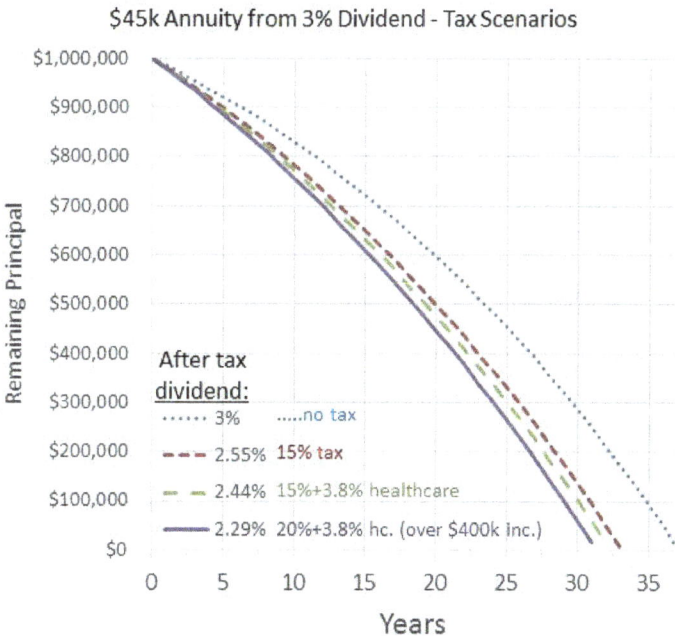

$45k Annuity from 3% Dividend - Tax Scenarios

After tax dividend:
- ...... 3%   .....no tax
- − − − 2.55% 15% tax
- − − 2.44% 15%+3.8% healthcare
- —— 2.29% 20%+3.8% hc. (over $400k inc.)

Let us suppose you have $1 million, not much now days (equivalent to $348,000 in 1980 or $125,000 in 1960, only 1/8th the wealth of a "millionaire" from the days of the old TV program *The Millionaire*). You anticipate expenses of $80,000 a year and have income from an employer retirement plan of $35,000 a year, so you plan to withdraw $45,000 annually from your investment account to meet these expenses. You have invested in an index ETF which typically yields 3%. Without considering taxes you estimate your funds will last 37 years (see dotted blue line on chart below). You are 55, and this would last you until you are 92. Can you retire early, and free up a slot in the workforce for someone else?

Now let's consider taxes. I found current tax brackets here:

http://www.bankrate.com/finance/taxes/tax-brackets.aspx

It looks like you will be in the 25% bracket. The 10% bracket only goes up to an income of about $9,000, twice that if you are married filing jointly, and the 15% bracket drops out at $37,000, also double that if you are married.

A good discussion of dividend taxes can be found at:

http://www.wsj.com/articles/SB10001424127887323689604578219952168695148

If you are not reading this on an eBook with click-able links, just search for "*dividend tax rate.*"

In the 10% and 15% brackets there is no tax on dividends. This is a dirty trick. The government can "sound like" they are giving a tax break, but in fact virtually no one in those tax brackets can afford to set aside money for investing. The 10% bracket is almost entirely below the poverty line and probably shouldn't be paying tax at all.

The rest of the brackets up to an income of $200,000 will pay a tax on dividends of 15%. Wealthier families will pay 15% plus 3.8% for a new Medicare tax implemented as part of healthcare reform. Over roughly $400,000 income, the tax becomes 20% plus 3.8%. I have included all these curves on the graph above in case you have more additional income than the example, or more than a million dollars invested, and you want to see how this is affecting you.

Assuming that you continue to withdraw the $45,000 despite the taxes because you have rent and other fixed obligations, and you worked all your life and don't want to give up your retirement and live poor, then it means you will draw-down the principal faster. Just the basic 15% tax reduces the effective dividend rate to 2.55% and your money will run out in 34 years instead of 37. Your retirement is reduced by about 8%, or 3 years.

If you have enough additional income to push you into the 3.8% Medicare tax, you lose another year. And if you have enough income for the full 23.8% tax you lose still another year, though at that level presumably you can reduce expenses somewhere.

Let's look at how much tax the government collects in each case. At the base 15% rate for the 34 years on the declining principle, the tax collected is $87,275.78.

At the 18.3% rate with the Medicare tax, over 33 years, the tax collected is $105,907.84. In this case the government does collect more taxes, about 21% more, while the family is paying 25% more (3.8% / 15% = 25%) and not living as long (apparently).

Taxing the goose that lays golden eggs

Consider a case where you inherit a million dollars from a relative at age 20, and plan to withdraw $35,000 a year as long as it lasts. That would be forever without taxes, 75 years with the 15% dividend tax, and 69 years at the 18.8% rate.

The total tax collected at 18.8% is $1,083,326. The total collected at 15% is $1,260,328.

That's not a misprint. For anyone withdrawing at a low rate to make their funds last more than about half a century, the slightly higher tax rate liquidates their funds faster, resulting in substantially less tax paid. If a person is allowed to build wealth, increasing instead of liquidating their nest egg, then the tax revenue obtained from them rises over time. It is possible the people who make these policies are not familiar with the old fairy tale about the goose that laid golden eggs, and how foolish people cut it open to get all the eggs and found none, killing the goose.

Will you kill the goose to get the "eggs inside?" [111]

Retirement & buyout decisions

Sometimes you will encounter complicated choices that are designed to induce you to do something you might not otherwise do. Evaluating them requires all the skills we have just learned about evaluating annuity-like payments, and then some.

Suppose for example your company is trying to get people to take early retirement and is offering a "buyout." Usually by retiring early you take a reduced retirement. With the buyout you also get a lump sum payment of cash, which is taxable. The first thing to do is to convert this lump sum to an after tax figure, and think only of that figure. If the buyout is $25,000 and you are in a 33% tax bracket, your net will be only

$$(100\% - 33\%) * \$25,000 = \$16,750.$$

If you were leaving anyway, it is a nice bonus. If you were not leaving anyway, it is not much. But what do you compare it to?

The comparisons are very personal. Are you planning on getting another job, and do you already have it in hand? Does the new job pay as well as your old one? Can you collect your retirement annuity while working at the new job? Then you probably do not need to do any further figuring to decide what to do, and don't need my help. In the 1980s this was often the case. In the 1990s it remained true for people in positions with specialized knowledge that wasn't easily cloned in a new employee. In the 2000s it gradually became a less frequent option.

Suppose you do not have another job lined up, and maybe you want to try some things that may or may not produce income, or maybe you want to just relax or travel. Keep in mind that the people who come up with these numbers like $25,000 do this for a living. They figure an amount that will induce a number of people to do what they want them to do, and the object is usually to reduce the employer's expenses. That means reducing what they pay to those who take the buyout over time. The point of confusion they use is an unequal comparison: $25,000 and your freedom *now*, versus a slightly higher annuity later while your current salary and job continue.

Suppose your salary is $90,000, and your retirement annuity is presently 70% of that, 70% x $90k = $63,000. We need to know how much your annuity increases with each passing year. Let us suppose 2%, which amounts to $1800 a year or $150 a month. How long do you think you would work if you didn't take the buyout? How long until you "break even" on the "work vs. take the buyout" decision?

Not considering the value of your time, i.e. assuming you truly retire, then we have the following two choices:

Buyout	Retire 1 year later
$16,750 lump sum	$0 lump sum
$63,000 annuity	$63,000 annuity
	+$1800 extra annuity

Can you compare the lump sum to the extra annuity? You would have to choose an interest rate, or an investment yield. Neither is certain. I know people who counted on a 4% bank interest rate and wound up with a 1% rate. If you choose investing over banks and stick with index funds, in the long run you may have a higher return but in the short run really all you can count on is about 3% dividends. At 3% the extra annuity a year from now is worth $1800 / .03 = $60,000. However, a payment a year from now must also be discounted, so $60k less 3% is $58,200. This is 3.4 times as large as the lump sum you are actually being offered, for a difference of $58.2k - $16.75k = $41,450.

The story is not ended, though. That's what it would be worth if you lived forever. Actually you will die at some point, and this makes the computation very complicated, requiring actuarial tables. I suggest that for back of the envelop computations you use the figure of 1/3rd that we already came up with for a crude estimate of the difference between an annuity tied to your lifetime, which your heirs cannot inherit, and an investment that continues forever. Subtracting 1/3 the value of $58.2k we see that the extra annuity is only worth 2/3 x $58.2k = $38,800.

That 1/3 figure was based on your being mid-60s. If you are male it goes to 2/3^{rds} in mid-70s and 100% at about mid-80s, where the life expectancy for many males ends (early 90s for women). If you have a spouse who will continue to collect some part of the annuity and is a few years younger, then cut my numbers about in half, e.g. 1/6th instead of 1/3rd.

http://www.allthingsclipart.com/retirement.clipart.htm (public domain)

In the table below we see the changing approximate value of working an extra year at different ages.

Value of $1800 annuity starting in 1 year at 3%

Age range	reduce for age	net value
Mid-80s	100%	0
Mid-70s	2/3	$19,600
Mid-60s	1/3	$38,800
50s or younger	0	$58,200

Immediately you may object that you currently make $90k a year. But actually what you make is kind of complicated. If you retired immediately (assuming they will let you) without the buyout, you'd have a pension of $63k. So in the next year you will only take in 90 − 63 = $27,000 more by working than retiring.

This is not your only reward for working a year, however. You will also get the extra $1800 on your annuity for each year worked, which we already figured was worth $58,200, so you could say you would be making $27k + $58.2k = $85,200 for working the next year. If you are in your mid-70s it's only $27k + $38.8k = $65.8k, and if you are in your mid-80s it's only $27k + 19.6k = $46,600.

According to this way of figuring, if you are mid-70s or older, you aren't really earning anything by working, or you may even be losing money in some sense. You are not losing immediate cash, however. It's just that your annuity is declining in value rapidly because you will not collect it for very long.

Since most employer retirement plans are annuity-like (so is social security), investing in them benefits no one except you while you are alive (and maybe your wife). Investment account retirement plans are more valuable if you have heirs.

If your annuity accrual is less than 2%, the future extra annuity is reduced proportionately. For example, a 1% accrual rate reduces it to $900 and cuts all the values in the table above in half.

If you figure an investment yield of greater than 3%, it has a similar effect. A yield of 6% reduces all values in the table by half also. If you figure both a 6% yield and a 1% accrual rate, the values in the table are cut 75%.

Higher yield is associated with risk. Total risk is proportional to the inherent risk of an asset, times the amount of time you own it. Inherent risk might be expressed as the likelihood of something going bankrupt in a particular year. Suppose the bankruptcy risk is 5% (which is quite large). That also might represent a risk of 10% for a decline in value of 50% (10% x

50% = 5%), which might be about the risk rate of some high yield securities in the 7% to 15% yield range. Probably if you are in your mid-80s you can go for a yield of 5% to 6% with only a slight chance of problems in your lifetime. Your heirs can then change to more long-term investments. But yields higher than that are risky for periods longer than 5 years. If your job is affecting your mental health, that is risky also. It is a tradeoff between risks.

The other aspect of a buyout or any unexpected opportunity is, "Are you ready?" If you were tired of your job, take the buyout. Few retirement plans have a 2% accrual rate anymore, and a 6% yield makes the buyout attractive.

If you are not ready, you can figure how many months to a breakeven point. In the example above your cash salary is $27k more than an immediate annuity, or $2250 per month. The annuity is rising at $150 a month while you keep working, which at 3% is 150/.03 = $5000 a month in present value. The total is $7250 a month, so after two and a half months you break even with the net after tax buyout of $16,750. If you figure based on a 6% yield, you are gaining at about $4750 a month and have a 3.5 month breakeven. If you have unfinished business at work, something you want to wrap up that takes two to four months, ignore the buyout.

Heck, if you just want three months to think about whether you are mentally ready for retirement, ignore the buyout.

The numbers above are not personal for me or for you. I did not want to produce a "formula" because there are too many factors and they are too uncertain, but I'm hoping that you will get the idea from this detailed example and will be able to intelligently adapt it to your situation. I know, I promised that accumulating wealth did not require brains or anything like actuarial tables. But this is not accumulating wealth, this is a retirement decision. The actuaries are sitting across the table from you playing the other hand, so yes, you will have to be a little bit on the ball to figure out what your options really are worth.

Training your heirs

Our exploration of the backgrounds of very wealthy people suggests that your children or other heirs might want to be doing some hands on investing by the time they are 12. It is very unlikely they will want to do this just because you ask them to. However, most children will attempt to emulate what they see their parents doing.

It is possible to set up a taxable trust account at a broker such as Scottrade. Some of the big discount firms such as TradeKing will not do it. A properly worded trust will make you the trustee and isolate the funds from your liabilities, but you will still have to pay tax on it at your tax rate. You can put much more in it than a tax exempt account, and avoid most taxes by using a buy and hold strategy with index ETFs.

You can set up a tax exempt education account in which you can hold stocks, and this tax deferred account would be good for active trading or dividend accumulation, but you can only add $2000 a year and only if your income is less than about $119k. The state 529 education plans have no income restriction, but you must invest in a limited number of state provided funds and you may be restricted as to the schools where you can spend the money.

I suggest both. The reason is that they serve the following two different purposes:

- The taxable trust account transfers wealth to your offspring on which the tax has already been paid, and they will not get hit with an additional estate tax when you die. This is mostly a consideration if you are very wealthy, in which case you probably already know about it. But as this book serves to inform either the curious or the would-be-wealthy, I thought I'd include the information.

- The education tax deferred account, not the state plans but the one you can set up with your broker if your income is sufficiently small, might be something you could use to educate your children by allowing them to choose some investments, and as they learn they can take a greater hand in it.

Speaking of taxes, you may be wondering why I don't address inheritance tax strategies. Currently more than $5 million per heir is not subject to federal estate tax, and only six states have an estate tax. Someone age 35 inheriting $5 million would be in the 99.48 percentile, far beyond the target audience of this book and able to hire specialized tax advisers. Why are more people not taking advantage of the privilege of easily increasing the wealth status of their children? Probably in part because they don't feel their children able to handle the nest egg wisely, which is what we are trying to correct with this discussion on training your heirs.

I suggest that you help your children get more educationally useful summer or part time jobs than I had - filling in on a newspaper route and helping out in a grocery store. Something like working at a bank or brokerage office would be ideal (think of Warren Buffett). Frankly I would not become an engineer again. At the time I chose the field, engineers were heroes in America and no one was thinking of sending these jobs overseas. Now the tech heroes have moved to Silicon Valley and their bosses don't even have degrees, and a lot of the Silicon Valley engineers come from overseas and use overseas engineers and programmers to develop their products. You can manage your investments from a computer or even a phone anywhere in the world, even Omaha Nebraska. You don't have to move to an expensive location.

You may find your child's account does much better than your own. Early in my career I shared an office with a guy named Buddy, a certifiable genius with an IQ of 150 who was exasperated by this problem. He would place complex and seemingly foolproof trades in his own account and something would go wrong. But accounts he set up for his children were the opposite, hitting the mark nearly every time. He felt cursed. Is there a logical (rather than a superstitious) explanation?

I don't now have data on Buddy's trades, but having recently set up an account for my own newborn son, I see one big difference between it and my own. The account will become his when he is 24. I was thinking of what will be worth something in 24 years, maybe a lot in 24 years, when I selected investments. I knew I would not find time to fiddle with it regularly, either. Despite my own advice to the contrary, much of my own account is invested only for the next 2 years. When thinking of myself it is hard to focus on 24 years hence, but easy when it comes to someone who will not be an adult until then. If this particular trick doesn't help you refocus, look for one that does.

Expanding your contacts

Our study of highly successful people suggested that receptive contacts and long-term trusted friends are essential to a rapid rise in wealth. Many of these were determined in your past, from your family's contacts, or from friends you made in school. You might attempt to enter a life context in which your children will make useful friends, such as by choosing a neighborhood or school or university. It might work, or it might entirely backfire if your children are not accepted by this new social community that is not naturally your own.

What is the style of your friendships?

Superficial friendships are useless. They take up one's time, but are not responsive when activities, projects or business ideas are proposed. Here is quick test you can use to determine the style of friendships you have from childhood. Think back to high school, and a group of your friends standing around talking. You propose an idea, maybe a movie to see or a restaurant or some game. Do the others:

- Build on your idea, making it something more interesting than any one of you individually would have thought of?
- Accept your idea without modification?
- Like your idea but don't take any action on it?
- Replace your idea with another in which they include you?
- Dismiss or ignore your idea?
- Argue with your idea?

Take a minute to genuinely remember several events that happened, if you can. If you had different groups of friends, you might want to compare the differences in how they respond.

If you have a group of friends that often makes the first response, spend more time with them. Obviously you are going to go farther as a group than any one of you individually, because your group ideas are better and you are natural collaborators.

If they accept your idea without modification, most of the time, whether it is a good idea or not, then you are perhaps destined to be dictator of a small country. Or an obnoxious boss. Or a petty crime lord. Or society queen. You surround yourself with yes-people who won't tell you if your idea is flawed. Perhaps you will be quite happy. I have no idea how to change the situation.

Research shows that trust in friendship is "*very important and is built through a series of signals and behaviors that have a cost to them on behalf of the sender.*" [112] Clearly the adult relationships you need for business require a lot of trust. If your friends in high school didn't take any action on your idea, they weren't willing to engage in behavior that had a cost to them - cost being the effort to act on an idea they admitted they liked, assuming they were telling the truth. Ah, assuming they were telling the truth. Do you see how willingness to exert effort builds trust? Without effort or cost, they are just making polite conversation. Paul Allen and Bill Gates, or Steve Jobs and Steve Wozniak, were not just making polite conversation.

It can be hard to make such friends over the age of 30. According to author Alex Williams, "*The workplace can crackle with competition, so people learn to hide vulnerabilities and quirks from colleagues. Work friendships often take on a transactional feel; it is difficult to say where networking ends and real friendship begins.*" [113] Susan Bryant writes on job finder site Monster.com, "*Most adults value the financial security of their jobs more than friendship with coworkers.*" [114] It's not impossible to acquire friends after 30, but it isn't the high percentage play. If you had great friends in school, the kind who built your ideas into something great, perhaps you should not be quick to move away from them. Maybe you should even move to where they are?

Effects of large cap growth on friendship

Corporate induced dispersal of friend and family networks was a huge phenomenon in the 1960s and 1970s. Corporations moved managers around deliberately so that they would not develop close ties to a community and possibly object to hurting local businesses or the local environment. Even government agencies (probably because they share consultants with the private sector) have picked up the practice of rotating managers with the effect that managers have no loyalty to the community around the facility where they worked when they raised their families and made adult friends. They can more easily be induced to downsize or close it. The Boeing company in response to a labor dispute with machinists in Seattle threatened to close the factory there and move it to a right-to-work state only after Boeing merged with several other aerospace companies and moved its headquarters to Chicago, where it has no factories or other installations. Boeing likely would not have been so quick to use this negotiating posture while their home office was located in Seattle.

Some interesting data was presented by Stacy Mitchell, speaking to the American Planning Association about how large chain stores with non-local management affect communities:

> *"Small-scale, pedestrian streets are giving way to massive, impersonal shopping centers. Street life has suffered, as our daily errands revolve increasingly around stores accessible only by car."*

> *"11,000 independent pharmacies have closed since 1990. Independent bookstores have fallen from 58 percent of book sales in 1972 to just 17 percent today. Local hardware dealers are on the decline, while two companies have captured 30 percent of the market. . . . Five firms control one-third of the grocery market, up from 19 percent just five years ago. A single firm, Wal-Mart, now accounts for 7 percent of all consumer spending."*

> *"Wal-Mart has been known to sell gallons of milk for 25 cents or to price entire departments below its own acquisition costs. This sets up a battle that local merchants cannot win. If they don't match the chain's prices, they risk losing customers. If they do match the chain's prices, they will lose money on every sale. While a chain can afford to operate a new outlet at a loss indefinitely, it's only a matter of time before the local business will be forced to close."*

> *"Once the chain has eliminated the local competition, prices tend to rise. In Virginia, a survey of several Wal-Mart stores statewide found prices varied by as much as 25 percent. The researchers concluded that prices rose in markets where the retailer faced little competition. A similar conclusion was reached in a survey of Home Depot."*

I already mentioned that I knew the owners of several small businesses when I was growing up. Either they had some involvement with school activities, or their children were my classmates. But I do not know the manager of the local Wal-Mart which replaced those businesses, and I doubt he or she would have the discretion to pursue some business idea if I proposed it to them. It's no one that I went to school with or otherwise encountered in an environment where we could become friends, and is likely someone from out of town. For example, I see local honey for sale up by the cash register in a locally owned hardware business. Have you ever seen such a thing in Wal-Mart?

Factors that encourage trusted friendships
What is the environment for making friends? Three factors have been identified: [Ibid. 113]

- **"Proximity**, which means being near enough to see each other or do things together."

- **"Repeatedly encountering the person informally** and without making special plans to see each other."

- **"Opportunities to share ideas and personal feelings** with each other."

Moving from place to place obviously disrupts this. Membership in small groups, or employment where the number of people interacted with is small and the interactions formal, is also obviously a deterrent. But the size of modern institutions, whether they be corporations or schools, makes interactions more formal and reduces repeated encounters. Few of the things movers can do will replace their abandoned social networks.

Did your friends replace your idea with their own, but include you? Then you are on the flip side of the small country dictator or society queen we discussed earlier. You are the assistant, better known as the lackey, or perhaps minion. It might work out very well for you, but don't expect it to change, or to be someday highly valued for your creativity and initiative. Only your loyalty is important. Any suspicion of initiative is liable to find your loyalty questioned.

Did your friends dismiss or ignore your idea and not even include you? I'm sure you already know the analysis of this one. Instead of feeling sorry for yourself, remember that it has happened to a great many people. But nothing else happens to them until they move on. You'll never win your way into this clique. If they suddenly find out you have some trait they desire, like wealth or skill at some sport, they may seem to include you but it may not be trusted and genuine. After all, they didn't expend any effort toward you, which is the criterion for trust. In this relationship you are expending all the effort, so sure, they trust you, but it matters not because you cannot trust them. Therefore it is truly not possible to win your way into a clique only by your own efforts no matter what you do. Trust requires two way initiative.

The kinds of friends who like to argue seem to multiply with age. When I was a kid only my cousin argued with me. (He doesn't actually do that anymore.) By middle age when people are competing for management responsibility, they argue pointlessly at work because it matters not who is right, only whose idea is adopted as that determines who gets credit and therefore who gets to rocket up the career ladder. In hierarchical corporate structure, fewer people move up at each level. Eventually you will be moved aside after losing an argument. Only one person "wins" the CEO job, and often it is an outsider. Forced retirement is the fate of virtually all ambitious managers. How many of our billionaires moved up within someone else's corporate structure?

Technology, friendship and collaboration
The attack on friendship by corporate culture has left a vacuum which of course technology attempts to fill. Facebook allows us to keep in touch with people we don't see regularly. Twitter supposedly allows us to expand our flock of admirers far and wide. International dating sites, despite the large number of fake profiles, allowed me to find an amazing and wonderful wife and to begin having children. LinkedIn allows us to form networks of people at our workplace or in our field that we have never even met and will never speak to except to learn that they are unemployed and looking for work.

But far and away the greatest use of the new social media, aside from posting selfies, is to argue. The older one gets the worse it gets. Some of this can be useful. Most of it is just killing time. An interesting website I have spent some time on is ResearchGate. It is a bit difficult to join. One has to have published some kind of technical paper, and it helps to have an email address at an academic or scientific institution. This is supposed to cut down on annoying contacts from unqualified people, like the fakes on dating sites. It only partly works. I have learned a great deal from certain discussions over two years, and almost had two collaborations form. But in the end, not quite. If you can't join ResearchGate you can find my journal papers also on Academia.edu or on my personal website listed at the end of the book.

There are websites devoted to promoting business activities and collaborations. One category is so-called crowdfunding. These aren't really collaborations, just funding, and the level of trust is not high. I have not found a way as an adult to develop trusted friendships that lead to collaborations, and I detailed my own experiences earlier.

How PowerPoint is like an AK47
Another piece of technology, PowerPoint, contributes to arguments in the workplace. Think about what PowerPoint is. It is a powerful tool for making a point. It is not an engineering tool or an accounting tool or a manufacturing tool or a marketing tool (would you buy a car from someone

who made you look at a PowerPoint presentation) or even a publishing tool. There are better software packages for all those things.

In days gone by when only the boss could afford to have presentation graphics produced by a team of secretaries and commercial artists (yes actually a good many positions in business carried the job title of commercial artist), then only the boss could be really persuasive. It is like a small village where only the chief has an AK47.

Everyone else was doing actual work, actual engineering (consisting of very large pieces of paper with blue-line drawings), actual accounting (long sheets with columns of numbers, or spreadsheets perhaps), actual manufacturing, actual marketing (talking to customers or producing advertisements) or actual publishing (with a page layout program).

Now give everyone in the village an AK47 and you will get no more work done.

I guess I should have put this in the "mistakes" chapter, but we were on the subject of technology enabled arguments and it was too good to pass up.

Your children's friends

I suppose we could draw a similar conclusion about children in regard to friends that we did in regard to career choices. After about the age of 12 or 13 how will you know which of the six types of friends your children have? They won't hang around you enough for you to see whether their friends are responding and building on your child's ideas, or whether your teenager is putting out all the effort without finding trust, or is in one of the dominant-submissive cliques.

The wayward friendship

I remember now one friend from my senior year in high school that I omitted earlier. We were great at collaboration and attracted several others into our schemes. Perhaps too good. Like Bill and Paul, we got into some trouble. Instead of a temporary suspension like Bill and Paul received, followed by offers of employment, we were permanently separated by our over anxious parents. Sometimes it is a difficult call to make as a parent, but now at least you are equipped to see more than one side of the issue, and more than one way to respond.

Mistakes Everyone Makes

Peter Lynch, myself, the government and big oil companies with high paid game-theory analysts all make mistakes - big mistakes. If a person, or a family, went just four generations without a mistake they would basically own the whole planet, so the lack of such a planet-owner (that we know of) proves everyone is making mistakes. Most of us make serious mistakes and keep making them over and over.

Hypothetically speaking, we earlier imagined a merchant in Rome who diversified and made no big mistakes. That does not mean he predicted correctly when Rome would fall, or which Roman cities would fall first. It means his investments (businesses) were prepared to survive unplanned disaster. We imagined that one of his descendants wound up in Lebanon, plausible, and was the ancestor of Carlos Slim, whose father emigrated from Lebanon to Mexico. Carlos is not only the richest man in the world, but seems to have a happy life and healthy attitude about leisure time, unlike some other billionaires.

Hathaway Mills in Bedford, MA - Wikimedia commons
Founded by Horatio Hathaway in 1888, a China trader and Pacific whaler. By 1917 108,000 mule spindles and 3400 looms produced fine cotton goods. Buffett was attracted to cash on the balance sheet.

Warren Buffett claimed his greatest mistake was his investment in Berkshire-Hathaway. It is hard for us to see his point of view on that given the current price of Berkshire-A shares of over $225,000 each. But perhaps he felt like the process of liquidating Berkshire's existing businesses was an unnecessary distraction - likely not very pleasant - and that he could have done better by just setting up a new shell company. This is a bit of second guessing success that is unnecessary, and not a mistake we will likely have the opportunity of facing. Let's talk about real mistakes:

- By ordinary people (beginner or experienced)
- By famous money managers giving advice (which you might hear and follow)
- By government in setting economic, tax and monetary policy
- By big corporations (which might affect entire economies & your investments)

Peter Lynch's mistakes

In the 1982 interview mentioned previously (I suggest watching the video clip before reading this), Peter gives two pieces of advice:

- Buy what you know, the industry you work in, because you will know a "turn" is coming before investment managers and other people know it.

- Do not buy a stock just because it has gone down 20% or 30%. It can keep going down (and he gives a disastrous personal example).

First notice that these two pieces of advice contradict one another. A "turn" refers to a turnaround in a company or in an industry. Since most of the movement of a stock price is related to the industry group, these are nearly the same thing.

Splitting hairs, you could say buying because you know a turn is coming is not quite the same thing as buying because the price is down. But consider the following:

- A "turn" cannot come without first a downward price motion.

- If the turn becomes evident in the price, then it is already public knowledge.

Spotting turns via charting (really?)

You can learn how to spot a "turn" (after the fact) and other features in pricing charts, called technical analysis, at http://stockcharts.com/. Click on "chart school." Their charts are very good, and free for the last two years or so of data, but relatively expensive for full services. It is possible to configure Yahoo Finance to produce "candlestick" charts by clicking the button with the zig-zag line, between the "custom" and "indicator" buttons. But in the chart below which one of the breakouts actually marks the turn? If you are living through events, rather than looking at past data, you can't see the future lower bottom that indicates a turn was not real.

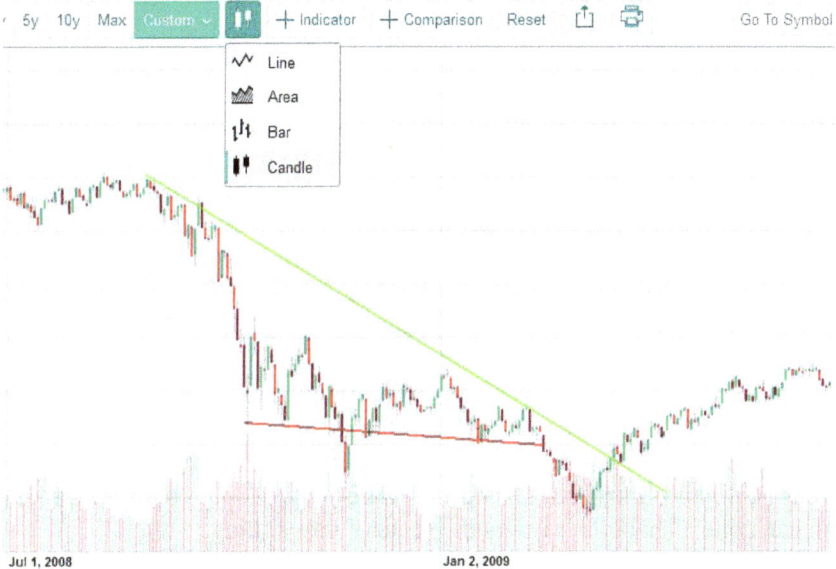

S&P 500 index near the 2009 market bottom
source: Yahoo charts - annotation lines added using PowerPoint

To control the dates click the "custom" button. Yahoo charts used to have bolder lines which were easier to see, and larger labels. For this book, so that all readers can easily use the methods described, we work with what is free.

The bottom of the financial crisis came in March of 2009. I began to suspect a turn in April, but was unwilling to commit large amounts of funds until mid-June, which is at about the end of the chart. Since I didn't have any cash left I used margin and negotiated a rate of 3% with my primary broker. This came about when a secondary broker called me asking why I was withdrawing money from that account and made me an offer, and I asked the primary if they'd match it. They came close enough.

There was an unnerving pullback in July, but the market continued up and by mid-2010 I had recovered from the "financial crisis."

A comment on day trading

As you can see, technical analysis is not nearly accurate enough for most purposes. It is like reading tea leaves. It is possible, just barely, to use this method to trade, or "day trade." I have done it, making money even when the market was going down in January of 2009 by betting only on the upside. But it was too stressful and I could not have kept my day job. The people I have heard of who did it successfully locked their doors and turned off their phones during hours when the market was open, did it for about a year or until they had about $1 million dollars, and then quit and switched to regular investing. It is very easy to slip up and erode your capital with either a series of ill-timed trades, or one big screw up.

There are numerous books on the subject which you can read, but take them with a grain of salt and don't bother paying for expensive seminar training or special day trading accounts. If someone really had a computer program that could beat the market, they would be using it and not telling you about it. TD Ameritrade has adequate tools. You will need a minimum of about $50,000 to even think about day trading. My own rule was never to buy anything I wouldn't like to be stuck with for a while if it went down. If you look closely at the stories of day traders, they make a living, like working a job, and rarely become wealthy. As their net worth grows, their trades get larger and soon begin to affect market prices. I quickly got to that point. To make money in a "day" and cover commissions, one has to trade volatile stocks, probably ETFs, and the volatile ones can be very thinly traded. With trades in the $20k to $100k range, order fills would often break down into dozens of smaller transactions and the share price would creep up noticeably with each one. That effect limits the scale of day trading.

The "spotting a turn in your own industry" mistake

Peter's first mistake was advising investors to use inside information from their own industry, not necessarily knowledge on which it was illegal to trade but just their experience of whether orders were picking up and so forth. Your own industry is actually the hardest on which to get perspective. You are too tied up in the details. Whenever I have tried to invest in "something I know" I have failed.

A second important factor is psychological. Companies must get workers, especially marketing and planning workers, *enthused and confident* to obtain good performance from them. A salesman cannot sell something he or she doesn't believe in. Nor will engineers do good work or factory workers happily put in overtime if they think the business is declining. Managers will paint the best picture possible most of the time to their own workers.

Zig Ziglar "Our land is developed because we are the land of sales people."
YouTube screen capture https://www.youtube.com/watch?v=tNEcsFDu7Bg

If you are high enough up or well connected enough to have actionable information, then you will probably go to jail for trading on it. Just ask Martha Stewart who lost her media empire after a 2004 conviction for insider trading.

Martha Stewart
Wikimedia commons

If you continue to believe that you know how your own company is doing, you should find and talk with some of the former employees of Enron who lost their life savings when this company proved to be as large a corporate scam as the South Sea Company.

The diversification mistake

An even worse mistake in the same piece of advice (two for one anybody?) is that investing in your own industry violates the principle of diversification. It is a 100% focused bet.

You have already invested the cost of your education, all your time and experience, your choice of location, nearly your whole life in the industry and company for which you work. Sooner or later it will go bad. Recall that the advantage of "equity" in the first place was the spreading of risk among not only many investors but also many business ventures so that total failure is avoided. If your plan for wealth is to accumulate it over time through investing, you must avoid wiping out by having all your eggs in one basket that breaks.

Actually, in the beginning you can experiment and try things when you have very little money, and you lose only some time. Your earnings will rise later, presumably, and you can replace your losses. But once you have more money than you can earn in your remaining career, what are you going to do if you lose it? Your children will have to start over from scratch, and your family will have lost an entire generation.

The stock picking mistake

Peter Lynch was all about stock picking. He would follow his daughters around in the shopping mall to see what they were buying to get ideas for what companies to buy. From 1977 onward it was hard to make a long-term mistake. The 1970s bottom had passed and the general direction of the market was up except for very brief periods until 2001.

The equity premium puzzle was discovered by my friend Rajnish Mehra and his mentor Ed Prescott in 1977. But it was so controversial, flying in the face of efficient market theory, that it was not published until 1985. Peter Lynch would not have known of it when he gave that interview. I heard of it vaguely in the 1990s as just another piece of investment advice, but did not appreciate it until 2002 when I began to ask Mehra about the theory behind stock prices and he told me it had been his life's work.

The statistics show that money managers who pick stocks rarely outperform the market for more than about 5 years. The Magellan fund was the best performing mutual fund in the world for many years, under several managers, probably due to statistical chance. In 1995 its performance went south. That was about the time it came to my attention.

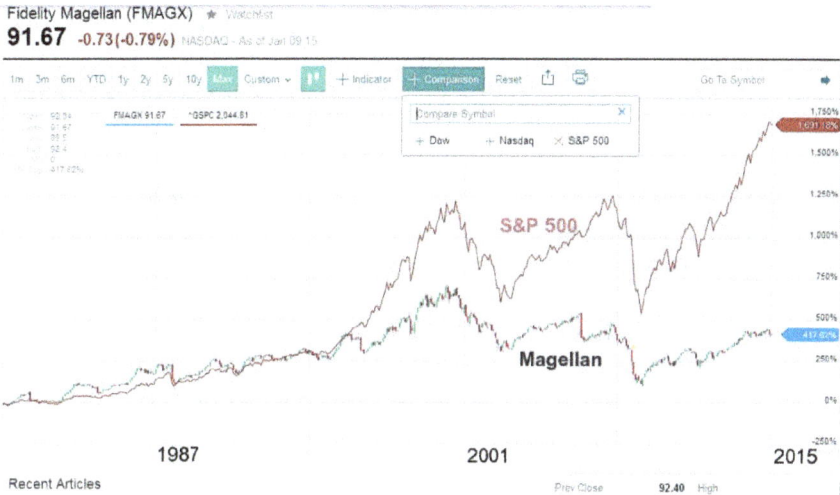

Fidelity Magellan (FMAGX) ★ Watchlist
91.67 -0.73(-0.79%) NASDAQ - As of Jan 09 15

Magellan fund (candlestick) vs. S&P 500
Yahoo charts

As you can see, since 1995 the Magellan fund's performance has been poor. However, if you happened to invest at one of the peaks it didn't go down as rapidly as the S&P 500.

My own mistakes

An unavoidable mistake, as far as I can tell, is to get interested in stocks generally when the market is doing well, and invest at that time. Like now. However, the past is already past. In 1983 I was 33 years old and the market had gone sideways since 1965, which was my entire memory of it. I made some money one year trading options during the energy crisis and thought I could keep doing that. The next year I traded options in the computer field, something I "knew," and lost two or three thousand dollars.

I did not trust the market rise that began in 1983. I continued to trade options thinking that markets basically must see-saw. By 1987 I realized my mistake just in time to experience a 25% market pullback. That kept me cautious. The 1987 pullback is barely visible on the chart above. Missing the great rise of the 1980s was the worst investing mistake of my life.

No one knew it was coming. I am not faulting myself for not knowing. The paper revealing the equity premium would not be published until two years later. I suppose I could fault myself for not having a strategy that provided for alternative scenarios, but that might be a little harsh.

One might look at the chart above and conclude either one of two things as of January 2015:

- The market has been rising for 5 years and is at a peak and will pull back.

- The market has been choppy with wars going on since 2001, like in the 1970s. The wars will resolve and the market will make up lost time by rising like it did in the 1980s. The current rise is not another chop, but the beginning of a so-called "secular bull market."

The investing style of the discoverer of the equity premium

Since Rajnish Mehra refuses to write a "popular" book, I will tell you a little about his personal investing, including his past mistakes, and how he invests now.

During the dot-com boom someone paid Mehra's son a fabulous amount of money for a web desktop homepage concept. Mehra felt he should be able to come up with some way to engineer a windfall, and in the dot-com bust when Microsoft's price fell by half, he bought Microsoft options. He told me he lost a great deal when Microsoft didn't recover in time for those expiring options. (I believe he gradually recovered his losses.)

His experience with options was unfavorable much like mine.

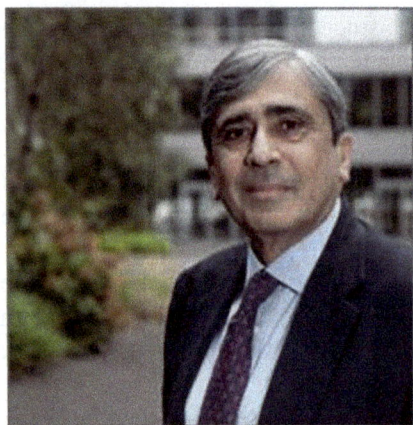

Dr. Rajnish Mehra at the University of Luxembourg
where he has a post-retirement appointment
http://wwwen.uni.lu/fdef/actualites/new_uni_lu_prof_dr_rajnish_mehra

Today Mehra invests in income derivative securities. They are more complicated than typical securities and achieve high income from leveraged lending. In leveraged lending, a company borrows money at a low rate, and lends it at a higher rate. Presumably diversification of the lending reduces the risk. But during a crisis, everyone will need to raise cash to cover losses, and will sell even good assets to cover losses. That is how a financial collapse spreads. Nothing which can be sold is unaffected, and the things that can't be sold are likely causing the crisis.

So I think Mehra's strategy is risky. He does not actually invest in the broad market. He is unsure himself if the equity premium will continue.

Another of his specialties is also retirement planning, and as he is already retired, he is following the standard economic wisdom to switch into income investments for the shorter term.

It is important to remember that if you are reasonably diversified, you will probably hold your rank among investors, i.e. you will keep your share even in a market downturn. Wealth is relative, and the absolute number in your investment account is not as important as that number relative to other investors.

The turnaround play

Confused by Lynch's advice to buy turns, but not falling stocks, and facing losses every time I tried to invest in my own industry, I began to follow Lynch's example of looking for consumer patterns. These are usually discovered too late. Perhaps on the west or east coast one might be able to spot emerging trends, but new chain stores seem to enter the Houston market only at the end of their expansion cycle.

Lulled by the perpetually rising markets of the 80s and 90s I began to buy companies in trouble which had a reputation for getting out of it, like Compaq. Every time Compaq (a Houston company) would get in trouble, the board would become active again and it would improve. But finally they hired a non-computer CEO who sold out to HP at a low price, and it was not favorable for me.

I tried a Fidelity technology growth fund, but it immediately quit growing, in about the mid-90s when the Magellan fund quit performing.

After that I had a mixed experience with turnarounds. Airlines like WestJet went right out of business taking my money with them. I had been very excited about low fares to Colorado, so that was based on Lynch's consumer popularity mentality. Apparently the management couldn't run an airline.

I invested in Korea after a crisis there, and Russia after the 1998-1999 bond default, and did very well with both countries. So I continued to believe in turnarounds. But which ones?

In the financial crisis, I bought a few mortgage companies, some of which I had owned for a long time and which had gotten out of trouble before. I lost half my net worth when they went bankrupt. But I continued to play the overall turnaround and continued to buy financial companies, among others, with the margin strategy I described earlier.

However, note carefully, there was nothing to prevent a second crisis. I got lucky. In the case of the Russia-Ukraine mess, there was a second crisis, the fall of oil, and that's what we'll talk about next.

Did big oil miscalculate?

At Rice I took a class in game theory. This is a mathematical approach to figuring out what your competitor might do in any possible situation, and plotting your best move. I got the impression that all large corporations used the technique to analyze competitors.

In 1983 after nearly a decade of investment in increased energy production and alternative energy in the U.S., Saudi Arabia abruptly caused a fall in oil prices and maintained low prices for more than 20 years. Many of my friends in Houston lost their oil-related jobs (mine is not oil related) and had to move away. The oil-based Soviet economy collapsed, resulting in the fall of the Berlin wall and eventual dissolution of the Soviet empire. My Russian wife assures me the only reason for it was the collapse of oil prices.

Just prior to the financial crisis, the price of oil again shot up, this time well over $100 a barrel.

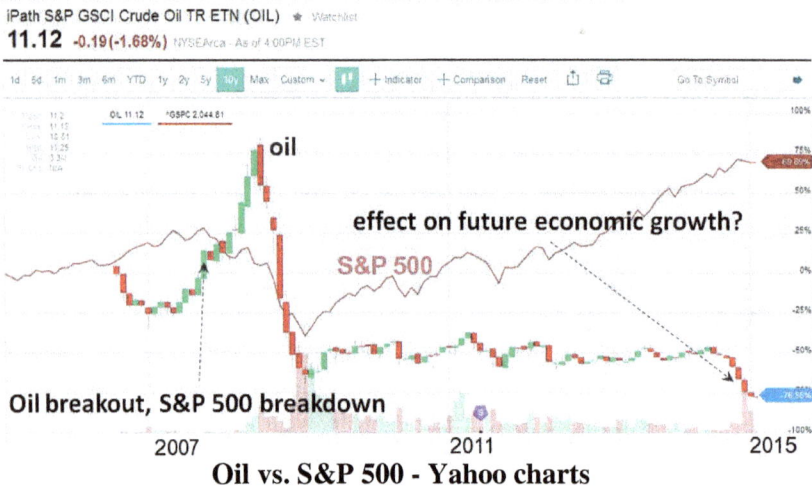

Oil vs. S&P 500 - Yahoo charts

If you subscribe to the view that oil drives the world economy - certainly plausible given the vast number of billionaires from Rockefeller to Koch who trace their fortunes to oil - then the mini-bubble of early 2007, on the left side of the chart above showing oil in candlesticks and the S&P 500 as a red line, coincided with a pronounced dip in the price of oil. Immediately as oil crossed above its former level the mini-bubble evaporated in the economy. But oil continued to climb until the S&P retreated to former levels.

Then in a circular dependency, combined with deflation of home prices in the U.S., both oil and the broad market collapsed and bottomed together. Oil never recovered. But all during this decade, before and after 2009, against the background of continual war in the Middle East, U.S. companies were investing in exotic methods of extracting oil and gas, some of them amounting to inducing mini-earthquakes, others amounting to digging up a continent of tar sand and sifting through it for oil.

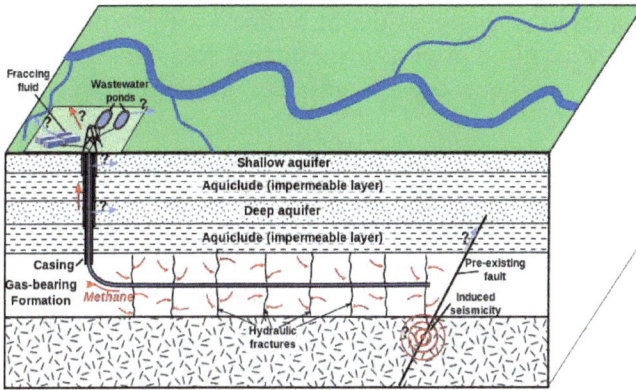

Hydraulic fracking - Wikimedia commons

Now we are easing tensions with Iran, Iraq production has come back online, and Libya is again producing oil despite the fallout from the Arab Spring not having led to stability. Oil can be used to finance war, and even ISIS is selling oil. Saudi Arabia is using the tried and true strategy it devised in 1983 to quash its competitors, only this time they don't have to increase production, they only have to hold steady. They have finally admitted it. Should that surprise anyone? Where are all the game theory analysts at the oil companies? Why have they not cut their own production?

The underlying reasons are closely related to the mechanism of the equity premium. The Federal Reserve made a lot of low interest money available since 2009. The idea was that businesses could borrow at low rates, stimulating them to engage in any business activity that had a higher rate of profit than their now low borrowing rates.

The game theory analysts looked at their competitors. They would have to borrow as much as their competitors in order to retain their own market share, their own "share of the world." Everyone raced to borrow as much as they could. Now they cannot just cut production because they need the revenue to pay their loans, even though the total rate of return has collapsed to a fraction of what they expected.

The oil companies have a new weapon, though – productivity in the form of rapidly declining costs. Some of the postponement of capital expenditure has been merely because it will be cheaper later. And some industry insiders think they can pump shale oil at any price the Arabian kingdom can stand. Either way my friends again lost their oil jobs.

Hold or fold?

When is holding an investment while the market declines a mistake? When is selling in a panic a mistake? We can find investment books and articles that make recommendations across the board on this one. Obviously if the market recovers, holding was correct and selling was the mistake. But if you have a security that goes out of business, or just permanently reduces its business, then selling even at a substantial loss would have been correct and holding would have been a mistake. However, we don't have this information.

While not simple, there is some clarity that emerges from studies of the equity premium and efficient market theory. But your personal situation also matters. Here are two questions:

- Are you wondering about whether to hold the whole market? Or just one stock or industry?

- Have you invested money that you will need in the next 5 years to meet known expenses, like mortgage payments, a car, or tuition?

It is rarely safe to hold a large amount of your portfolio in one company or industry. Beware also of hidden connections between industries, or between countries and industries. Also, if you hold individual stocks and mutual funds or ETFs, check the largest holdings of your funds. You can do this on Yahoo Finance by clicking the "holdings" link on the left side of the company summary page. If you own Apple and the NASDAQ 100 (e.g. QQQ), you own practically nothing but Apple, because QQQ is weighted by capitalization. That is, the dollar amount of Apple it contains is proportional to the total value of all Apple stock, its capitalization. Since it is currently the highest capitalization company in the world, it is the largest holding in QQQ.

There is an equal weighted version of the NASDAQ 100 you can hold if you wish. But the NASDAQ 100 itself omits financial stocks, such as banks. Banks are an important part of the economy. Even to hold the broader based S&P 500 or Russell 2000 under weights certain industries. These are U.S. indexes. There are not many U.S. container shipping companies, for example.

It is a bit safer to hold a country fund than individual companies, but not to hold it indefinitely. If you hold a country which comprises a large portion of the world economy and whose companies have operations all over the world, this is more like holding the whole world economy. Countries which have less corruption (none have zero corruption) will likely do better over the long run. Corrupt cultures may spurt ahead for a while, but they can collapse suddenly, like Russia has done a couple of times.

In The Equity Premium Puzzle I devote a long section to analyzing Japan. You might want to read that before committing to a country focus strategy. I have had good luck so far with betting on countries to recover when I had other signs that they were working hard to do so. In the late 1990s there was a financial crisis in Korea. It was reported that Korean Americans were sending money home to help out with the crisis. The Koreans have a long reputation as smart, hardworking, and largely honest people. So I did well investing in Korea. But I did not leave it there. Korea has certain issues, such as nearby North Korea, that keep it from reaching its full potential. The families that own Korean conglomerates also tend to be arrogant.

After NAFTA (the North American Free Trade Agreement) was signed I invested in Mexico. This was mostly neutral, and after a few years I sold out. If an investment does not behave as you expect, then something in your basis for buying it was not understood. You should probably sell.

If you have a focused investment, then if it goes down your share of the world decreases. Everyone else will not have the same problem. However, if you own the whole market, everyone's share will decrease and you will hold on to your share of the world. Eventually prices of goods and services you buy will come into line with equity prices, because the companies you own, after all, are doing business providing those goods and services.

Professional management

With Brazil I also did well anticipating a recovery, and with Russia in 1998-1999. The Russia story illustrates one big disadvantage of mutual funds. A bond fund I owned sold its Russian bonds at the worst possible time. Russia did not default on the international bonds. But the fund management had made the loss permanent. We saw with ProShares and Fidelity Magellan that professional management, other than Warren Buffett who is getting too old for you to count on for the next 20 years, is capable of making mistakes and often does.

It is possible to get good results from professional management. But I do not know how to choose and it is also possible you are giving your money to Bernie Madoff, or more likely a team of young hot shots who aren't as experienced as you are, and who will take unnecessary chances to achieve their own success.

People can mislead even themselves, so that in their own minds they are being honest about their records. Often when you hear gurus claiming success, they are not telling you about all their wrong predictions. They likely just don't remember their wrong predictions. I have deliberately given you enough information about my own blunders so that you can evaluate and use the information in this book objectively.

I have a friend who is a professional money manager, Nat, whom I mentioned earlier. I think he is probably as good as any, and certainly honest. He works for a big bank. I have looked over the portfolios he offers. They will indeed produce good returns, I believe. They contain the possibility of both growth and income. They have a lot of partnerships in them which we already discussed. If you hold ordinary mutual funds, these too have tax implications. If they have done a lot of trading in a year, they may declare short-term capital gains on which you will owe taxes.

Tax mistakes

It is, of course, a mistake to make a mistake on your taxes and fail to correct it, or hide income from the IRS. They can send you to jail for that easier than for many more morally reprehensible activities, or they can simply seize your property. Due to the limited partnerships I once had, I got a $22,000 bill from the IRS for back taxes a few months ago. I immediately re-calculated my taxes, did my very best to figure what I owed, and paid them about $13,000 (less than they asked for) after filing some additional information I had failed to notice before. In the end they said I overpaid, based on the new information, and gave me about half of that back. So the IRS is not necessarily evil or out to get you.

There are several incentives under current tax law to be a long-term holder rather than a trader:

- You can only deduct $3000 a year in capital losses. This number is antiquated. I still have half a million in unused losses carrying over from mortgage companies I owned that went bankrupt in the financial crisis. It's possible I'll never have enough capital gains to offset that loss. A market-oriented strategy would not wind up with such a bankruptcy unless the whole country goes bankrupt, in which case we are all in the same boat.

- Capital gains on stocks held a year or more are taxed at a lower rate, with a maximum of 20% currently (plus the Medicare tax of 3.8% if your income is over $400,000). The ordinary income tax rate is closer to 40% for most investors.

- Most dividends on stocks held 6 months (the actual rules are a little complicated) are taxed only at the long-term capital gains rate of 20% (less if you are in a low tax bracket). Not all companies are eligible, but most are.

These incentives can color your decisions about whether to sell when trouble appears. I think this is an unfortunate effect of the tax code. They also cause inefficiencies in the market by adding non-market costs to transactions that would otherwise equalize prices that ought to be equalized.

Foreign taxes can derail the value of some otherwise good investments. Some countries levy income tax on dividends paid by their companies, regardless of your citizenship. In theory you can deduct these from the tax you owe on those dividends, but in practice if the amount is over

$500 (a very small amount) you will be subject to too much scrutiny. The IRS is very suspicious of people with foreign income trying to avoid U.S. taxes, and they will automatically require additional documentation. There are also some limits on how much you can deduct.

Using other people's money

Using other people's money is not by itself a mistake. Most wealthy people do a lot of this. If they are persuasive like Warren Buffett or Michael Bloomberg, they get it as investment capital. Most people will probably only be able to get it as debt. Failing to manage the debt will inevitably result in forced sales, permanent losses, and possibly bankruptcy.

If you use margin, i.e. borrow money from your broker to buy stocks, the rules are now set up such that you are unlikely to go bankrupt. Your broker will sell enough securities from your account to cover any liability. But your losses will be permanent.

Unfortunately, debt is most useful when you are first starting and have little money. But that is when it is hardest to obtain and you will be charged the highest rates, currently around 7.5%. It is hard to find stable stocks that yield more than that. If you are already a millionaire and can negotiate with a broker to give you a 3% rate, you can use the strategies we discussed to increase dividends to cover your interest. But you should keep it to no more than about 1/3rd of your total account balance. Pullbacks of 40% in the market are not that uncommon. If you have 50% of your account balance as margin, a pullback of 40% takes the total margin plus equity down to 60% and leaves you with only 10% of the original amount or 10%/60% = 16% equity in your new reduced account balance. The minimum required equity is 30% to hold and 50% to buy. So you will get a margin call for the missing 14% and will have to sell a lot of stocks. Until your equity rises to 50% you will not be able to buy them back, so you will miss most of the recovery.

If you never exceed 30% margin, then a 40% pullback in the market leaves you with 60% of your original account balance and you still have 50% equity (30/60). At this point you should begin selling things to maintain at least 50% equity, so that when the recovery comes you can buy them back.

You will need to sell the things that retain the most value, and are the least likely to recover. Of course if you only hold an index fund, you only have one thing to sell. But the prospect of buying it back on recovery leads to the next common mistake . . .

Trading in and out

Nervously selling and buying usually leads to small losses which accumulate and ruin your long-term performance. You avoid going broke. That is the upside. But you can get relatively poorer pretty fast. This is the best argument I know for buying and holding a diversified portfolio of the whole economy and not adjusting it too often. Any stocks you add for income will be exceptions that may from time to time decline and you should not hold so much of one that a decline ruins you.

Of course if you find you like buying and selling, then quit your job and become a day trader. I just find this too stressful. I can't point to a wealthy person who did this with stocks. There are probably a few. I have never been a currency trader like George Soros and it seems to me he did this only a few times. Warren's investment in Berkshire-Hathaway was not a timed trade. He could see the cash on the balance sheet and it was just sitting there waiting for him. Warren has never claimed to be a market timer, though sometimes his value-seeking approach leads him to buy when prices are down. But he is not buying because prices are down, rather because he sees some long-term value that is under priced. If you aren't sure what the difference is, then don't try this at home.

The lure of excess returns

You might be cautious enough to realize that investing a lot of money in things that have just gone way up in price is a classic mistake. It might be less obvious that securities yielding greater than 3% with growth, or 5% to 6% without growth, are risky. They often go along just fine for a while and then fall out of the sky. But these general comments are not likely to help. Let's look at a couple of examples, one that happened to me and one that happened to a friend.

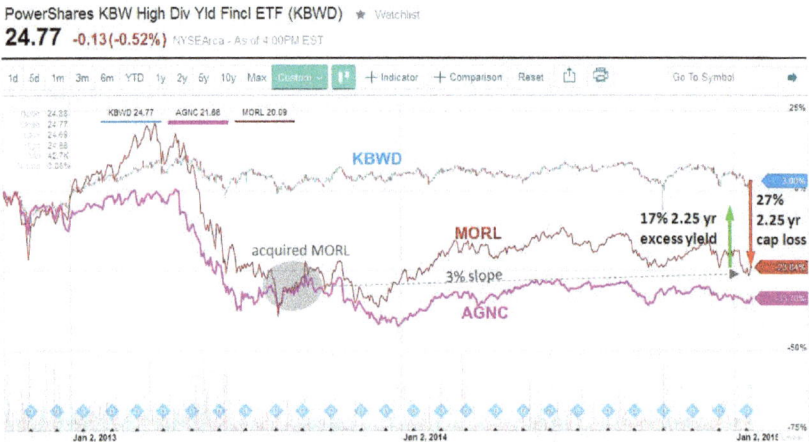

KBWD, MORL & AGNC 2.25 years
Yahoo Finance

There are only two ETFs I am aware of at present which hold high dividend financials. Both are relatively new. The primary one is KBWD which holds both REITs (Real Estate Investment Trusts) and BDCs (Business Development Companies). Both types of companies are organized under special laws that escape most corporate tax provided they pay their income as dividends. This limits their ability to grow by reinvestment, but results in much higher than normal dividend yields.

The other one is MORL, which we discussed earlier, actually an ETN not an ETF. You can find an explanation here:

http://www.investopedia.com/financial-edge/0213/etf-or-etn-whats-the-difference.aspx

- ETNs hold a note, not any actual stocks.
- The note is issued by some backer such as a large bank.
- The note is at risk if the backer were to go bankrupt.
- The note's value has some fixed relation to the stocks you might expect a similar ETF to own.
- Since the ETN's value is not based on buying and selling, there are no tracking errors.
- Tax treatment is like ETFs, but they are new and there is some uncertainty as to whether or not holders may incur some capital gains distributions in the future if the underlying note is sold.

So, MORL doesn't hold anything except a note backed by UBS. It is based on certain types of REITs which derive income from mortgages. MORL is 3x leveraged, attempting to get three times the dividend of a similar ETF like KBWD, and it mostly succeeds, yielding around 21%, vs. currently around 8% for KBWD. You would expect it is also more volatile, and it is. In the chart above we see that in the 2 and 1/4 years since the inception of MORL, its price relative to KBWD has declined 27%, and short-term ups and downs are much greater. The dividend has barely made up for this loss. I estimate about a 19% dividend over the period, for a total of 2.25x19=43%, giving a net of 43-27=16% which over 2.25 years is an annualized gain of only 3.4%.

If you had acquired MORL at inception, as a new investment and not a replacement for something already in your portfolio, that would have been marginally attractive, at least up to the present time, since the price loss was almost as much as the dividends paid.

However, what most people seeking dividends had at that time was AGNC. This is a particular mortgage REIT which was widely held and paying dividends in the 12% to 14% range. It held up well during the financial crisis when others were failing. Then in the spring of 2013 it cut its dividend and began to collapse. Since both KBWD and MORL have AGNC as a component, they also declined. In the short run, MORL declined more than KBWD as it is based only on mortgage REITs whereas KBWD is more diversified. Overall, it would have been better to hold MORL than AGNC.

In spite of the leverage, MORL has an advantage of diversity over a single REIT like AGNC. And so it has recovered better than AGNC. Are any of these a mistake? Only time will tell. AGNC might recover further. You can see on the chart that I acquired MORL over a two month period when it was down, and it is higher now than where I bought it, so I am feeling pretty good about it. But I'll be regretting it if something goes wrong with housing again, or there is a negative effect from eventual rising interest rates. At the moment, it looks like the Europeans are going to force us to keep rates low a little longer. These are probably not the sort of things you want to be worrying about though. If you do enjoy worrying about them, you are not so much a generational wealth builder as a would-be-hedge-fund-manager.

Because mortgage REITs are not diversified, and because of the leverage involved in MORL, I can't be sure it is better than KBWD as an income supplement to the 3% dividend index fund strategy. But it is very interesting that it avoids tracking error and worth watching closely and perhaps experimenting with as a small fraction of holdings.

BBEP & RUSL 6 months ending January 2015
Yahoo Finance

Brietburn Energy, shown above, is one of those limited partnerships in oil and gas I warned about. RUSL is a 3x leveraged version of the Russian index RSX, which is heavily dependent on oil. Brietburn, which a friend of mine laments she didn't sell when I warned her about the tax consequences a year ago, has declined as much due to oil prices as a highly leveraged country fund based mostly on oil. That is because most smaller energy companies borrowed a lot of money at the Fed's low interest rates in 2009 to develop fracking-based oil production, so they are just as leveraged as the 3x fund. This company is focused only on production of oil, not on refining or retail marketing, so it has no compensating benefit from low oil prices like the vertically integrated major oil companies.

I had several oil holdings I disposed of in the spring, thinking that with Iran and Iraq increasing production the price might drop. I kept only BP and RUSL. I was thinking BP was an integrated major and still recovering from the Gulf oil spill. It has declined more than Shell or Exxon but is now yielding over 6%, so I'm not complaining. Russia started a war, the effects of which are not shown on the chart above (they occurred earlier in the year), and then oil collapsed while the sanctions from the war were in place - not a good scenario.

My friend was hanging on to BBEP for high dividends, and I was investing in RUSL because of the potential high capital gains from the world's most undervalued stock market. In each case it was the lure of excess returns.

You have friends and read books and listen to financial news that will tell you about opportunities for excess returns. Investors like Warren Buffett seem to provide examples that they can be found. I cannot tell you not to do it. But why did I claim that 2-3% yield from growing index funds and 5-6% from non-growth investments (KBWD is 8% but seems to decline a bit each year, making the net return closer to 6% or 7%) was what you should expect? Because few people I know have done better than that. I know only one person actually who did better, a chain smoking Chinese engineer who invested in small companies in corrupt foreign countries, using his local knowledge of those countries to try and pick companies that he thought had the best political connections.

If I tried that, I'm quite sure they'd steal my investment. I know indirectly of one woman who locked herself in the house and day-traded her way to a million dollars in the year prior to the dot-com bust. Then she retired from day-trading. This amounts to a market timing decision, and against her example stand the millions of investors who did not exit the market before the dot-com bust. So I do not tell you not to do this, only that you are not following the scientifically investigated strategy of generational wealth building using the equity premium.

Update as of April 2016

Brietburn has come down from the $25 range to around 30 cents per share, essentially a total loss. AMLP, an ETF of similar MLPs, is doing fine. Even RUSL, which has the leveraged volatility losses, is recovering at least some of its value having doubled over the last few months. RUSL is very inefficient. Not all leveraged ETFs are the same. UPRO, a 3x version of the S&P 500, is relatively more efficient. One may determine the efficiency of a leveraged ETF by comparing the long and short versions, to see how much the average line goes down (it will always go down, representing the volatility losses).

Below are the efficiency charts for RUSL and UPRO, as well as for OIL which though not leveraged, has some inefficiency since it is a tracking fund and cannot simply hold stocks (after all, oil in storage incurs fees).

RUSL (Russia 3x long) vs. RUSS (3x short) 6 mo.

UPRO (S&P 500 3x long) vs SPXU (3x short) 6 mo.

OIL (crude oil long) vs. SZO (crude oil short, or inverse) 6 mo.

The annual inefficiency is double what these 6 month charts show. It suggests that if you are not "right" about the timing, it is not wise to hold either the leveraged ETFs, or the commodity tracking ETFs (or ETNs). UPRO pays a small dividend. It is relatively less dangerous, BUT, if you are caught in a downdraft you are stuck holding it because nothing else is going to recover at 3x. So it is not for most people. You could lose 30% to volatility losses over a 2 year downturn (4 x 8% semi-annual loss, adding back about 2% in dividends). The more dividends such an instrument pays, the less you have to worry about losses during the downturns.

Can you recover from a mistake?

There are many kinds of mistakes. Did you simply type the wrong stock symbol, or share amount? I have done this several times. You can reverse the mistake immediately by executing the reverse transaction (e.g. sell if you just bought). It will cost you two commissions, plus whatever the price movement has been, less the bid-ask spread (difference between what you can sell for and buy for, usually small). This is the smallest loss you will ever encounter, and avoids a great deal of anxiety.

Is the whole market simply down? That is not a mistake because it affects everyone and you do not lose your share of the world. Try not to react to it.

Did you invest too much in stocks when you had upcoming expenses, and then the market went down? This is tough luck. You will need to reduce the expenses, as one always seeks to reduce expenses when the market is down. We learned this from the annuity analysis. Then you will need to sell enough to meet your expenses.

Did you make a focused bet in a particular industry, company or country that has gone down? Will it recover? If so, what are you worried about? Was it in a leveraged ETF like RUSL in the chart above? Then it may not recover due to volatility compounding in leveraged ETFs. Was it in a particular company like BBEP in the chart above? Then it is a gamble. The company might go bankrupt, or more likely it could scale back its operation meaning it no longer has the potential to reach the value it once had. Or you might have bought it during a bubble.

Let me ask you a question. If you flip a coin can you make it come up heads? If so, then you can absolutely recover. I never met anyone who could do this without using a two-headed fake coin. In the stock market it is more likely you'd find a two-tailed coin than a two-headed one.

Noticed that I have placed the "recovery" discussion in the "mistakes" chapter. I know that I cannot talk all of you out of trying it because I cannot talk myself out of trying it, so I will attempt to moderate your mistake.

If you have a loss in a particular company in a good industry, and the whole industry is down, don't double down on that company. Succeeding at this just once is the worst luck you can have, because then you will try it over and over. Instead use an industry index fund so that the recovery, if it happens, is not subject to the fortunes of one particular company.

If you have a loss in a leveraged ETF, get out with a smaller loss if you have the opportunity. In theory one could cancel compounded volatility by buying small amounts on the way down and selling those amounts on the way up. But almost no one has the discipline to do this, or the money to keep buying if the situation keeps getting worse and stays there like with Russia, or even the mathematical sophistication to decide when and how much.

To recover from a loss like Russia, look at the industry causing the loss. It is oil. Russia is like a single-company investment in this regard. It has other unique problems in addition to its basic industry problem that will hold it back, such as sanctions. Recover from the loss in Russia by investing in oil production - if, that is, you think oil production will ever recover. Remember that at this writing, while oil appears to have bottomed, Iran is talking about $25 oil. By the time you read this, the outcome for oil will probably be old news. I am attempting to explain how the reasoning goes before you know the future data.

Since BBEP is an oil and gas exploration and production company, the recipe for recovery is the same as for Russia. Wait for the bottom and invest in an oil production ETF. If you search for "oil ETF" you will get ETFs keyed to the raw price of oil, not actual collections of companies, and such ETFs pay no dividends. They also may not experience long-term growth. By searching for "oil company ETF" I got several relevant lists, including this one:

Top 3 Oil & Gas Exploration & Production ETFs [119]

XOP   SPDR S&P Oil & Gas Exploration & Production ETF
IEO   iShares Dow Jones US Oil & Gas Exploration & Production Index Fund
PXE   PowerShares Dynamic Energy Exploration & Production Portfolio

These do not include integrated oil companies with refining and retail operations. Those kinds of companies have not suffered much from lower oil prices, because their refining and retail operations are profiting from low oil prices. Thus they won't recover much. Maybe you should have invested in these kinds of companies (via ETFs) in the first place (which a broad index strategy does), but we are assuming you already made the mistake and it is too late. Below is a chart of these three ETFs versus the S&P 500 over a five year period.

5-year Oil exploration & production ETFs vs. S&P 500
Jan 2010 to Jan 2015

All of them have fallen and if oil recovers they will rise again. If it doesn't, they won't. Don't try to recover everything. Remember the Joyce Brothers test? Trying to recover the entire loss or even make a profit is like standing in the next room and shooting for the target around a corner. Satisfy yourself with a good long-term investment which pays some dividends. Then even if there is no recovery at all, you will not have actually made a second mistake!

We need to know the dividend yields of these ETFs. Without doubt the dividends will be cut soon, but all we have to go by is the history:

XOP   1.41% yield
IEO   1.3% yield
PXE   2.04% yield

I also looked at the top holdings of each, and didn't see any known problem companies or other surprises. That doesn't mean there aren't any. We see that the top dividend payer is the PowerShares ETF PXE. We already know they tend to vote the shares that they hold and we own progressively on issues like executive compensation and shareholder initiatives. Over five years PXE has performed better, but there is no guarantee this will continue.

You don't actually know if the turnaround in oil has come or whether there is another drop due. So instead of betting the farm immediately (anytime you could plausibly use the word "bet" there is a mistake brewing), divide the amount you might like to invest into several parts, perhaps three. Spread the purchases out over time, even weeks or months, and wait if more trouble develops instead of a recovery.

If you are lucky enough to reach the point where the selected ETF is 30% to 40% above the S&P 500 in long-term performance (5 years or greater), you might want to consider selling some of it. This is the part where I have the most trouble. I sometimes feel it will keep going, and I always hate figuring out what to buy instead.

Short-sighted tax & stimulation policy

A business news article offers the following definition of "quantitative easing:" [115]

1. Central bank creates money...
2. ... to buy bonds [*debt*] from financial institutions ...
3. ... which reduces interest rates ...
4. ... leading businesses and individuals to borrow more [*debt*] ...
5. ... so they spend more and create jobs ...
6. ... to boost the economy.

And this is supposed to be good to encourage all this debt? When some bubble develops, maybe even in only one sector, interest rates are raised. Since interest rates are slow acting, maybe they are raised out of habit when the economy is not even fully recovered (like the Fed plans to do sometime in 2015 unless the EU central bank makes it impossible for them to do so). What happens to all those loans, some of them long-term? Those are expenses which cannot be arbitrarily trimmed back. Actual consumption will take the full brunt of the stimulus withdrawal, and instead of leveling out the economy will unevenly contract. Investments in education and careers will be ruined by the uneven nature of the contraction. Companies will be conditioned by this cycle to expand cautiously, using automation instead of workers. Nothing about this is good.

We have pretty well established several things regarding government policy:

- Two out of three stimulus methods (interest rates and quantitative easing) *produce more individual debt.* In turn, debt increases instability when contractions occur. Debt obligations are not optional expenses that can be cut back. We even see American businessmen continuing the old practice of using debt to confiscate competitors and even the resources of other countries, increasing the chance of political instability and war.

- Incorrect tax policy may liquidate investment capital, ultimately *reducing the tax base in the long-term, requiring even higher tax rates* which in turn cause faster liquidation.

- There is a strong degree of *equivalency between dividends and capital gains.* Virtually without exception, investment vehicles (companies, funds, notes) that pay high dividends give up growth, or experience negative growth, in proportion to the dividends paid.

- The pressure to grow encourages corporations to reinvest most or all their profits, even if they don't really have a new idea and must grow by *cannibalizing existing markets.*

- The firewall between capital gains and other types of income was necessary due to different tax rates. Now that dividends are taxed at the same rate as capital gains, there is *no compelling reason to maintain the firewall between dividends and capital gains.*

- Due to the penalty for negative capital gains (not deductible as a business loss in any meaningful way), and the necessity for losses in dividend paying companies to show up on the other side of the firewall as capital losses, *the firewall maintains pressure on companies to grow even in unproductive ways* in spite of moves toward equalizing treatment of capital gains and dividends.

We further conclude that large corporations like debt because:

- They can expand using low cost debt capital, increasing returns on equity.

- Indebted employees are more dependent and compliant, less likely to strike out on their own and open competing businesses.

- A debt crisis is more likely to hurt smaller competitors. In fact, if a corporation is large enough then its employment cannot be sacrificed and the government will bail it out. This is a consideration only for managers, because shareholders do not get bailed out. They are liquidated. Only the GM management was bailed out. The old shares are worthless.

In view of these considerations, it seems to be a *mistake for government to continue to treat capital gains separately, at least separately from dividends.* Because of the equivalency between them, we could at least allow capital losses to be counted against dividends. This would reduce the incentive for cannibalistic growth and the resultant social ills, which we have well documented. It would not reduce the incentive for healthy growth, because that still provides an equity premium that exceeds anything possible with a purely income strategy.

It also seems a *mistake for government policy to favor stimulus which results in debt.* The unexpected effects of that debt, in terms of either instability or transfer of power to the largest corporations, has not been considered. Tax policy stimulus has been criticized as transferring wealth mainly to the very wealthy, but let me ask you two things. Can you not imagine a tax stimulus policy which would encourage moderate wealth building and the establishment of more small businesses, which everyone concedes provide the most jobs? How many of you felt less confident about the economy and the future in the 1980s when we had a tax stimulus policy than you do today?

The Regan tax cuts can be criticized on the grounds that they did not immediately reduce the budget, in fact it went up. But as we have seen, the compounding effects can easily take ten or twenty years to reach maximum effect. Capital grows so slowly that we resort to making a "generational" wealth building plan rather than a rapid one. Then is not the balanced budget achieved in the Clinton administration attributable to the Regan tax cuts? Have we allowed anywhere near enough time to judge the Bush tax cuts (which might not have been ideal, but at least equalized capital gains and dividend rates) given that a trillion dollar war intervened?

Borrowing money to meet expenses

An exaggerated version of the borrowing mistake is running up credit card debt and paying 18% or higher interest on it. I'm assuming you are not in that category if you are reading this book. If you are, stop it immediately, regardless of what it takes.

My friend considered a $100,000 line of credit using the equity of her home as collateral, to replace the income lost when BBEP cut its dividend. A banker relative of hers told her about HELOC loans but did not recommend them because the payments suddenly balloon in a few years when the principal payments kick in. This is very close to the same kind of excess home lending that caused the financial crisis. If the money has gone for expenses and anything happens to the value of her home, there is no way she can repay the $100,000. It would be less crazy to take the $100k and buy MORL. Even though MORL would also crash with housing, at least there would be some residual, and the income from $100k would in the near term be $20k per year (less taxes).

I offer this not as advice, but just to illustrate that the risk in using the money for expenses is far greater than even a non-diversified and leveraged investment. If the $100k comes at an interest rate of less than 3%, it would be okay to invest it in a broad market index fund. Probably. Except that since it is not a margin loan, the interest may not be deductible from the dividend income. So it would only be okay if she is in the 10% or 15% tax brackets which have no dividend tax.

The trouble is, people in that tax bracket tend to have financial emergencies and think they "have to" use any money they have access to in order to solve them. Then they have inadvertently used the money for "expenses" despite intentions otherwise. If you have an emergency expense, first repay all your debt, then deal with the expense. You don't "have to" do anything except pay taxes.

Your equity protection firewall

What if borrowing in your case is not risky at all? What if you only tap a tiny amount of your equity? You are still liquidating your equity. The principle of the thing is this - there is a situation in which the equity in your house is not very useful to you. You think. Equity in the market would be earning income, which you could spend, and going up in value, which your house may be doing, but not as much as the market. There is no difference between selling your stocks to meet expenses, and pre-selling your house to meet expenses. That's what the loan is. It is admission that you aren't planning to keep this house and you are going to get the sales money early. But it is equity money, not expense money.

Without a firewall between equity and expenses, how are you going to accumulate equity for a generational wealth building plan? Without a firewall that will withstand all the disasters, emergencies, diseases, house fires, car wrecks, weddings and other normal expenses of life, it won't happen. That's right. Not even a house fire, a car wreck, or someone dying can be allowed to erase the equity and force the next generation to start over. Otherwise it is not a generational wealth building plan at all.

Small leaks can sink a big ship

Figure the cost of everything in terms of the investment capital you need to finance it with a dividend yield of 3%. A $200 a month cable TV bill absorbs the income from $80,000 invested (12 x 200 / .03). Is that what you would really do with $80,000 if you had it in your hand? It is now possible to watch most of your favorite shows much cheaper over the internet from a variety of sources, if not as convenient.

Your $80 a month iPhone 6 is costing you $32,000 (12 x 80 / .03). Trade it for the $7 a month Android from TracFone which only takes $2800 of investment capital. If you even have a home phone, exchange it for an internet phone from Ooma for about $4 a month.

Instead of a new Honda or Toyota, buy a 5 to 7 year old Mercedes on eBay. I still have one I bought that way in 2006 and it still conveys more status than a new car of lesser brand. If you drive a sufficiently old car you can drop the comprehensive insurance coverage and have liability only. The comprehensive probably won't pay as much on an old car as you would pay in premiums.

Personal and emotional factors

How will you handle it when the value of your portfolio goes up or down in a month, or a day, more than you make in a year? If you have a $2 million portfolio, it only takes a move of 5% to change the value by $100,000. About once every three years there is a 5% up or down day for the S&P 500.

Will you be able to remain interested in your job when the fluctuations in your portfolio dwarf your salary?

Once you have accumulated more than you can earn in your remaining career, how will you feel if you lose it?

If you start life with a nest egg which is more than you'd earn at an ordinary job, what kind of career will you choose?

If your friends, brother, sister, etc. can no longer afford to pay their share at the places you now want to go on vacation, will you go without them? Pay their way? Will you still go somewhere that they want to go?

You probably have heard that *greed and fear* are the emotions to watch out for. I have never felt either one in connection with investing. That advice is inaccurate. Greed is when you take someone else's share just because you can and you want it. Fear is when you are afraid something terrible is going to happen. Greed might lead you to break the law, for example to commit insider trading, or it might lead you to cheat on a contract. But if you follow the law, every investment transaction is freely entered by both parties and the concept of taking someone's share, of greed, doesn't apply.

If you become fearful, you'll probably just sell out. So?

The emotions that appear for me are *confidence and defeat*. Defeat is when the loss has seemingly already occurred, and it is apparent that it is unrecoverable. This might lead to selling at a bad time. Generally the strategy is to focus on rational decisions, and stay the course unless there is concrete data to act on. If you are invested in a whole market index, the only ways you can be defeated (other than your country being invaded by an enemy nation) are through theft or through withdrawing at too high a rate and thus liquidation.

I feel I have made some progress at handling defeat. Generally the strategy is to focus on rational decisions, and stay the course unless there is concrete data to act on. If you are invested in a whole market index, the only ways you can be defeated (other than your country being invaded by an enemy nation) are through theft or through withdrawing at too high a rate and thus liquidating.

When the market is down X%, then decrease your annual withdrawal by the same X%. This means of course that you should not be living so close to the edge that you cannot reduce expenses. Remember that you might not be able to sell real estate or cars during a downturn.

Guarding against theft is mostly beyond the scope of this book. As far as your broker running off with your money, if you use a major firm it is less likely than failure of a bank. Your broker is not allowed to lend against your assets in the same way that a bank lends against deposits. Broker margin lending provides for liquidation of assets before the collateral drops too low. But if you are worried about it, open accounts at two different brokers, using different passwords. And don't allow transactions to be initiated from your bank account. That way, the cracking of one single account cannot wipe you out.

There are many other personal and family factors to consider. The subject of personal and emotional factors in wealth building is more general than investing, and deserves its own book. I am not at all qualified to write such a book. There are lists of possibly applicable books on the internet. By and large I find them unhelpful. I did enjoy reading Freud and Jung many years ago, but they are a very indirect way of getting at it. Still, that's the best recommendation I have. Freud was a very popular writer, but be warned he is no longer in vogue in psychology circles, most of whom have turned to behaviorism. Jung was extremely oblique, and has many interpreters who write popular books, some of which are good and some of which are ridiculous. You just have to hunt around and find things to which you can relate. I find that being honest and flexible with my immediate family is very helpful. With my friends I'm flexible, but we rarely discuss financial status as it can lead to envy, consciously or unconsciously.

And the number one mistake everyone makes is . . .

Drum roll please. ...

If you were paying attention, I already listed the biggest mistake Americans make. Do you remember what that was?

It was "*thinking only of themselves, and trading away their share of the world economic pie for temporary comfort*" at the beginning of the previous chapter. In other countries I believe there is more consciousness of the longevity of family. People still fight over land for their children to have, for example.

Everyone, every culture, makes "the number one overall mistake." We see it so easily in other people. *They give up their land and way of life and take jobs.*

After that they might, or might not, raise their standard of living. But it is always uncertain. They can never relax. Any slip and they fall into poverty. In the ancient world, employment was beneath slavery. Employees are expendable. They represent no capital investment.

In the middle of the 20th century in the U.S. it wasn't as bad. In Japan prior to about 1990 it wasn't so bad. Companies invested in their employees and so were not willing to lose them. Competition in the world labor force, engineered by both liberal and conservative wealthy interests, has destroyed the negotiating power of employees around the world.

There are many tricks that will deceive you. Free education for everyone through junior college? Then everyone will be qualified for most jobs. Society will have made the investment in all that education even if the job market doesn't utilize it. Many countries such as India and China have excellent education systems, but lower standards of living. And so education has undermined even professional jobs. If you want to cheapen something, mass produce a lot of it. Anyone want a $199 laptop with solid state disk? How about a $19,000 a year PhD? If you position yourself as a commodity, you can be cheapened. Owners are not commodities.

Manufacturing jobs were undermined by massive investment in the infrastructure of transportation, both aviation and shipping. It is no coincidence that it is the primary beneficiary of shipping, China, which wants to build the new Nicaraguan canal.

Intellectual service jobs were undermined by massive investment in communications (internet) infrastructure. Now cheap educated labor anywhere can be brought immediately to bear on a local task.

But mostly by depending on a job you give up your freedom - and your right to govern yourself. That means when other things go wrong, you cannot really change the government. The American founding fathers believed an educated and independent citizenry of landowners was a requirement for a democratic government to succeed.

Any employer will eventually try to completely control you, even off the job. If you are doing something they really don't like, they will feel they are stupidly opposing themselves by continuing to employ you. With lots of other qualified people wanting your job, eventually they will take the easy way out and just replace you. I have seen it. Even the government does it. And you will too if you become an employer. It is a disease of humanity that the concept of employment has spread and corrupted all thinking and made most of us willing, dependent slaves.

You might not immediately agree with me. It is a startling concept. But think about it. It is impractical for all of us to own land. But we can all own public companies, and can gain our financial independence. Then the tables will be turned and it will be possible to have democratic nations.

Misjudging large scale calamities

There are two common mistakes regarding large scale calamities. One is worrying about disasters that either aren't likely in the near future, or that you will survive. For example, contact with extraterrestrial aliens is unlikely in the near future. Or if there is a severe economic downturn and you are holding companies that produce essential goods and services, don't worry, you'll survive. Another is obsession with catastrophes that are the unexpected results of our own collective action, such as misguided trade and monetary policy, much the subject of this book, and ideological or religious philosophies, such as an obsession with "end times" prophecies

Doomsayers have always been with us, and they are right whenever doom arrives, which it does periodically. But they have no clue when it is coming. They are like the stopped clock which shows the correct time twice a day. That does not mean you should not worry about calamity at all. That would be the other kind of mistake. It means you should be prepared for it to strike at any moment. For example, you should not be using so much margin or living on such tight finances that loss of a job or a 40% decline in the market will ruin you. And yes, they are more likely to happen at the same time.

In this book we dwelt on financial calamity. It is beyond our scope to address in detail other potential problems such as, what if life span increases? Then you might not die and pass wealth to your children. This isn't in my opinion likely in the current generation, but it is possible within the next century, and perhaps you should endeavor to move your family up the ladder a few percentile points while it is still possible by our simple method. But it is not as urgent a concern as simple replacement of jobs by automation, which is ongoing at a rapid pace.

Another calamity that befalls us is our own guilt at becoming wealthy. We may not even be consciously aware of it. Keep in mind that the strategy of investing creates jobs, which most people want even if you have decided it is time to become less dependent on them. Becoming wealthy causes you to pay more taxes enabling lower tax rates for everyone. Many social ills become less acute.

Speaking of guilt, there are certain ideas we get if we live in a wealthy culture that are not quite factual, or only partly so. For example, much has been made of European exploitation of colonized areas in the 18th and 19th centuries. The worst part was the unintended death of around 90% of indigenous peoples in the western hemisphere due to disease. This has led to a general "conclusion" that a less developed culture will always disappear when contacted by a more developed one.

But that only happened in the western hemisphere. In Africa it did not happen. The indigenous people are still dominant there. They have regular contact with the most threatening new viruses, such as Ebola, and are developing immunity to them gradually. Pandemic may be the greatest threat to humanity. If so, less developed regions that have had previous exposure may be the survivors. They may also be better able to cope when complicated trade and commerce systems break down.

A Mississippian mound-builder settlement in Illinois [116]
Settlements with populations as large as colonial cities were encountered by early explorers, but disappeared without explanation or conflict.

Conclusions

Regarding war in relation to economies

Massed warfare appears to have arisen about the same time as massed wealth. Agriculture enabled larger settlements, which supported mining, manufacturing, trade and mutual defense. Agriculture may even have been adopted because of the need for larger settlements capable of defense. Groups or nations will attempt to obtain what they want through trade. If they cannot, they will consider whether the cost of war is less or greater than the value of what they want. If a people become desperately poor, the cost of war seems very small to them and war becomes more likely. An example of this is the Sea Peoples who contributed to the end of the Bronze Age.

Disputes between two parties can sometimes be resolved by raising the cost of war and lowering the cost of trade, then getting them to move into reconstruction and rationalization of their monetary and trading systems. Disputes in which the parties want conflicting things, which become more likely as more parties get involved, are just plain hard to resolve.

We are not absolutely beyond risk of a crash of civilization today through poverty-fed terrorism enhanced by modern exotic weapons. Managing economies and trade so as to move to more stability where people can plan their lives, and a reasonable level of global prosperity so that impoverished people are not tempted to blow us all up, seems a prudent course, and a necessary prerequisite to any personal wealth building strategy. It is likely, for example, that the dot-com bust might have rapidly cleared up, and our economy may have resumed growth in response to the Bush tax cuts, except that after 9/11 we engaged in a trillion dollar war that as far as I can tell is still going on. The current president, Obama, is simply in denial about the level of conflict. War is not over until your enemy sues for peace, or decimates you. You don't get to declare unilaterally when war is over.

The course to a stable world economy is not obvious and policy makers and central banks are struggling with changes in trade and advances in technology which bring unheard of levels of productivity.

Cultural factors also run deep, and melting pot countries might not be well served by imposing their values on everyone. But neither should melting pot countries necessarily allow themselves to be "colonized" by immigrants who don't want to blend in. The attraction of the economically stable countries should be addressed by exporting stability, otherwise it is likely that instability will be imported. Current western leaders seem to be encouraging other countries to change governments in response to protest rather than elections. Then they take in massive numbers of refugees from the wars triggered by such extra-constitutional actions. What are they importing?

Unemployment and instability? They should be exporting employment and stability.

Alexis Tsipras
leader of radical left Syriza party which won Greek elections 2015
Wikimedia commons - Lorenzo Gaudenzi

    The seven stages of war, trade and currency management continue to grind in a long cycle in which humans seem to reinvent the old problems in new unrecognized forms, like substituting a unified European currency for gold with the same deflationary effects. The photo above shows Alexis Tsipras, former communist, and as of early 2015 leader of the radical left Syriza party and prime minister of Greece. At first he seemed to want to be prime minister of all of Europe and appealed to the jobless and nearly jobless. Electorates are nearly always somewhat balanced between right and left philosophies and the degree of economic despair or prosperity easily tips them in one direction or another. Only Germany is doing well at the moment.

    As of mid-2015 Tsipras dismissed his economic minister and seemed to cave to the demands of German bankers for more austerity. German companies took over the operation of 14 Greek regional airports as part of the collateral for additional loans. This is not too different from the behavior of bankers in any country or culture who are less concerned with the financial ability of their clients to repay loans than with what assets they might acquire through default.

    The way Germany and other northern EU countries are treating Greece is also not too different than the way the Allied Powers treated Germany after WWI with regard to the payment of war reparations, in gold, which Germany could not "print." Euros may as well be gold to a Greece which cannot print them. While this doesn't excuse Greece's spendthrift past, it is not in anyone's interest to prevent Greece from recovering. It is about as useful as debtor's prison to confiscate their assets. Hitler seized on the reparations as a means to gain legitimate political power. Greece has a thriving fascist group already, the Golden Dawn Party.

In 2012 the Golden Dawn Party got 7% of the popular vote and 21 seats in Parliament, later reduced to 18. In areas where immigration, especially of Muslims, is high, it has garnered up to 20% popular support. While this is a far cry from winning a national election, the enormous influx of migrants escaping war in Syria, Iraq, Afghanistan, Yemen and elsewhere in the Middle East will only increase support for Golden Dawn. Tsipras has called snap elections after losing some of his party's support in the latest round of austerity. It bears watching how Golden Dawn will fare. They might attain some measure of influence through a coalition.

Mario Draghi, current president of the EU central bank, seems as determined as Alexis Tsipras to reduce unemployment in Europe. Though the EU bank is not chartered to address anything other than currency stability, Draghi has embarked on a program of quantitative easing which rivals that which the U.S. Fed just concluded. He will fill the EU with debt, he hopes postponing the crisis to some future time, when "he hopes" it can be dealt with.

Mario Draghi
president of the EU central bank
Wikimedia commons - Epizentrum

What do members of Syriza and the rebels in Donetsk People's Republic have in common? Both have said they will take Berlin next. But I think Russia's ambitions are for the natural gas in Ukraine and possibly Poland. This is the biggest challenge to date of the WTO's theory of settling such matters through trade rather than war. If we are to preserve the trade regime that has so far ended global war, then the Ukraine gas cannot change hands as the result of a war.

The WTO constraint of trade considerations to price and quality encourages trade based on the cost of labor, and a downward spiral toward exploited labor exported to all nations via equalization. This should be fixed. What works about the WTO is its dispute resolving power backed by the advantages of membership and the costs of being thrown out. Russia must accept trade dependence on other nations, not just the dependence of other nations on it, so that being thrown out is a deterrence.

The floating currency system in effect since 1971 works. There have been no disasters from it. The disasters are traced to either foolish attempts to unify currencies, or debt that nations like Argentina take on in currency other than their own.

Because lenders cannot contain themselves against the temptation to seize assets through financial manipulation, and because the WTO is the only effective method of regulating international commerce at the moment, I recommend that selling bonds denominated in other currencies than a nation's own be recognized as international trade and essentially forbidden, or at least escape clauses be forced into the bonds. Retroactively. Otherwise socialists and religious radicals will seize the resources in the chaos that develops.

Will this keep working?

Do not think I am suggesting the WTO will *continue* to prevent war. See *The Equity Premium Puzzle...* (preview follows) for my analysis of trade and conclusion that trade based on labor cost is bad for everyone, and the only viable trade is based on uneven geographic distribution of resources.

If a single large economy is inefficient or corrupt, and money pouring into it does not raise the standard of living of its workers, then its workers will bring the rest of the planet down to their level via trade pressure. Mexico, China and many nations come to mind as potential threats. When citizens of any country, Syria or the US, find themselves losing what they have, they will become upset and look for heroes like Tsipras or Sanders on the left, and Putin, Trump, Cruz or London mayor Boris Johnson on the right.

I have started a blog to post thoughts on current events and give readers a place to react with their own comments, which would be very interesting and useful to me. See *http://ShulerResearch.Wordpress.com*

Regarding your personal wealth strategy

It is not obvious how an economy should work if human labor is not the primary component. As a hedge against upheavals in the coming century it might be wise to diversify if you are currently depending on employment, and adopt a policy of generational wealth building in lieu of simple retirement. It also might be wise to support moderate political and economic policies, stoking neither liberal inflation (printing money to redistribute) nor conservative deflation (holding the money supply fixed while goods and services increase at fantastic rates). Either can lead to employment collapse and war.

Assuming the economic environment is stable enough to support personal wealth building, it is possible to move up by adopting a generational strategy in combination with a whole-market investing strategy (e.g. by index funds). We have discussed ways of doing this which preserve at least in a limited way your corporate voting preferences, and which use some of the techniques of successful wealthy individuals like Warren Buffett by practicing what he does (extracting cash) rather than what he preaches. Finding an ETF that does either without giving up growth has not really been possible, leaving us with holding broad index ETFs and supplementing with a small allocation to a high income ETF. There is relatively little cost difference, perhaps 1/3rd or less, between a retirement plan and a generational wealth plan.

Americans and Europeans have been misled by the emphasis on accumulating wealth only for retirement. This does not benefit families, which keep having to start over, nor does it benefit governments, which are constantly liquidating their tax base. It does benefit two surprising groups. It benefits extreme liberal ideologues by approximating their desire that all persons (other than themselves) be not just politically equal but born into equal physical circumstances, meaning neither knowledge nor resources are acquired from their families. It benefits extreme conservative ideologues by preserving the existing wealth hierarchy and protecting it from new blood rising into its ranks.

Regarding society

The wealthy, especially the moderately wealthy, are socially valuable, not enemies of the people or of the state. They pay most of the taxes to provide government services, open and operate most of the small businesses which account still for half of all employment, and provide the most rational and independent voice in government since they are not beholden to the interests of large, powerful corporations or slaves to welfare. We should get over the moral stigma attached to wealth. And, something I have not said much about, wealthy people should get over the idea that they are much smarter than everyone else. After a few years of investing you will realize that your intelligence will cause you to deviate from the strategy and trip up, and perhaps that will remind you to be humble. The account in which I had a choice of only five funds, and put it all in "small cap" and left it there, has been by far my most successful investment account.

There is a need for global diversification, but we were unable to settle on a good strategy for it. In the last five years (which is really still short-term, no matter how long it seems to Wall Street), global markets have done poorly. U.S. companies are globally diversified in many cases, and provide some exposure to global markets. As more central banks learn that they should manage not only inflation/deflation, but also employment (as the U.S. does) and possibly growth (as China does), the situation should improve somewhat. The EU experiment is a risk because the consolidated currency amounts to a "gold standard" for Greece, Italy, and other countries that are not well matched to Germany.

Building generational wealth would be accessible to far more people if dividends were paid by the largest companies with the highest profits. Most of these companies pay no or very small dividends, implying that the only value of their shares is in growth. This growth by the biggest companies, to the extent it exceeds growth in population and increases in the standard of living, must cannibalize small and medium sized businesses. This increases the wealth inequality gap, and decreases the number of self-reliant citizens that are not beholden to a job, possibly endangering the principle of a democratic government guided by free citizens. Some attempts by Congress have been made to encourage dividends, including a leveling of the tax rate between capital gains and dividends, and the establishment of special classes of corporations (REITs and BDCs) which must pay most income as dividends. But the latter has come entirely at the expense of growth. Instead of increasing tax rates, encouraging large corporations to pay more of their income as dividends would increase the tax base. At the same time the larger circulation of money into the hands of consumers would stimulate demand and counter deflation.

Investors continue to be pressured to seek mostly growth companies, otherwise they are stuck with losses they cannot deduct. These losses are real cash out the door, not some paper accounting scheme. At $3000 a year they hardly count against anything. There is no symmetry. If a company gets in trouble it cannot issue a negative dividend to raise capital. It can only experience capital losses. If we allowed all or some of capital losses to count against dividend income, would it reduce the pressure on companies to cannibalize small and local businesses when they cannot find ways to actually grow the economy? This could be tried in phases and the results monitored to see if it has the desired effect. Potentially the economy and the tax base would grow and more than compensate for any lost revenue, without the socially undesirable effect of growing only the largest businesses.

Closing thoughts

Anyone who tells you the universe is limited and you must constrain your possibilities has their head in the sand. There are 55 times the Earth's entire stock of hydrocarbons in one lake on Titan. We've only just learned to read DNA and look for extrasolar planets. The idea of using the trading concepts of early manual agriculture (which led directly to massed warfare) for our future needs and automated economy is absurd. The idea of basing money on a silver-gold alloy that happened to be abundant in a river in Lydia but not elsewhere is even more absurd. To wait for governments or religions or liberals or conservatives to figure this out is infinitely absurd. It is time to take matters into your own hands. You will, of course, need to accumulate the power and influence and wealth to do that.

Overview of: *The Equity Premium Puzzle, Intrinsic Growth & Monetary Policy*

Thank you for reading Money, Wealth & War. Please leave a review at your favorite bookseller or book review site. You can find additional information at *http://amazon.com/author/robertshuler* or on my website *http://mc1soft.com*. To contact me use *http://ShulerResearch.Wordpress.com*.

If you have enjoyed this book and are curious to explore further the principles of money, trade, economies, risk, the equity premium and economies of the future, then you might also enjoy the book described below. I write other types of books as well, and plan to write a lot more.

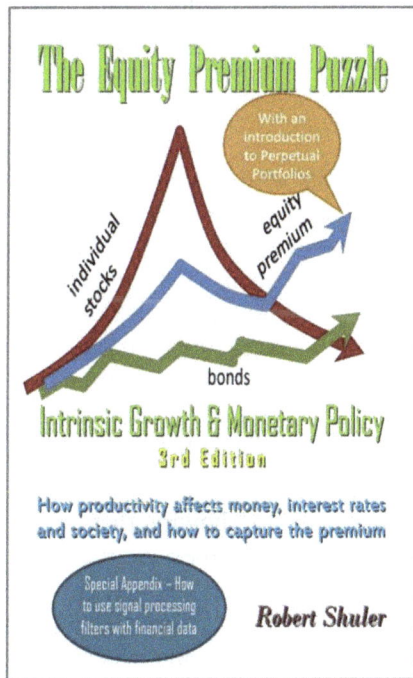

The Equity Premium Puzzle, Intrinsic Growth & Monetary Policy

In a new introduction for the Second Edition I summarize a few of the points made in the book you just read, and discuss the "oil war." There are only a few other things the two books have in common. Following is a brief summary of each chapter. It is not a picture book like this one, but there are plenty of graphs and several figures.

PART I - MONEY & RATIONAL MARKETS

Portfolio Logic - Everyone is an investor, making choices about a job, education and housing by default if not by financial logic. The nature of randomness in markets causes a majority of investors to fall behind. That is, the median performance is lower than the average. To capture the average performance one must invest in all available securities.

Finance Dawning - More detail on the psychology of money and its origins is given, with extended examples to show the role of favor returning, the basis of inflation and the way people organize money as backed by a "strong man" more than by any commodity.

Minimally Rational - Discusses the theory of rational markets and also behavioral economics, so that the reader can understand why the equity premium is a puzzle. The performance of individual investors is discussed, and the process of equalization of returns, in much more detail than the book you just read.

Risky Business - Interest rates and discounting are discussed also in more detail, and various methods of statistical analysis and their flaws. Modern economic analysis uses only risk as a price determinant in equilibrium systems, which explains why economists have so much trouble explaining the equity premium. The Capital Asset Pricing Model (based on risk) is qualitatively discussed, and Zheng's objection to it, along with proposed solutions to and estimates of the equity premium.

PART II - INVESTING IN THE EQUITY PREMIUM

Perpetual Portfolios - I unearth data showing that the lifetime of companies is growing dramatically shorter, perhaps presaging an era in which jobs are very unstable. Problems with trusts and partnerships are discussed in more detail, and explanations are given for BDC's and REIT's which we only briefly mentioned here. The permanent portfolio simulator is discussed with an example.

Pros & Cons of Perpetual Portfolios - Provides a discussion of market timing, comparison perpetual portfolios to mutual funds and bonds, discussion of rents vs. earnings, and a comparison to other historical periods since 1871.

Hazards in the Equity Premium - What to do when something goes wrong. How to use and not to use leverage (margin). More analysis of country diversification, the Euro and gold. A much briefer mention of war and monetary policy than here, primarily analyzing Germany.

Pitfalls of Windfalls - A sudden influx of money can be hard to handle. Some people buy property that has high expenses they cannot maintain. Jealousies and squabbles can break up marriages. I look at what happens to lottery winners and analyze one that has kept his money and done well, showing his portfolio and comparing it to an equity premium portfolio.

PART III - SOLVING THE PUZZLE

Intrinsic Returns - This chapter looks at the difference between equalized returns, the apparent return over a fixed period based on a price intended to equalize that return, and intrinsic returns which are based on the growth rate of the equity that may extend beyond any equalization date. In fact equalization cannot be accomplished without an end date because the value of even a small amount of non-terminating growth is infinite. It is like a "black hole" that would suck everything in if one tried to equalize it. The price would go to infinity.

Volatility & Competition - The effects of industrialization and stock companies on economies using the hypothetical Land of Zo are discussed, with an analysis of Japan including a recommendation of what they should do. A general theory is developed for equalizing a declining currency.

Lending Friction & Supply (of lending) - Discusses equity and debt ownership patterns, rational banking, how theoretical methods of equalization hypothesized by economists face limits in the real world, and the era of free banking in the U.S.

Evolution & Sustainability of Productivity - Views of prominent industrialists Henry Ford and Thomas Edison about money and productivity, and the problems that result from not increasing money supply are presented, along with growth and free trade.

Conclusions - Summarizes arguments and concludes that monetary policy must permanently adapt after a change in productivity, rather than expect the lowering of rates or other stimulus to be temporary. The natural "set point" of an economy is changed when productivity changes.

Utopian Visions - Surveys various rosy visions of how economies ought to work but don't.

Realistic Approaches - Makes practical suggestions for providing incentives for an economy to value human growth and individuality, not just anonymous money.

About Writing This Book - Tells the story of how I met Rajnish Mehra in college, how we kept in touch and I learned of his discovery of the equity premium puzzle.

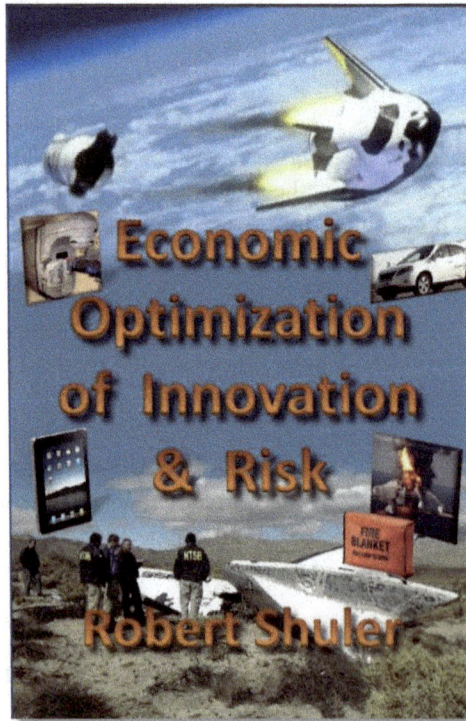

Excerpt from: *Economic Optimization of Innovation & Risk (Crash Rate Theory)*

Project Management Example

The goal of our hypothetical Space Tourism Transport (STT) is to visit an orbital hotel, presumably a future version of Bigelow Aerospace's efforts. Tickets will be $1 million, or 5 times the original price of Virgin Galactic's suborbital tickets. Market surveys indicate 5000 or 1% of the 640,000 people in the U.S. in households of over $20 million net worth will be interested over the next 10 years, and many more outside the U.S. So for individual passengers $V_F=\$1$ *million*, presumably. The objective is to hold recurring costs (M) to $750,000, giving a net revenue of $250k per passenger, times 10 passengers, or $2.5 million operating profit per flight. In 2015 launch costs are about 6 times higher than this for an 11,000 kg payload. Our exercise is set a few years in the future when a reusable launch vehicle (RLV) is available with 10x lower launch costs and 400x improved reliability. Our analysis does not include the RLV or the stay in orbit.

Two vehicles will be built at $250 million each. One flight a week gives an expected operating profit of $125 million per year. Investors expect to go public at the end of the first year of operations at a price to earnings (PE) multiple of 40, giving a capitalization value of $5 billion dollars, a ten-fold return on their $500 million investment, typical of venture capital expectations.

Passengers sign a waiver of liability, but it is not expected to hold up in case of vehicle systems failure. At-fault accident liability is estimated at $120 million dollars (~$10 million per occupant including pilots), which no one will insure at a reasonable price. Investors insist on an $R_o<1/(25\ years)$ to insure public confidence and some profit after recovery of development and liability costs. Five year operating net revenue yields $625 million, vs. development costs of $500 million, and $120 million liability once in 25 years in the worst case of $R_o=1/25yr$.

The reliability goal of less than one crash in 25 years, or R_o $<=1/1250\ flights$, is still 1000 times more risky than a 1000 mile automobile trip, but it is 50 times safer than a WWII bombing run over Germany and 25 times safer than riding on a NASA Shuttle.

The dilemma to be solved

Test flights are $10 million, slightly more than the $7.5 million of operational flights because of instrumentation and engineering costs, and general startup inefficiency. After 10 test flights the team finds 5 major but ultimately fixable problems. This gives C_d = *$500mil / 5 = $100 million per major defect.* You are the project manager. You have to do some guessing at this point. By that I mean you have all your engineers conduct a traditional risk analysis, using all the data you have found, and you conclude that most likely *D<=.1*, that is, you think in the next 50 flights (one year of operation) only two and a half serious problems are likely to show up. (D of .1 times 5 defects per ten flights times 50/10 = 2.5) In crash rate theory risk analysis still essential, but assigned the more circumscribed role of forecasting the defect ratio.

We now have all the parameters necessary to calculate Ro, so we plug in to the crash rate equation:

$$R_O \approx \frac{V_F - M}{C_C + C_d / D}$$

$$R_O \approx \frac{\$1M - .75}{\$1B + \$100M / .1} = \frac{.25M}{2B} = \frac{1}{8000}$$

At first glance you are quite pleased with that number. But immediately two things happen:

- After you enthusiastically reveal the calculation at a press conference, a space.com reporter who is on the ball realizes that you have used the V_f for a single passenger, so you really expect a crash in every 800 flights, not 8000.
- A competing spacecraft fails spectacularly, driving up the perception of risk, and ticket sales top out at 100.

The crash rate is not bad for a spacecraft, about once in 16 years, but worse than the original requirement of 1/25. What if the crash comes sooner rather than later? And of course the real problem is public perception. Ticket sales barely account for two months of operation and no or few new tickets are being sold.

What do you do?

End Notes

[1] http://www2.vcdh.virginia.edu/civilwar/index.php?section=Exhibits&page=War
[2] http://www.vintag.es/2011/02/35-years-after-fall-vietnam-war-in.html
[3] http://www.hwysafety.com/hwy_montana.htm
[4] http://www.rand.org/pubs/research_briefs/RB9505/index1.html
[5] http://en.wikipedia.org/wiki/German_autobahns
[6] http://commons.wikimedia.org/wiki/File:Highway_20_Kuusamo_Finland.jpg
[7] http://www.treasurenet.com/forums/what/386585-arrow-heads-spear-heads-age.html
[8] http://www.livescience.com/7794-human-stabbed-neanderthal-evidence-suggests.html
[9] http://en.wikipedia.org/wiki/Prehistoric_warfare
[10] http://all-free-download.com/free-vector/vector-clip-art/bow_with_arrow_117570.html
[11] http://en.wikipedia.org/wiki/Agriculture
[12] http://mannaismayaadventure.com/2013/10/11/in-photos-lost-prehistoric-code-found-in-mesopotamia/
http://www.usu.edu/markdamen/1320Hist%26Civ/chapters/16TOKENS.htm
http://prehistoricarch.blogspot.com/2013/08/5000-year-old-gaming-tokens-found-in.html
[13] http://unenumerated.blogspot.com/2008_08_01_archive.html
[14] http://www.ancient.eu.com/image/144/
[15] http://www.dailymail.co.uk/news/article-2486251/1bn-haul-art-Picasso-Renoir-Matisse-squalid-Munich-flat.html
[16] http://en.wikipedia.org/wiki/Ottoman_Empire
[17] http://www.topkapisarayi.gov.tr/
[18] http://en.wikipedia.org/wiki/Topkap%C4%B1_Palace
[19] http://en.wikipedia.org/wiki/Age_of_Discovery
[20] http://www.motherjones.com/politics/1999/11/top-10-reasons-shutter-wto
[21] http://en.wikipedia.org/wiki/World_Trade_Organization
[22] http://wiazowskisec5.blogspot.com/2013/02/cold-war-communist-vs-capitalist-bloc.html
(original source Wikipedia)
See also: http://en.wikipedia.org/wiki/File:New_Cold_War_Map_1980.png
[23] http://khude.wordpress.com/category/knowledge/mobile-phone/
[24] http://europa.eu/about-eu/
[25] http://en.wikipedia.org/wiki/Indo-Pakistani_wars_and_conflicts
[26] http://en.wikipedia.org/wiki/Outline_of_war
[27] http://en.wikipedia.org/wiki/Toyota_Camry
[28] http://en.wikipedia.org/wiki/Magnetic_resonance_imaging
[29] http://en.wikipedia.org/wiki/List_of_countries_by_military_expenditures
[30] http://spectrum.ieee.org/riskfactor/at-work/tech-careers/stem-crisis-as-myth-gets-yet-another-workout/
[31] http://www.businessinsider.com/tuition-costs-by-country-college-higher-education-2012-6
[32] http://en.wikipedia.org/wiki/List_of_countries_by_incarceration_rate
[33] http://news.yahoo.com/mexican-drug-cartels-now-money-exporting-ore-050325576.html
[34] http://en.wikipedia.org/wiki/Shepherd
[35] http://en.wikipedia.org/wiki/Hittites
[36] http://en.wikipedia.org/wiki/Jacob_%28sheep%29
[37] http://en.wikipedia.org/wiki/Bronze_Age_collapse
[38] http://en.wikipedia.org/wiki/Minoan_civilization
[39] http://en.wikipedia.org/wiki/Bronze_Age_collapse
[40] http://en.wikipedia.org/wiki/Currency
[41] http://en.wikipedia.org/wiki/Ark_of_the_Covenant
[42] http://en.wikipedia.org/wiki/Battle_of_Jericho
[43] http://en.wikipedia.org/wiki/Coin
[44] http://www.travellinkturkey.com/phrygia.html
[45] http://pixdaus.com/golden-river-river/items/view/23545/
[46] http://en.wikipedia.org/wiki/Ama-gi
[47] http://en.wikipedia.org/wiki/Babylonian_law

[48] http://answers.yahoo.com/question/index?qid=20100217081102AAGB7az
[49] http://ancienthistory.about.com/od/neareast/ss/052909Mesopotamia_2.htm
[50] notably Michael Hudson at the University of Missouri, see
http://www.washingtonsblog.com/2011/07/we-have-forgotten-what-the-ancient-sumerians-and-babylonians-the-early-jews-and-christians-the-founding-fathers-and-even-napoleon-bonaparte-knew-about-money.html
also views on parasitic financing http://en.wikipedia.org/wiki/Michael_Hudson_(economist)
[51] http://www.travelocafe.com/2011/06/last-free-people-on-earth.html
also http://en.wikipedia.org/wiki/Uncontacted_peoples
[52] http://en.wikipedia.org/wiki/Lydia
[53] http://en.wikipedia.org/wiki/Croesus_and_Fate
http://en.wikipedia.org/wiki/Croesus
[54] http://en.wikipedia.org/wiki/Sumer
[55] http://en.wikipedia.org/wiki/Assyria
[56] http://en.wikipedia.org/wiki/History_of_banking
[57] http://www.mckinsey.com/insights/global_capital_markets/118_trillion_and_counting
[58] http://www.businessinsider.com.au/warren-buffetts-father-howard-2010-11#howard-on-the-gold-standard-1
[59] https://en.wikipedia.org/wiki/Howard_Buffett
[60] https://en.wikipedia.org/wiki/Bill_Gates
[61] http://www.dailymail.co.uk/news/article-2698361/The-richest-man-world-says-working-THREE-days-week.html
[62] http://finance.yahoo.com/news/russias-richest-man-responds-putins-124548540.html
[63] http://www.therichest.com/rich-list/world/the-15-wealthiest-women-in-china/
[64] https://en.wikipedia.org/wiki/J._Paul_Getty
[65] http://www.cnbc.com/id/102174296#.
[66] Discover Magazine, August 5, 2010 http://blogs.discovermagazine.com/gnxp/2010/08/1-in-200-men-direct-descendants-of-genghis-khan/#.VJegxeAA
[67] Frank, Tenney, An Economic History of Rome,
http://socserv.socsci.mcmaster.ca/econ/ugcm/3ll3/FrankTenney/EcHistRome.pdf
[68] http://en.wikipedia.org/wiki/Rise_of_Rome
[69] http://ancienthistory.about.com/od/marius/p/Marius.htm
[70] http://en.wikipedia.org/wiki/Colour_revolution[71]
http://abcnews.go.com/blogs/entertainment/2013/07/paula-deens-cook-alleges-racism-slurs-by-celebrity-chef/
[72] http://www.vanityfair.com/politics/2012/04/vladimir-putin-mikhail-khodorkovsky-russia
[73] http://en.wikipedia.org/wiki/Bank_Menatep
[74] http://en.wikipedia.org/wiki/Argentine_debt_restructuring
[75 – 82] deleted
[83] http://en.wikipedia.org/wiki/History_of_the_United_States_dollar
[84] http://www.let.rug.nl/usa/essays/general/a-brief-history-of-central-banking/the-first-bank-of-the-united-states-%281791-1811%29.php
[85] Galbraith, John K., A Short History of Financial Euphoria, New York: Penguin Books, 1990.
[86] http://www.let.rug.nl/usa/essays/general/a-brief-history-of-central-banking/states-in-charge.php
[87] http://www.let.rug.nl/usa/essays/general/a-brief-history-of-central-banking/depository-safety-and-economic-safety.php
[88] penxv 11/28/2007 http://www.ronpaulforums.com/showthread.php?42656-CPI-graph-since-1800-to-illustrate-inflation
[89] Federal Reserve Bank of Minneapolis, via http://www.economics-charts.com/cpi/cpi-1800-2005.html
[90] http://en.wikipedia.org/wiki/Long_Depression
[91] https://www.census.gov/const/C25Ann/sftotalmedavgsqft.pdf
[92] http://www.census.gov/const/uspricemon.pdf
[93] http://www.washingtonpost.com/blogs/fact-checker/wp/2014/01/27/do-9-out-of-10-new-businesses-fail-as-rand-paul-claims/
[94] https://www.boundless.com/business/textbooks/boundless-business-textbook/small-business-

and-entrepreneurship-7/small-business-owners-the-disadvantages-57/low-success-rate-278-1212/
[95] http://www.statisticbrain.com/startup-failure-by-industry/
[96] http://www.forbes.com/sites/jasonnazar/2013/09/09/16-surprising-statistics-about-small-businesses/
[97] http://en.wikipedia.org/wiki/Corporation
[98] http://riskencyclopedia.com/articles/corporation/
[99] http://www.ribbonfarm.com/2011/06/08/a-brief-history-of-the-corporation-1600-to-2100/
[100] http://elreporterosf.com/?p=1626
[102] Jan. 19, 2015, http://www.bbc.com/news/world-europe-30878406
[104] http://www.marketplace.org/topics/economy/true-biography-davos-man
[105] "Davos town" by Biovit - Own work. Licensed under Public Domain via Wikimedia Commons - http://commons.wikimedia.org/wiki/File:Davos_town.jpg#mediaviewer/File:Davos_town.jpg
[106] http://www.economist.com/news/business/21570684-global-leadership-industry-needs-re-engineering-davos-man-and-his-defects
[107] http://www.vanityfair.com/online/daily/2015/jeff-greene-davos-lifestyle-expectations
[108] http://en.wikipedia.org/wiki/Jeff_Greene
[109] http://www.nydailynews.com/life-style/real-estate/billionaire-real-estate-mogul-jeff-greene-lists-195m-home-article-1.2003369
[110] http://uselectionatlas.org/FORUM/index.php?topic=98954.0
[111] "The Goose That Laid the Golden Eggs - Project Gutenberg etext 19994". Licensed under Public Domain via Wikimedia Commons -
http://commons.wikimedia.org/wiki/File:The_Goose_That_Laid_the_Golden_Eggs_-_Project_Gutenberg_etext_19994.jpg#mediaviewer/File:The_Goose_That_Laid_the_Golden_Eggs_-_Project_Gutenberg_etext_19994.jpg
[112] http://journal.webscience.org/237/1/websci09_submission_145.pdf
[113] Williams, Alex (13 July 2012). "Friends of a Certain Age: Why Is It Hard To Make Friends Over 30?". The New York Times. Retrieved October 25, 2012. Via http://en.wikipedia.org/wiki/Friendship
[114] Bryant, Susan. "Workplace Friendships: Asset or Liability?". Monster.com. Retrieved October 25, 2012. Via http://en.wikipedia.org/wiki/Friendship
[115] http://www.bbc.com/news/business-15198789
[116] "Chromesun kincaid site 01" by Herb Roe. Licensed under CC BY-SA 3.0 via Wikimedia Commons - http://commons.wikimedia.org/wiki/File:Chromesun_kincaid_site_01.jpg #mediaviewer/File:Chromesun_kincaid_site_01.jpg
[117] http://www.bbc.com/news/technology-31023741
[118] http://www.bbc.com/news/31047780
[119] http://etfdb.com/type/sector/energy/oil--gas-exploration--production
[120] http://www.history.com/topics/cold-war/berlin-airlift
[121] http://en.wikipedia.org/wiki/Flag_of_Novorossiya
[122] http://en.wikipedia.org/wiki/Alexander_Zakharchenko
[123] http://www.pecob.eu/shale-gas-pl-ua
[124] https://consortiumnews.com/2014/04/24/beneath-the-ukraine-crisis-shale-gas/
[125] While the plural of index can be either indices or indexes, indices usually refers to statistical tables. As an active collection of companies which pays a dividend, I prefer indexes.
[126] Various articles in 2014 announced China had overtaken the U.S. economy:
http://www.foxnews.com/world/2014/12/06/china-surpasses-us-to-become-largest-world-economy/
http://www.marketwatch.com/story/its-official-america-is-now-no-2-2014-12-04
http://www.businessinsider.com/china-overtakes-us-as-worlds-largest-economy-2014-10
But the BBC points out that even Chinese officials admit GDP numbers are made up:
http://www.bbc.com/news/magazine-30483762
[127] http://www.economist.com/news/essays/21609649-china-becomes-again-worlds-largest-economy-it-wants-respect-it-enjoyed-centuries-past-it-does-not
[128] http://www.vanityfair.com/news/2015/01/china-worlds-largest-economy

www.ingramcontent.com/pod-product-compliance
Lightning Source LLC
Chambersburg PA
CBHW072100040426
42334CB00041B/1493